THE EVOLUTION OF ECONOMIC SYSTEMS

Ota Sik, 1987
(photo by foto lautenschlager, St Gallen, Switzerland)

The Evolution of Economic Systems

**Essays in Honour of
Ota Sik**

Edited by
Kurt Dopfer
Professor of Economics
University of St Gallen, Switzerland

and

Karl-F. Raible
Assistant to Ota Sik
University of St Gallen, Switzerland

MACMILLAN

First published 1990

Published by
THE MACMILLAN PRESS LTD
Houndmills, Basingstoke, Hampshire RG21 2XS
and London
Companies and representatives
throughout the world

Phototypeset by Input Typesetting Ltd, London

Printed in Hong Kong

British Library Cataloguing in Publication Data
The evolution of economic systems: essays in honour of Ota
Sik
1. Economic systems, history
I. Dopfer, Kurt II. Raible, Karl-F.
330.12
ISBN 0–333–51153–0

Contents

Ota Sik   *frontispiece*

List of Figures   viii

Preface   ix

Notes on the Contributors   x

1   Introduction: Sik's *Third Way* of Economic Evolution   1
    Kurt Dopfer

Part I   An Interdisciplinary View

2   Changing Priorities   21
    Jan Tinbergen

3   Limitations to the Interdependence of Systems   32
    Gerhard Schwarz

4   Economics, Environment and the Faustian Imperative   43
    Hans Christoph Binswanger, Malte Faber and Reiner
    Manstetten

5   Systems Reproduction in Interdisciplinary Perspective   59
    Leonhard Bauer and Herbert Matis

6   Why Some Reforms Succeed   68
    Gerhard O. Mensch

7   A Cognitive-evolutionary Theory of Economic Policy   77
    Alfred Meier and Susanne Haury

Part II   The Evolution of Market Systems:
           (1) Principal Aspects of Market Evolution

8   Evolution and Stagnation of Economic Systems   91
    Ernst Heuss

9   The Self-organisation of the Economy   100
    Michael Hutter

10 Evolution and Innovation   111
    Jochen Röpke

11 Waves in Long-term Economic Development   121
    René Höltschi and Christian Rockstroh

Part II   The Evolution of Market Systems:
            (2) Reproduction,Institutions and Governmental Planning

12 Plan, Market and Banking   133
    J.A. Kregel

13 The Market and the Classical Theory of Prices   141
    Bertram Schefold

14 Some Thoughts on Plan and Market   155
    Alec Nove

15 An Institutionalist View of the Evolution of Economic
    Systems   165
    Marc R. Tool

Part III   The Evolution of Planning Systems:
             (1) General Evolution of Planning Systems

16 Socialist Experience and Ota Sik's *Third Way*   177
    Jírí Kosta

17 Socialism as a Socio-economic System   186
    Branko Horvat

18 On the Reformability of the Soviet-type Economic
    Systems   193
    Leszek Balcerowicz

19 Strategic Reappraisal and Short-term Adjustment: The
    External Economic Policy of Socialist Countries at the
    Crossroads   202
    András Inotai

20 The Technological Gap in the CMEA Countries:
    Missing Incentives   213
    Friedrich Levcik

Part III   The Evolution of Planning Systems:
             (2) Evolution as Reforms in Eastern Countries

21 Innovation as the Crucial Problem of Perestroika 225
    Harry Maier

22 Gorbachev's 'Radical Reform' and the Future of the
 Soviet Planning System 235
 Hans-Hermann Höhmann

23 Success and Failure: Emergence of Economic Reforms
 in Czechoslovakia and Hungary 245
 Tamas Bauer

24 The State of the Debate on Planning in Hungary 256
 Jan Adam

25 The Evolution of Socialist Economic Theories and the
 Strategic Options of Reform in China 265
 Jinglian Wu

26 The Evolution of Economic Systems: A Summary 276
 Karl-F. Raible

Index 283

List of Figures

1.1   Reproduction scheme with key variables   12
6.1   Wave model and metamorphosis model of economic evolution and transformation   76
7.1   Individual behaviour under certainty   79
7.2   Characteristics of bureaucratic and political decision processes   84
7.3   Basic model of politico-economic processes   85
9.1   The flow of the economy   103
9.2   Transactions   104
9.3   Observing the economy from the 'science position'   105
9.4   Observing the economy from the 'economy position'   106
11.1   The hexagon of economic dynamism in the United States   122
11.2   Development of the profit rate and the prime rate, 1950–85, in the USA   126
18.1   Reform thresholds   197

Preface

The Evolution of Economic Systems is dedicated to Ota Sik on the occasion of his seventieth birthday. It honours Ota Sik's economics, his political life and his social and humane concerns. His commitment to truth, his challenging of established politico-economic structures and ideological borderlines as well as his search for solutions aiming to improve the life of humans in the economic, social and political realms, are all deserving of our deepest respect.

We think that Ota Sik may in some way be considered as an 'evolutionist' whose work has always been stressing economic and societal change. He succeeded in analysing with competence developments in both the Eastern and Western systems and in combining what he considered the best of both worlds. Looking back fifty years from now, quite a few economists may feel that Sik was, with his vision of a *Third Way*, on the right track.

The *Evolution of Economic Systems* brings together contributions from economists from East and West. While this naturally implies a comparative view, we have attempted to overcome static comparative economic analysis by viewing the different economic systems in evolution.

The first part attempts to establish some interdisciplinary perspectives and to discuss principal aspects of the analysis of economic systems. The second, 'Western' part highlights market evolution as well as planned reproduction and institutional change. The third, 'Eastern' part focuses on the evolution of planning systems, highlighting various reform movements in Eastern European countries including the USSR and China.

KURT DOPFER
KARL-F. RAIBLE

Notes on the Contributors

Jan Adam is Professor of Economics at the University of Calgary.

Lescek Balcerovicz is at the Central School of Plannings and Statistics, Research Institute of Economic Development, Warsaw.

Leonhard Bauer is Professor of Economics at the Institute for Economic Theory and Economic Policy, University of Vienna.

Tamas Bauer is Professor for Socialist Economic Systems at the University of Frankfurt/M.

Hans Christoph Binswanger is Professor of Economics at the University of St Gallen.

Kurt Dopfer is Professor of Economics at the University of St Gallen.

Malte Faber is Professor of Economics at the University of Heidelberg.

Susanne Haury is at the University of St Gallen.

Ernst Heuss is Professor Emeritus of Economics at the University of Erlangen-Nürnberg.

Hans-Hermann Höhmann is at the Bundesinstitut für ostwissenschaftliche und internationale Studien, Cologne.

René Höltschi is a former assistant to Ota Sik, Zurich.

Branko Horvat is Professor of Economics at the University of Zagreb.

Michael Hutter is Professor of Economics at the University of Witten-Herdecke.

Andras Inotai is at the Institute for World Economics, Hungarian Academy of Sciences, Budapest.

Jinglian Wu is Professor of Economics, Senior Adviser, Research Centre for Economic, Technical and Social Development, the State Council, Beijing.

Jiri Kosta is Professor Emeritus for Socialist Economic Systems at the University of Frankfurt/M.

J. A. Kregel is Professor of Economics at Johns Hopkins University, Bologna Center.

Friedrich Levcik is Professor of Economics at the Vienna Institute for Comparative Economic Studies.

Harry Maier is Professor of Economics at the University of Flensburg.

Reiner Manstetten is at the University of Heidelberg.

Herbert Matis is Professor of Economic and Social History at the Institute for Economic Theory and Economic Policy, University of Vienna.

Alfred Meier is Professor of Economics at the University of St Gallen.

Gerhard O. Mensch is Professor of Economics at the University of Munich.

Alec Nove is Professor of Economics at the Centre for Development Studies, University of Glasgow.

Karl-F. Raible is Assistant to Ota Sik, at the University of St Gallen.

Christian Rockstroh is a former assistant to Ota Sik, Zurich.

Jochen Röpke is Professor for Economic Theory at the University of Marburg.

Bertram Schefold is Professor for Economic Theory at the University of Frankfurt/M.

Gerhard Schwarz is editor of *Neue Zürcher Zeitung*, Zurich.

Jan Tinbergen is Professor Emeritus of Economics at the University of Rotterdam.

Marc R. Tool is Professor of Economics at the California State University, Sacramento, Ca.

1 Introduction: Sik's Third Way of Economic Evolution

Kurt Dopfer

THE ORIGINS

A scholar's theory is part of his biography. It may be different perhaps in physics, but few economists would disagree entirely with this opinion. In any case, it is hard not to recognise the connections between the eventful life of Ota Sik and his theories.[1] Demonstration of this is facilitated by the fact that his biography falls into two easily distinguishable parts: the 'Eastern' and the 'Western'.

His biography opens, naturally enough, with his birth in Pilsen, two years after the October revolution in Russia. The poverty of his youth brought him to Marx, and Marx, in turn, brought him into the concentration camp at Mauthausen. This is the sad prelude to the two main chapters of his biography.

The 'Eastern' main chapter starts with his role as Communist activist (together with his wife Lilli), and ends with his emigration to the West as a former Economics Minister and Vice-President of the CSSR after the invasion of the Warsaw Pact troops in 1968. In between there lie fruitful years devoted to the study, research and teaching of Marxist theory and Party work that allowed him to measure his theoretical insights against actual economic and political events.

The second, 'Western' chapter starts with Sik's role as a refugee – and even a famous refugee is still essentially a refugee. He had accumulated much experience of the Eastern politico-economic system: a valuable background for interpreting and assessing his newly acquired knowledge about the Western market system. He became acquainted with Western scientific literature and took the opportunity to study the wealth of economic theories, thus gaining a more differentiated picture than he already possessed. He has

1

now been teaching and researching at the Universities of St Gallen and Zürich for twenty years.

Sik possesses in many ways a unique knowledge of two different theoretical and actual worlds. So it cannot come as any surprise that his theories have grown out of this distinctive theoretical competence and empirical knowledge. It seems, with hindsight, that he was almost destined to become a *bridge builder*. His bridge is a brilliant synthesis put forth in his *Third Way*, attempting nothing less than a vision of a better society: one based on the firm grounds of his knowledge and experience of two major politico-economic and social systems.

This chapter attempts to provide an idea of Sik's major theoretical contributions, their philosophical and empirical origins, compatibility with, contradictions of, and promises for the Eastern and Western worlds.

HUMANE ECONOMIC MAN

Any economic theory starts with a *model of man*. Part of neoclassical theory's triumph has been that its proponents succeeded in convincing a significant number of other economists that man can be reduced to his typical *economic* features. It has been argued that economics deals with economic phenomena and therefore requires behavioural assumptions that, self-evidently, rely on *economic man* – implying that not only this reduction to economic features but also the type of reduction suggested are valid. Neoclassical *homo oeconomicus* comes out as a rational decision-maker who maximises his or her utility, basically as a trading agent in a market.

Sik's model of man is much broader, relying on the early anthropological writings of Marx. At the core of the model are latent human *needs* that become effective in an individual's exchange with a specific *natural and social environment*. Sik first drew attention to this relationship between man and environment in his doctoral dissertation, *Economics, Interests, Politics*:

A need is usually connected with a concrete object, an activity or a relationship or certain groups of objects, activities, etc. It emerges therefore not as a specific state in man himself but always in connection with man's relationship to his environment, in particular to the societal products and the impact of the environment on man . . . Even the state of hunger is not only an expression of specific changes in the human organism but also of the growing contradiction between the living organism and the external sources of its nutrition without which no living organism may develop.[2]

He took up the needs issue again two decades later in his seminal *A Humane Economic Democracy: A Third Way*. Extending a comprehensive chapter on Maslow's Hierarchy of Needs, he objects to the psychological bias in Maslow's approach emphasising the necessary co-evolutionary nature of needs.

Self-realisation of man takes place in the process of *production*: a basic need to realise one's creative potential is satisfied by participating in a work process. This *process-need* is concealed in the neo-classical context where only tradable end-results come into the picture, while their generation is discounted in its welfare theoretical significance. A further major class of needs refers to the *end-results* themselves, particularly consumer goods and leisure time.

Individuals have an *interest* – the second conceptual pillar of Sik's economics – in *satisfying their needs*. They try to materialise their interests by shaping socio-economic processes in a way that allows them to satisfy their needs. It may be noted that Marx shares with Adam Smith the premise that *self-interest* is a key characteristic of human nature. Thus, the articulation of individual self-interest has, in the classical context, a theoretical rationale since it is based on human needs. In a neo-classical context, however, self-interest is typically related to a *preference function* that may or may not be based on human needs. An individual 'chooses' his or her wants, and thus requires additional choice criteria. One may suggest that wants depend on value judgements but this is only a sophisticated way of saying that nothing can be said about preferences scientifically. Needs – particularly if their nature is demonstrated by comprehensive biological and cultural analysis – have an objectivity of their own. Individuals may utter value judgements on various needs, and they may change those judgements. But they will be unable to change the needs themselves; man can suppress needs, but he cannot eliminate them. The classical model can do without neo-classical refinements, but the neo-classical model is left without substance in its basic explanation of human behaviour unless it relies on the classical model of man – its concept of needs.

An understanding of the substantive character of needs is useful for an understanding of Sik's focus on *interests* rather than on value judgements. Given the objective character of needs, a *relationship between interests and socio-economic environment* may be established scientifically. On the one hand, there is an objective dynamics of need-propelled interests; on the other, there are ascertainable regularities in the developmental dynamics. The relationship is thus one which may be defined by two scientifically ascertainable sets of variables.

These two variable sets may be in *harmony* or in *contradiction*. It is a major claim of Marxism, a claim which Sik accepts, that a capitalistic market system generates objective contradictions. In a theoretical view that features preference functions and value judgements, such frictions do not become so easily apparent since man appears to behave more adaptively. Any conflict between individual interests and environment appears as relative, since the relationship between preferences and environment is more one of a logical (decision-making under assumed constraints) than one determined by actual necessity. Individuals may always be able and willing to adjust their decisions and wants. In a needs model, contradictions are not resolved primarily by changing individual value judgements or preferences but by changing socio-economic conditions. This explains Sik's emphasis on institutional and economy-wide change.

The 'determining interest' is, according to Sik, the *economic* one. He criticises, for instance, Kautsky's narrow interpretation of interest as bourgeois 'profit interest', and suggests that the interest notion should be given a broader meaning.[3] Yet this meaning is still predominantly economic:

> We cannot deny that material interests together with other economic interests are the strongest immediate motive for the development of economic activities. The economic interest corresponds always to a specific economic status of man, is intrinsically connected to it, and characterises directly specific social groups.[4]

Concerning the actual application of this belief in Eastern economies, the editor of the German version of Sik's book recognised in the foreword the importance of the interest concept and concluded that the road to economic progress has been opened up in the German Democratic Republic since it has succeeded in resolving the stated fundamental contradiction:

> As for the comprehensive building of socialism in the German Democratic Republic we may start from the fact that by now the correspondence between societal requirements and the material interests of individuals, groups and collectives of the socialist society constitute the decisive motive forces of the economic and societal development.[5]

Sik's assessment of the politico-economic system of the GDR differs profoundly from this self-assessment by a GDR economist. There are obviously several possibilities to achieve an 'optimal' correspondence between 'material interests' and 'societal requirements', even in a socialist society.[6]

MICRO THEORY: NEO-CLASSICAL ECONOMICS WITH MARXIST SUBSTANCE

It comes as no surprise that Sik is prepared to acknowledge the validity and usefulness of Western microeconomics. He has witnessed an economy shaped by policies that largely failed to recognise the relevance of the market. For Marx the spontaneity of the market generates anarchy and its resource allocation is grossly inefficient. And though Marx did not provide a new micro theory, his statement was persuasive enough to hold communist politicians back from applying a market theory. As a result, actual systems have emerged that are based on the premise that spontaneity of markets leads to disproportionality and that governmental planning endows the system with increased order. The actual result, however, was a planned disproportionality rather than a planned proportionality:

> While Marx assumed that the continuously disturbed proportionality in the capitalist production that he called for that reason anarchic production can be substituted by a planned proportionality in socialism, there are much larger disproportionalities that,

additionally, may be overcome more slowly and less consistently, in socialist reality.[7]

The key problem of allocative inefficiency in the Eastern economies consists not only in price rigidities or a lack of 'fine tuning' on the basis of relative price adjustments, but in gross misallocations of production that fails to meet basic human needs. The superior results of the market system become apparent by demonstrating its performance record:

> The fact is important that in highly developed market economies an excess of supply or demand does not occur for many products and that therefore the prices do not fluctuate frequently since . . . producers anticipate micro disequilibria curbing them before they actually occur.[8]

A gourmet of equilibrium theory may look for the fine differences in the application of specific theories. Marshall's equilibrium theory relies in its adjustments on the quantities supplied. Prices may be adjusted, of course, but in the medium or long run the firm will also adjust its cost and supply functions. Aspects of historical time enter the model explicitly. Walras, on the contrary, in his static general equilibrium theory keeps the factor and supply quantities fixed. The tradable quantities are the same before and after exchange, and the equilibrium state is reached via an iterative process of price adjustments. Sik's work is basically in the spirit of Marshall. He talks of 'production corrections', or uses a terminology that refers to physical or technological magnitudes, and recognises (implicitly) the importance of real time.

How can a Marxist *needs* approach be reconciled with neoclassical micro theory? Sik succeeds in matching marginal utility theory and a needs approach and while this may look like bringing fire and water together, a closer look reveals that the two are complementary rather than contradictory. First, the marginal principle is, as a formal instrument, independent in its validity from empirical application. Marginal calculus has proved powerful, and it would be inappropriate not to use it whenever we derive demand schedules from individual behaviours – irrespective of the supporting rationale. Neither the Marxist nor modern humanistic needs approaches apply the principles of marginalism. The needs approach has often been discarded, therefore, on the grounds that it fails to apply appropriate analytical tools.

However, it may be recognised that a needs approach provides *empirical* substance for microeconomics. The first law put forth by H. Gossen states that marginal utility decreases the more the needs are satisfied. A needs approach, says Maslow's Hierarchy of Needs, provides additional information about the nature of needs, and is therefore able to add scientific backing to the argument of decreasing marginal utility (given increasing marginal needs satisfaction). Some economists argue that neo-classical micro theory does not need any empirical support of this type; some even state that the entire body of microeconomic statements is redundant, since the 'realism of assumptions' does not matter at all. One may take the opposite view, claiming that empirical substance always counts in an empirical science. As for the present case, an important conclusion is that a Marxist or humanistic needs approach is consistent with marginal utility theory. At best, a needs approach improves neo-classical assumptions, at worst, it is not inconsistent with it.

The question is, however, whether this would be sufficient reason to introduce an additional concept into marginal utility theory. There remain arguments in favour of Ocam's razor, the formal rigour and elegance of theoretical reasoning. The discussion may be open-ended as far as microeconomics is concerned. An additional argument for applying a needs approach may, however, refer to the potential it holds for *macro*economics. Generally, macroeconomics takes as a starting point the market process (described by microeconomics) and subjects that process to *additional performance criteria*. Macroeconomic performance criteria are (i) the overall use of available resources and (ii) the stability of the market process. If one assumes, as J.B. Say does, that the market process fulfils itself by meeting those performance criteria, there is no need for a macro theory, since micro theory alone may describe a process that meets all performance criteria. However, as Keynes has shown, the full use of resources is a special case within a broad range of macroeconomic possibilities that include a gross underutilisation of resources. Harrod, in turn, has demonstrated that the dynamic stability of the market process depends on rather special assumptions.

Using the concept of neo-classical preferences, a macro-economic consumption function represents an aggregate of individual consumer preferences. Preferences are conceived as basically exogenous; they fall, particularly in the 'new microeconomics', under the verdict of *non est disputandum*. Or, if discussed at all, they are viewed as wants in their volatile subjectivity. Consequently, the preference approach does not provide a scientific base for a consumption function, but rather supports the opposite view that meaningful scientific statements about consumption functions cannot be made. The consequences of this conceptual deficiency will be different, depending on the use that one intends to make of macroeconomics. If no macro policy is envisaged, deficiencies in the theoretical foundations of macroeconomics will matter little.

This may explain why Sik, in turn, relies on a needs approach. His approach stresses the importance of policy intervention, and, accordingly, requires appropriate macro theoretical foundations. Furthermore, Sik's humane vision laid down in his *Third Way* also includes non-market needs. A needs approach is particularly important for cases of 'unrevealed preferences' since it provides (consumers absent) the only way for a theoretical 'revelation'.

In an analogous vein, the question may be asked why a Marxist *interest* concept should be introduced into neo-classical micro theory. Specifically, why should the *maximisation* principle not suffice as behavioural assumption for a theory of firm? We may state, in defence of the interest concept, that the maximisation principle allows us to discuss relative allocative efficiency but fails to provide foundations for a similar consideration of macroeconomic magnitudes that determine its overall scope.

In conventional micro theory, the typical firm minimises its costs, given a competitively determined sales price. In any real economy, the firm will make profits; but in an equilibrium approach profits are ruled out by the assumption of perfect competition. This approach demonstrates thus not how profits are made but rather how they are not made. There is, hence, no profit function – a bad starting point for macro theory.

There may be profits, however, even in a static equilibrium model. On the one hand, the process towards the equilibrium state allows, temporarily, differentials, assuming that some of the agents start trading before equilibrium is reached. On the other hand, there are differentials in the performance ability of the agents that allow them to garner profits from market exchanges. In a real life economy, where information imperfections and risk and uncertainty are the rule, there is always a surplus to be earned somewhere. Generally, imperfections of any kind lead to Pareto suboptimality. Paradoxically, profits – and thus a potential for growth – emerge in a static equilibrium model if it portrays a Pareto suboptimal state. Sik's analysis shows high esteem for the allocative capacity of the equilibrium model, and it would run into contradictions if it were to accept a profit function on the basis of challenging the normative power of that model.

There are various ways of arriving at a profit function without support from the allocative inefficiencies of a static model. The safest is to rely on a theory of firm. This is where an interest approach becomes relevant. Sik views the firm basically in its *social* properties. Employees cooperate in a productive unit and social interactions generate a productive result distributed as wages and profits. All participating individuals have their specific interests. The efficiency of a firm depends on its capacity to provide for an organisation that allows it to take advantage from the motives that result from those interests. The institutional arrangements become a major production factor and engine for generating surplus.

The *property rights* concerning the means of production play the key role in the institutional set-up: workers will be motivated if they own a fair share of the means of production. They will, hence, increase the firm's efficiency in the short and long run by being motivated to work and by taking care of the firm's assets. Sik's approach is in the spirit of Leibenstein's *X*-efficiency theory that relies analogously on the assumption that a firm's internal efficiency is improved by increasing worker motivation.

Sik does not cope particularly well with Schumpeter's notion of an entrepreneur as a *creative destructor* nor with any 'subjectivist' constructs of Austrian origin. A reason for this may be that he views innovational change to be driven basically by objective technological forces rather than by the ingenuity of individual entrepreneurs. Sik may feel some sympathy for Saint Simon's idea of an invention office, and he may view in the concentrated R & D efforts of large companies confirmation of his preference. One may leave it to further inquiry to decide whether Sik's profit function properly catches the nature of capitalist dynamics. He may always counter that it has not been his ultimate scientific aim to describe capitalism but rather to set up a viable alternative – the *Third Way*. He may consider it his task to outline a 'normative profit function' leaving further theoretical refinement to economists who rely on the premise of capitalist profit-making.

MACRO THEORY: RECONCILING ACCUMULATION AND DISTRIBUTION

Macroeconomics deals with an overall assessment of the relative allocative efficiency of the market considering the stated macroeconomic objectives.

Sik trusts the *self-regulating* forces of the market as far as *relative* allocational efficiency is concerned. He objects to orthodox Marxist thinking for being unable to distinguish properly between the micro and the macro aspects of the market. Here Sik is in accordance with Keynes who argued that the system broke down only in determining the overall volume of investment but not in deciding its directions. Sik – relying on the advances of Keynesian analysis – distinguishes clearly between the microeconomic validity of Say's analysis and its macroeconomic fallacies. In fact, he defends Say's analysis as far as microeconomics is concerned:

> Of course, we have to assume first of all that all the various types of goods will be produced in quantities in which they are needed and demanded. Say does not contradict the view that there may be disequilibria between supply and demand of various commodities in the short run, that there may exist also some micro disequilibria . . . The view according to which a well functioning market mechanism can overcome micro disequilibria relatively quickly and that they exist only in the short run and exceptionally, may be generally accepted.[9]

Say's theorem, however, may be challenged on macroeconomic grounds. Sik considers the major shortcoming of Say's macroeconomics that it propounds that supply creates its own demand not only in the consumer goods but also in the *producer goods* sector. Say assumed perfect proportionality between the consumer good and the producer good sectors. Keynes challenged the synchronicity between savings and investments but failed to see the interrelation of the consumer and the producer goods sectors. Developing his arguments, Sik is faithful to *Marx's reproduction scheme.* The two mentioned *meso* production sectors are at the very heart of Sik's macroeconomics.

His theory is composed of *three pairs of macro variables.* Aggregate income is subdivided into income out of profits and of wages, employment of income into investment and consumption, and finally aggregate demand into demand for producer goods (A) and consumer goods (B). The key macroeconomic problem is to secure a *proportional development* between a *structured aggregate supply and a structured aggregate demand*. The structure of the aggregate supply function is defined by the relation between the output of the A- and B-sectors; the structure of the aggregate demand function is determined by the relation between investment and consumption. A *macro equilibrium* is reached if the two macro structures fit. The macroeconomic equilibrium conditions are stated thus:

> The total supply of production goods must equal the sum of replacement investments in A and B, of the profit shares in A and B, which are used for net investment used directly in the enterprises (self-financing), of public expenditures as well as credits required for the acquisition of production goods. The total supply of consumer goods thus equals the sum of wages and profit shares in A and B, the public expenditures as well as credits required for the purchase of consumer goods.[10]

Level and structure of aggregate supply are basically determined by the interdependency between the two production sectors:

> There exists between A and B a complementary relationship in a sense that the A-production can develop in the long run only in a technically determined relation to the growth of the B-group. And equally, the B-group can grow in the long run only on the basis of a specific growth of the A-group.[11]

Technological progress, another key variable of any dynamic supply function, is treated on a theoretical *ad hoc* basis. From an Austrian point of view, entrepreneurs' innovational capacity will be the driving force, leaving the investment rates as dependent variables. In a Marxist interpretation, technological progress will depend on the investment in the production goods sector. In Sik's interpretation, the level and structure of the aggregate demand function are determined by the levels and structures of the partial aggregates of investment and consumption. The major (income) determinant of the two partial as well as the total aggregate demand functions is the relation between wages and profits:

I am of the opinion that the primary distribution of wages and profits predetermines the relationship between consumptive and productive demand in a significant way. The public and credit related re-distributions may influence the proportion between consumption and net investment but will not change them fundamentally.[12]

The interrelationship between the key macro variables and the equilibrium conditions may be summarised in a diagram (Figure 1.1).

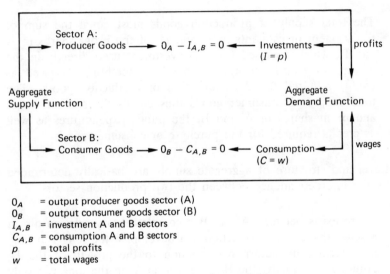

O_A = output producer goods sector (A)
O_B = output consumer goods sector (B)
$I_{A,B}$ = investment A and B sectors
$C_{A,B}$ = consumption A and B sectors
p = total profits
w = total wages

Figure 1.1   Reproducing scheme with key variables

The macro model presented may be seen to be very much in the line of conventional *economic dynamics*. There is the familiar circular resources flow; similarly, changes are brought about by a self-propelling resources determination or by exogenous events. Together with its equilibrium conditions, the model resembles the self-perpetuating golden age dynamics. The resources dynamics of the model is also present in the consumption and investment functions. Consumption is determined by wages, investment by profits.

Sik's microeconomics, however, does allow us to give his consumption and investment functions a *behavioural* meaning. As for the former, we may recall his substantive needs approach; as for the latter, the investment function may rely on his profit function. It is difficult to see why the Sik model could not be improved by introducing Keynes's propensities to consume and to invest. In turn, there are few plausible reasons why Keynesian economics could not benefit from integrating the sectoral characteristics of the Sik model.

PLANNED REPRODUCTION

In his micro and macroeconomics Sik reaches specific conclusions about the performance of a capitalist market system. It performs well in the microeconomic domain but less well in the macro domain, failing to meet optimal allocative efficiency and stability. Accordingly, governmental planning must supplement the macro performance of the market system.

For the *micro* performance, Sik emphasises the importance of *maintaining competition* and suggests applying effective *antimonopoly policies*. This policy proposal is much in the line of the Freiburg School's 'ORDO-liberalism' (although he criticises this approach for expecting macro proportionality and stability from competitive markets alone).

For the *macro* domain, *governmental planning* is required in two major areas:

(1) *Normative directions* of the socio-economic process;
(2) *Proportionality of the macro variables* to achieve macro allocative efficiency and stability.

Sik's approach, which he calls *Distribution Planning*,[13] may best be evaluated by contrasting it with three basic requirements that any planning approach must meet. First, governmental planning must rely on a positive theory with *deterministic* features. Any actual decision-maker must operate within a causal world that allows him to predict the consequences of decisions taken. A problem of applied Marxism is that Marx provided a model of 'deterministic chaos' (Capitalism), but not one of 'deterministic order' (Communism). The requirements for determinism make Sik's emphasis on deterministic resources dynamics understandable.[14]

Secondly, a planning approach requires that a distinction be made between a set of *endogenous* and *exogenous* variables. A non-interventionist model features only a set of endogenous variables. Governmental planning or policy, in turn, attempts to influence that process 'from outside' and therefore relies on an additional set of 'intervening' variables. The two major pairs of independent variables are, on the one hand, *wages and profits*, and on the other, *investment and consumption*.

Thirdly, a planning approach requires *appropriate institutions* that allow decision-making to affect both the endogenous and exogenous variables. A non-interventionist model may rely on the existing market institutions and ignore decision-making in the governmental domain and in micro institutions designed to bring about policy-conforming decisions. Sik's model of a *Third Way* explores the institutional possibilities required to implement a decision-making process that supports the resources policies envisaged.

As for *resources planning*, the overall resources scheme may be divided, following Tinbergen's criteria, into *goal and instrumental variables*. One may group the various normative issues that Sik discusses into three sets of goal variables. The most general and central goal variable is the *relationship between aggregate consumption and aggregate investment*. This relationship represents the *time-preference* of a society. Present consumption has opportunity costs in terms of investment foregone. Consequently, future consumption is reduced. Sik does not make statements about an intergenerational distribution function. Communist dogma has a strong bias towards future generations by sacrificing present welfare. Sik does not emphasise that type of time-preference on an aggregate level, thus rejecting a most crucial dogmatic corner stone of the Marxist – particularly Stalinist – heritage.

A second goal variable is the apportioning of *private and public consumption*. Sik has in mind some needs-based 'selective consumption planning' rather than selective investment planning (which he rejects). The non-market consumption planning includes environmental conditions, lifestyle and work conditions, as well as life quality in general. The distributional conflicts are expected to be reconciled by a planning procedure that is highly iterative.

Thirdly, having stated the normative direction of the macro process, an additional goal is to secure the *stability and efficiency* of that process. Sik views the capitalist system as a dynamics of *continuous upswings* and *downswings* generated by disproportionate developments between the consumption goods and production goods sectors. In an upswing phase there is an overshooting of profits and investments and consequently an overproportionate growth of the production goods sector (A). In a downswing phase, the process is reversed with an overshooting of wages and an excess demand in the consumer goods sector (B). Sik has attempted to provide empirical support (particularly for the FRG) for his cycle theory in recent years.[15]

A normative statement of time-preference must accept corrections, if it is to be optimal in *performance* terms. Instrumental efficiency aspects therefore enter the normative realm of distribution.

The notions of propensity to consume and propensity to invest receive a specific meaning in the planning model presented, different from any that applies to a non-planned market economy. The propensities still represent individual decisions but they are influenced by a social consensus.

The key *instrumental* variables are *wages and profits*. Based on classical reasoning, the wages fund will determine consumption, and profits will determine investment. Consequently, any control over the change of wages will directly influence consumption, or similarly, any control over profits will directly influence investments. The social institution that has command over this key macro relationship possesses most economic power in an economy. This relationship represents the *principal distributional conflict*.

Traditionally, the wages and profits are distributed on the basis of bargaining between the social partners labour and capital. Labour has self-interests and capital has self-interests, which cannot be easily reconciled. This inner contradiction prevents a policy that is oriented towards other important normative issues, such as intergenerational time-preference, the apportioning of private and public consumption, and macro stability.

Sik comes up with the proposal to 'neutralise the capital', and thus to resolve the principal distributional conflict. The concept of 'neutralised capital' relies basically on the Marxist concept of collective ownership of the means of production – the only but crucial difference being that the property is now not owned by the State but by the workers of a company. The returns from capital thus accrue directly to the employees of a firm. In contrast to the Yugoslav model the internal distribution is influenced directly by the State.

Resolution of the old distributional conflict between Capital and

Labour leads to an improvement of the macro efficiency of the overall economic process, without disturbing claims from interest groups. A marriage between efficiency and distribution seems in sight.

INSTITUTIONAL CHANGE FOR ALTERNATIVE DECISION-MAKING

For the *implementation* of the resources plan Sik suggests a restructuring of capitalist institutions that would allow decision-making to support the macro goals stated in the plan.

Regarding the *macro institutions*, he envisages a governmental 'Central Planning Commission' that is composed of a 'Production Commission' and a 'Life Quality Commission'. Both commissions are to be supported by a 'Council of Economic Advisers'. The task of the Production Commission is to plan the aggregates of consumption and investment, foreign trade and money supply. The Life Quality Commission is a subcommission for the consumption sector, planning private consumption as a whole, its relation to collective consumption, and environmental and regional issues. The Production Commission receives empirical data from the 'Industry Research Institute', and the Consumption Commission accordingly gets scientific support from a 'Needs Research Institute'.

Besides the scientific support, a major feature of planning is the *democratic spirit* in which it is conducted. Sik has devoted a book to *The Communist Power System*[16] and he does not fail to draw relevant conclusions from the pitfalls of actual power systems. The Central Planning Commission is composed of representatives of political parties, social groups, industry sectors, regions and individual firms, and is subject to democratic control by the parliament. Its major task is to assess the effective societal needs and to contrast them with the economy's productive possibilities. A set of *alternative plans* is set up and submitted to the people's decision in a direct vote.

On a *micro level*, the shareholding company – as the prototype of capitalist enterprise – is replaced by a 'Labour Sharing Company'. Similar to its capitalist counterpart, it is composed of a 'Managing Organisation' and an 'Asset Holding Organisation'. Unlike it, however, the agents representing the Asset Holding

Organisation are the employees of the firm itself; there are no 'capital representatives' that would control the firm, by controlling the management, for instance, or by executing decisions concerning the sale of the firm's assets.

The *capital market* withers away. We may distinguish between an internal and an external allocation of capital. Neo-classical and Keynesian theory is concerned with *external* capital allocation and expects efficiency by distributing capital according to its marginal productivity or efficiency. Internal allocative efficiency enters the picture only to the extent that the value assets of the firm as a whole are concerned. In contrast, Sik rates highly efficiency gains from optimising *internal* capital allocation. The lack of an external capital allocation mechanism is reconciled by two aspects of his model. Saving is made primarily inside the firm; investment is made out of profits. There is no Keynesian 'inequality' between savings and investments. It is assumed that there will be little external financing. The second external allocative device for capital is the government's control over investment. Interestingly, Sik does not favour a selective investment policy, as suggested and employed in some Western European countries. Sik might not view the lack of an external finance device as a grave shortcoming of his model.

THE FUTURE

Sik's approach provides much scientific nutrition for economic theory in East and West which in many ways has tended to become sterile and outdated.

In the present reactionary mood of politicians in his mother country, the CSSR, the seeds of his work may not fall on fertile ground. Nevertheless, Sik's work reveals the inner contradictions of the centrally planned systems of the East with lucidity and concern. If the waters of Gorbachev's Perestroika succeed in nourishing the soil of scientific thought and if the hopes are not exaggerated that some day an actual transformation of the polit-economic systems does occur, then Sik's approach will also have a chance to flourish.

In considering the West, Sik's theoretical insights are only one voice in a pluralistic chorus. Political repression of thinking, though sometimes attempted, is not notoriously successful, and the main battle field is the scientific community. Sik's views open up broad vistas for a research programme, aiming to contribute solutions to the most pressing problems of our times, such as gross macro inefficiencies, unemployment, and large-scale intertemporal misallocations.

Notes

1. O. Sik has recently published his autobiography *Prager Frühlingserwachen – Erinnerungen* (Prague Spring Awakening: Memories) (Herford: Busse Seewald, 1988).
2. O. Sik, *Oekonomie – Interessen – Politik* (Economics – Interests – Politics, edited by Otto Reinhold (Berlin: Dietz, 1966), p. 306.
3. Ibid., p. 364.
4. Ibid., p. 6.
5. Ibid.
6. Sik presented his *Weltanschauung* and principal theoretical position clearly in his *Der Dritte Weg* (The Third Way), (Hamburg: Hoffmann and Campe, 1972); this is the first book he published in the West after emigration.
7. O. Sik, *Wachstum und Krisen* (Growth and Crisis), (Berlin: Springer, 1988), p. 6.
8. Ibid.
9. Ibid., p. 5.
10. Ibid., p. 41.
11. Ibid., p. 12.
12. Ibid., p. 41.
13. Sik has given a full account of his *normative* theory in his *Humane Wirtschaftsdemokratie – Ein Dritter Weg* (revised English edition: *For a Humane Economic Democracy*, New York: Praeger, 1985) (Hamburg: Albrecht Knaus, 1979).
14. Compare, for instance, O. Sik, *Wachstum und Krisen* (Growth and Crisis), p. 104, where Sik emphasises the importance of *repeatable* processes and the *regularities* derived therefrom as contrasted to *concrete* historical processes.
15. O. Sik, 'Zwei Wirtschaftskrisen in der Bundesrepublik Deutschland' (Two Economic Crises in the Federal Republic of Germany), *Jahresbücher für Nationalökonomie und Statistik*, 1983, vol. 198/5, pp. 185–408.
16. O. Sik, *The Communist Power System* (New York: Praeger, 1981).

PART I

An Interdisciplinary View

2 Changing Priorities

Jan Tinbergen

MAIN MARXIST THESIS

Since we have had the pleasure of having Professor Sik in our midst some important events have taken place. They are important enough to reconsider the relationships between the centrally planned and the market economies. Until recently the first priority for the former was to establish a communist society and for the latter to prevent that from happening. The centrally planned economies were and are governed by the Communist Party and this party's main vision of socio-economic history is that a country's social order is moving from a feudal to a capitalist and from a capitalist to a socialist order. In the latter the means of production are owned by the community and the production and distribution processes carried out along the lines stipulated by the Central Plan. Whereas Karl Marx felt strongly convinced that these main features of social development could be anticipated on the basis of scientific research, he added that 'recipes for the future' on details could not be given.

Marx recommended the worker class to organise itself both in trade unions and in political parties, his well-known slogan being 'proletarians of all countries unite'. During his own lifetime such organisations were established and constituted important innovations in political life. After his death in 1883, his successors were unable to maintain unity and increasingly two currents showed, as often happens, how difficult a task 'uniting' is. Radicals and moderates reached different interpretations of 'their master's voice'.

DEMOCRACY OR EQUALITY

The split between radicals and moderates had a variety of aspects. The radicals attach more importance to the final aim, equality, and are in a hurry; they want to accelerate the evolution, if necessary with violence. Often they are the representatives of the

21

most serious victims of capitalism. The moderates want to attain
the ultimate aim by persuasion, not by violence. Essentially they
are convinced that the evolution towards a socialist society is
unavoidable and, for that very reason, cannot be accelerated. They
recognise the rights of all citizens to participate in the decision-
making process and reject imposing their own ideas, because they
also reject the prospect of being the victim of imposed ideas of
other parties.

Perhaps as a consequence of the internal debate the labour
movement was unprepared to prevent the outbreak of the 1914
war – later called the First World War. The French leader Jean
Jaurès was murdered before it started. The German leaders made
the serious mistake of not resisting the war. The Russian socialists
took the lead in the February 1917 revolution. German conservatives created the possibility for Lenin to return to Russia and to
assume leadership of the bolshevik (majority) socialists, who were
radical and seized power in the 'October' (on our time-scale:
November) 1917 revolution.

In Germany, the moderates participated in the democratic
government in which the non-socialist parties were also represented. The radical leaders Karl Liebknecht and Rosa Luxem-
burg were murdered. In 1918, the radical minority established the
Communist Party. In France, in 1920, the moderates left the party,
which became the Communist Party.

DEVIATIONS FROM THE MARXIAN POINT OF VIEW

After the First World War a new Europe emerges, different in
some essential respects from pre-war Europe. In Western Europe,
the governments are conservative or coalitions of conservatives
and democratic socialists and considerable social improvements are
obtained. The Versailles Peace Treaty, however, imposes on the
new German Republic a war indemnity which is much higher than
the economy can bear. A hyperinflation results and France occu-
pies the Ruhr area.

Socialists are in full power only in the Soviet Union – as the
result of the October revolution, which establishes the dictatorship
of the Communist Party. Democracy was an unknown concept in
Russia as a nation.

This constitutes a deviation from the Marxian thesis that socialism is the phase following capitalism. Socialism, according to that thesis, should have been attained first in the most advanced industrial countries, which at that time were the Western European countries. The leading position of England had already been taken over by Germany; but in Russia capitalism had only started and the country still had important feudal elements. German democracy also was new and vulnerable.

Another deviation occurred after the Second World War when the United States of America became the leading industrial country. In that country socialist ideas never had much influence, but democracy had.

COMMUNISTS AND VIOLENCE

Communists and communist-ruled nations used violence on many occasions; so for many observers their image is linked with violence. Part of the violence they used was, however, imposed by others. In the civil war after the October revolution the initiative was with the Whites. In the Second World War the initiative was Hitler's. The majority of the new types of weapons first used by the Soviet forces had been introduced earlier by the Americans. Once an armament race develops it becomes difficult to trace the originator.

As radicals the communists introduced violence into the class struggle autonomously, characterising it as an answer to the 'structural violence' of the police and occasionally the military, and used to maintain law and order. They also used violence in the class struggle when it was unnecessary. This gave an easy excuse for fascists to use it as well; and to the fascists violence was part of their philosophy of life.

The introduction of violence into class struggle and into the life philosophy of an internationalist movement was a regrettable step since it alienated the communists from groups – such as the Gandhians – which made remarkable contributions to decolonisation, in particular to the decolonisation of the largest colony of the world – India.

The strategy to introduce Lenin, a citizen of an almost feudal nation, where the hopelessness of the poor almost automatically leads to a radical attitude, into the world evolutionary process was a strategy of German conservatives and militarists. It forced world history into a roundabout process of unification with an enormous amount of human suffering – most of all in Russia – that could have been avoided.

CAPITALISM'S SUPPOSED AND ACTUAL ROLE

The broadminded view of Karl Marx is illustrated by his positive evaluation of the economic role of capitalism, namely, to raise productivity in an unprecedented way, creating the possibility of welfare of the masses of advanced countries. However, the necessary complement of a better distribution in his view is the task of socialism.

The role of capitalism in international relations, as Marx saw it, was biased. Since socialists were internationalists, their opponents were to be held responsible for the scourge of war. But this supposed negative role was considerably overestimated. It is the predecessor of capitalism, the feudal world, that is answerable for the origin of war: with nationalists and militarists. Capitalists, or rather managers of large enterprises, had mixed interests. To be sure, weapon producers are interested in war, but the production of weapons even today is far less than that of non-military goods and services. It is true that in the period of colonialism business profited from what nationalists and militarists had contributed to colonial structures. But colonialism is a phenomenon of the past. Today, business is strongly in favour of European integration, one of the strongest instruments against war.

MILITARISTS AND NATIONALISTS

As noted, present society is not only composed of employees and employers, or workers and capitalists. We still have remnants of previous social orders, among whom are militarists and nationalists. The same individual may be an employer and a nationalist, of course; for a limited number of functions only his nationalism may exert a strong influence on society. For functions in government and parliament in particular the nationalist or militarist preference for an individual may strongly affect society.

Militarism grew out of personal fights between knights in feudal societies, where they played a positive role in the sense of giving satisfaction to the fighters. With the growth of political territories individual fights were transformed into struggles between groups of soldiers, guided by officers. With the development of technology and the invention of explosives the nature of military activities changed again and also hit non-combatants. Another aspect developed as the consequence of conscription: individuals were forced to fight, even though they disliked it. The result of these processes and the destruction of the environment increasingly changed the character of military activities into criminal ones. An illustration of this is the way in which younger generations were sent into the hell of modern war by their politicians, so becoming the prisoners of older generations with a justification based on nationalist arguments. Nationalism is the idea that the citizens of one's own nation are better than the citizens of other nations. It is an irrational concept. If the quality of a nation's citizens is indicated by a figure, it is impossible for all nations considered this figure is higher than all other national quality figures.

The arguments used to justify a war have often been misleading. In essence, the Second World War was a war of ideologies; in Russia, between fascism and communism. The Russian soldiers were not told to fight in defence of communism, but the war was baptised by Stalin the 'great patriotic war', since the mass of his soldiers, being of rural origin, did not like communism. American soldiers, having a worker background, were not told to defend capitalism, but 'freedom' (whose?).

FASCISTS AND RACISTS

Ideologies other than nationalism are fascism and racism. Fascism is the extreme and openly violent form of capitalism, often combined with nationalism. Racism is comparable with nationalism but concentrates on racial differences instead of differences between nations. Racism is also close to religious fanaticism, known from the crusades, but reaching into the present conflicts between Shiites and other Moslems or Sikh extremists and Hindus. The criminal character of wars such as Hitler's aggression is the clearest of all, especially if the number of victims is considered. A recent example of young generations being in thrall to older generations is seen in Khomeini's hold over Iranian youngsters.

PRIORITIES BEFORE THE SECOND WORLD WAR

After this brief description of the groups that played a role in the sociological dynamics of the last century, we arrive at our main theme – the changing priorities of the parties involved. The change, we think, has occurred as a consequence of the mass production of nuclear weapons. Therefore, we start our argument with an account of priorities in the pre-nuclear era. Since the most important aim of international policy today is security and the establishment of a peaceful world, this also being one of the goals of socialist policy, we will concentrate on two important aims – the establishment of a socialist social order and the banning of war as a means of solving international conflicts.

Before the Second World War, the first concern of socialist parties was the establishment of a socialist society. The type of socialism – democratic or dictatorial, for instance – varied with different socialist parties. For non-socialist parties the corresponding aim was also another society, varying among the parties but essentially of a non-socialist order.

The intention of avoiding war was important but of a secondary nature. For most socialists that would be attained automatically once socialism had been established.

NUCLEAR 'WEAPONS' NOT THE ONLY ARGUMENT AGAINST WAR

The technological development of armaments made them increasingly murderous. A quantum jump in that development was, of course, the introduction of nuclear energy. This jump was so large that Professor Hannes Alfvén thinks we should not use the word weapon for nuclear 'weapons', but rather 'annihilators'. The creation of annihilation has the advantage that its use has become out of the question to rational individuals and governments. Such use would be senseless: any other activity would be made impossible and discussions about activities other than maintaining peace superfluous. So even for the most enthusiastic militarist war has lost its sense.

As a non-militarist I think that long before the invention of nuclear energy war had become a phenomenon to be banned. In my opinion, the trench war in Flanders in 1917 became so monstrous that war should have been banned. In other words, the need for other instruments to solve international conflicts existed long before the moment when nuclear energy was discovered. Be that as it may, the advantage of nuclear weapons is that even the most outspoken militarists are now forced to give up their hobbies, such as heroism, patriotism and so on. Their power has evaporated.

The remaining danger is the possibility of an accidental war. The unreliability of complicated electronic devices constitutes a mortgage on our civilisation and hence requires an alertness not yet organised.

TODAY'S HIGHEST PRIORITY

All this implies that a change in priorities has been imposed on all social reformers: communists, democratic socialists, conservatives, and all others, even ecologists. Priority number one has now become the non-use of annihilators, in Professor Alfvén's terminology, or the banning of war, in traditional terminology. Even the most fervent reformer of any type will have to cooperate with the organisers of peace, including their opponents, otherwise nothing remains to be reformed.

For the extremists on either side, communists and fascists, this constitutes a fundamental change not yet understood by many of them. It is largely due to the personal initiatives of Mikhail Gorbachev, the Secretary General of the Communist Party of the Soviet Union, that this change in priorities begins to be understood.

For many adherents to the traditional views, whether Marxist or anti-Marxist, the change in priorites will be hard to swallow. It may even be too difficult for them and this would create a dangerous situation. Members of peace movements and of peace research institutes may like to give thought to the assistance they could offer to such doctrinaire politicians so that they comprehend the 'new thinking'. It was already understood in Einstein's and Russell's time and has now been emphasised eloquently by Gorbachev.

COOPERATION WITH ALL WHO UNDERSTAND THE SITUATION

As a consequence of priority number one, mentioned in the previous section, and of the widespread lack of understanding of the situation, the cooperation of all who do comprehend the risk of a nuclear conflict is needed, even though there are many types of bourgeois politicians. The new thinking is bringing social democrats and communists more closely together, as illustrated by the contacts between Willy Brandt, Egon Bahr and Mikhail Gorbachev. It is tragic that such a roundabout way has been necessary for the conflicts of 1917 to be transformed into more mutual tolerance.

A few words should be added about the ecological threat. The improvement of the quality of the environment also constitutes an urgent aim and one of common world interest which requires a high priority, as well as world-wide cooperation. Unfortunately, this was not understood by politicians of most parties in and around 1970 and as a result 'Green' parties were established in several countries. This occurred in the German Federal Republic and, remarkably, it was necessary even in Sweden – which hosted an international congress on the subject in 1972. In this context the Dutch were surprisingly more advanced than the Swedes although most parties understood the necessity of a cleaner environment. Perhaps population density is the reason for this. (The outcome of the 1988 Swedish elections might have been adversely affected, but fortunately was not.) The environmental issue seems to be the best example to persuade all peoples of the world of the necessity of a reliable global decision-making structure. This may be the best expression of what we also need for security.

THE NEED FOR A RELIABLE GLOBAL DECISION-MAKING STRUCTURE

In order to satisfy what clearly has become the first priority of all international political activity, we need a reliably operating world decision-making structure. By 'reliably operating' we think of a system which consists of institutions with clearly defined competences for each of the aims chosen and with the power to have their decisions carried out. The system may be thought of as a reconstructed United Nations and the recent change in attitude *vis-à-vis* the UN of both superpowers indicates that their thinking also goes in that direction. Adapting our language to that assumption, what we need is a Security Council that operates 'reliably', a UN Environmental Programme (UNEP) with the power to have its decisions carried out, a World Bank which is empowered to decide how much each donor country must contribute, and an institution in the field of trade policy with similar competences in its area. This list is not complete.

Since the security aspect has first priority, the Security Council must not only ban war as a security instrument, but cooperate with the International Court of Justice as the competent institution to solve international conflicts.

More reforms will be necessary; one being a change in the voting system of virtually all UN institutions. Another will be the creation of some new institutions such as a world police force, a world treasury, and maybe more. An essential feature is that the system must be 'complete', leaving no loopholes. The world security structure must become as reliable as the internal security structure within a well-governed nation. In many respects the architects of a world decision-making structure may check their task by looking at how things are done at a lower level. Another check is to look at how serious integration operations are carried out at the Western European level. The authorities involved, in turn, should look at how their member nations are governed.

A reliably operating structure is probably also characterised by a clear hierarchy, comparable in some respects to well-run transnational enterprises.

SOCIAL REFORMS IN A SECURE WORLD

Once the first priority is taken care of, that is, once we live in a secure world, we can take up priority number two. For socialists of all kinds this will be the establishment of an equitable order. In several respects this aim can be achieved only with the aid of a class struggle, but one without the use of violence by people or institutions not in charge of security. In other words, violence may be used only by policemen. The class struggle is a struggle of arguments; arguments in parliament and arguments in court. Arguments may be supported by strikes or lock-outs.

The reforms should not stop at national frontiers. More important are those concerned with cooperative development. Inequality in incomes is much larger in the international community than in, for instance, the 'First World' – the world of industrialised market economies. If we wanted to reduce income inequality in all the market economies of the world (developed and underdeveloped), we would have to transfer 'development assistance' from the developed to the underdeveloped market economies of about 29 per cent of national income of the developed nations. It is clear that some discussion would be needed before an agreement on this subject could be attained.

Similarly, reduction of the protection of the United States, Japan and the European Community will also be a subject requiring a thorough debate.

One source from which part of such social reforms may be paid is the reduction in armament expenditures that becomes possible because the first priority has become security.

CONVERGENCE

In a secure world, the evolution of market economies and centrally planned economies will continue. Whereas around 1850, when Karl Marx developed his views on sociological dynamics and forecasted the change of capitalist nations – as they then existed – in the direction of socialism, the difference between capitalism and an (imagined) socialist order was very large indeed. In addition, the communist countries, as they evolved in the 1920s and developed up to 1980, showed an order which differed considerably from that in the West. But both systems are not immutable: from experience and comparison they learned how to improve the operation of their systems so as to attain their aims by better means or with less effort. They discovered that some of the means used by the other system contributed more to their own aims. They also learned that their aims gradually became less different and could be defined as maximum welfare distributed as equitably as possible. All this led to a converging movement of the two social systems.

Thus, the 'capitalist' market or order introduced a redistribution of incomes with the aid of social security institutions, income and wealth taxes, and the extension of education. The market economies also introduced a certain amount of planning, but not in such detail as in the centrally planned countries.

The latter learned that productivity is higher if producers own private means of production, for instance, private lots of land, and are permitted to sell them directly to potential consumers. They learned that part of their detailed central planning could be done better by the production units (factories, shops, etc.) themselves, and less in the centre.

Recently, this convergence of the two systems made further progress. In particular, in the fields of environmental policy and of international security they both came to understand the necessity of supranational decision-making, partly through the institutions of the United Nations. Both superpowers changed their attitude *vis-à-vis* the United Nations and paid the amounts they owed that organisation.

Convergence will enhance mutual understanding and make a reduction of armament possible. A first step has been made and a next step is being discussed. A reduction in the tremendous stockpiles of armaments will make available the means to improve welfare in communist countries and, even more urgently, in underdeveloped countries.

The nature of the socialist order as anticipated by Marx will prove to be less extreme than that which Stalin tried to establish, and even less extreme than Lenin's. This latter point may be a matter for future research and discussion – activities which will become possible once we have satisfied our first priority, a secure world. The recipes for the future could not in fact be given during Marx's lifetime and Russia was not the most advanced country at Lenin's time. But the most imaginative politician of the last few years is a Russian.

3 Limitations to the Interdependence of Systems

Gerhard Schwarz

INTRODUCTION

The theory of the Interdependence of political and economic systems is one of the most important 'dogmas' of ordoliberalism which considers the market economy as a willingly created – and by the visible hand of the state controlled – system (or order) and not as an automatic mechanism. Walter Eucken outlined this theory on several occasions,[1] claiming that knowledge of it was 'essential' for understanding present-day problems in the fields of economics, law and politics.[2] As a result, Eucken's thesis has almost become an integral part of general knowledge – at any rate as far as the German-speaking area is concerned, and at least as regards mainstream economics. It constitutes an essential analytic instrument in understanding the susceptibility to reform of Eastern systems, in judging socialisation trends in the West and within the context of convergence considerations.

The assertion that 'inevitable interdependences, inevitable reciprocal associations and dependences are to be found' between economic and political systems,[3] or that they proceed 'in inner harmony with one another'[4] would indeed, in its generality, appear to be very intelligible – although perhaps almost commonplace. However, closer examination reveals that although possibly correct in general terms,[5] this theory requires considerable differentiation. Evidence for the opinion that interdependence is not inevitable is also provided by Ota Sik's struggle for a *Third Way* between the planned and market economies – maintaining that a combination between planned and market economies, or better, between socialised systems of ownership and a market economy 'with a political system organised in a scientific and democratic manner'[6] is feasible. That is why we shall attempt here to set a number of limitations

32

as regards the concept of 'interdependence of systems', in particular with regard to the connection between a market economy and democracy – without, however, making any claim to completeness. These limitations are based on constant intellectual grappling with this topic, as well as on observations made in the First, Second and Third World.

THE DEFINITION OF ECONOMIC AND POLITICAL SYSTEMS

An answer to the question as to whether the interdependence of systems is really valid depends on how these systems are defined – for example, how the terms 'market economy' and 'democracy' are defined. This statement may at first seem commonplace, and yet the immediate plausibility of the 'interdependence of systems' probably has mainly to do with the fact that market economy and democracy are two very broad and flexible expressions. We could with the same assertion maintain that politics and economics are interrelated. For this reason the 'thesis of interdependence of systems does not say very much, when expressed in these general terms'.[7] Even Walter Eucken himself recognised this when he said there was not much point 'talking generally of the fact that politics determines economics while others retort that economics determine politics'.[8]

If we define the economic and political systems with the aid of two criteria, instead of simply as market on the one hand and democracy on the other hand, we realise that the interdependence is more complex than generally thought. Here we shall use the following basic criteria:[9]

- on the economic side
    the system of ownership
    the price formation and the degree of regulation associated with this

- on the political side
    the rule of law
    the electoral system

These criteria are not dichotomic but dimensional. We can

imagine one criterion plotted on a horizontal axis and the other criterion plotted on the vertical axis. We then get four possible quadrants for classifying the various economic systems and four quadrants as well to classify the political systems. In the economic field we could, for example, on the basis of the large share of the nationalised sector combined with relatively free price formation, classify France under Mitterrand[10] or Austria in a different quadrant from Switzerland, which combines greater freedom in price formation with the dominance of private ownership. The *Third Way* economic system with its collective, though not nationalised form of property belongs somewhere in the first group. Traditional, planned economies (with their far-reaching state control of the means of production and of prices) form a third category, while the fourth possible combination – price controls alongside largely private ownership – is probably most characteristic of temporary interventionist policies (e.g. price controls imposed to check wild inflation) in a fundamentally market oriented economy.

Concerning the political side, only in the classical Western democracies are both criteria largely fulfilled. In the Soviet Union, in contrast, they are not fulfilled. Hong Kong provides the best example of a country in the third category or quadrant, since although the rule of law is safeguarded to an exceptional degree there are no elections.[11] It would hardly be possible to find stable examples existing over a longer period which fit the criteria of the fourth combination– free elections in a democratic party system together with a despotic legal system. Perhaps the examples closest to this combination are states on the way to an authoritarian system – possibly one or other of the South American countries.

It is, of course, evident that the interdependence between political and economic systems is dissolved where there are so many different combination possibilities. Thus economic systems as largely market oriented as those of Hong Kong or Chile (under Pinochet) do not coincide with a particularly democratic political system – in one case there are no free elections while in the other the rule of law is also missing to some degree. On the other hand, mixed economies like those of France and Austria are clearly consistent with far-reaching individual rights and the rule of law.

THE NUMBER OF SYSTEMS LINKED TO ONE ANOTHER

A further limitation to the rigid concept of interdependence is that there are more social subsystems than just the economic and the political systems. That is why it is difficult to see why these two alone should be bound up with one another. Milton and Rose Friedman's rather slogan-like designation of 'freedom as one whole'[12] expresses the fact that there are a great variety of reciprocal effects which exist between the fields of politics, economics and society, not just dependences and links between the political and economic systems.

If one takes into account the social and cultural fields in their widest sense, it becomes particularly clear that a judgement on interdependence must differ greatly from one country to another. Thus the French are far better than the Germans at being both Étatists and market economists at the same time, because there are many things that they do not take nearly as seriously as the Germans do. The fact that the thesis on interdependence on systems is linked principally with German-speaking economists – the Ordoliberals who have already been mentioned, or F.A. von Hayek's famous book dating back to 1944[13] – may well be indicative here. Living in and with contradictions would seem to be more than just imaginable and practicable to people from the Mediterranean cultural area, it would even seem to hold a certain attraction. Regarding a strong, interventionist state as sensible, while at the same time constantly endeavouring to escape its encroachment, hardly seems to constitute a contradiction in the Mediterranean countries, or at any rate it would seem to be a bearable one.[14]

THE CLOSENESS OF INTERDEPENDENCE

If the number of theoretically possible combinations between different versions of political and economic systems is not four but sixteen, and only two of these combinations are 'pure' or thoroughly consistent combinations; if reality confronts us with numerous mixed systems and the reciprocal effects are also additionally complicated by taking cultural components into account, we may easily assume that in general interdependence is 'relatively loose' and that it only excludes 'extreme combinations',[15] at the very most. At any rate, it can hardly be an indissoluble marriage. A similar idea can also be found in the writings of Jöhr as regards the interdependence between the individual elements of the socialist economic system, where it is held that this linkage is only valid under complete or 100 per cent adherence, but not under half or three-quarter adherence. Thus complete management of all production by a central authority would make private owner-ship of the means of production illusory, even if this were retained in formal terms. In the case of mixed forms, however, central management might well be more advanced than the socialisation of ownership, and vice versa.[16]

THE RECIPROCAL NATURE OF INTERDEPENDENCE

The relationship between the market economy and democracy must not necessarily be in equilibrium. The combination of the two systems may be a product of match-making where one area is clearly dominant, i.e. the mutual connection need not be logically symmetrical. The early fathers of the ordoliberal school examined this question repeatedly.[17]

Thus we would need to examine the question as to how the four criteria of a liberal system – free elections and the rule of law, private ownership and the market economy – are related to one another. Based on experience in South-East Asia, Green-wood[18] concludes that the rule of law is more important than free elections if a country is to be economically successful, and that private ownership is more important than the market economy. In our view, private ownership is also dominant in so far as interventionist economics encounter difficulties and can scarcely be maintained over a longer period in places where private ownership is safeguarded. For this reason private ownership is likely to be one of the best institutional guarantees of a free market. Thus renouncing this guarantee represents a scarcely justifiable risk – an opinion which probably goes against the ideas embodied in the *Third Way* – and in particular in cases where the market economy is seen as instrumental in overcoming totalitarian, although not necessarily authoritarian,[19] regimes.

As far as the relationship between the market economy – seen as a system entailing private ownership and free price formation – and democracy (in the sense of both the rule of law and free elections) is concerned, a great number of authors – like Roepke and Usher,[20] for example – believe that the market economy is a necessary but not sufficient condition for democracy. After all, in recent times there have scarcely been any examples of democracies which were not at the same time market economies, while market economies could certainly be located (e.g. in South-East Asia) where structures were not very democratic. On the other hand, democracy – and in particular its rule of law aspect – is a sufficient condition for the market economy. It would be difficult to imagine a 100 per cent democracy in combination with a 100 per cent planned economy.

However – as opposed to Josef Schumpeter's view,[21] for example – the socialist economic system would appear to be a sufficient but not a necessary prerequisite for an authoritarian political system. That means that whenever the economic system is socialist to an extreme degree, the political system is organised in a correspondingly non-liberal manner, but democracy deficits appear not only when the economic system is socialist. As early as Hayek, attention was drawn to this political and cultural determination of a socialist economy. 'However Hayek is not only taking a stand against Schumpeter's thesis on indetermination, he is also opposing the theory of a middle or Third Way argued by Neoliberals in particular.'[22]

THE PROPORTIONALITY OF INTERDEPENDENCE

Generally, the interdependence of systems is seen as a one-way street, a positive feedback, in the sense that market economy and democracy harmonise with one another, that they are mutually advantageous. However, 'reverse proportionalities', i.e. counteracting movements – which are also interdependencies, of course – are banished from the scene, despite the fact that the famous Hayek polemic is based on precisely this point. What is meant here is the tendency of democracies to move towards a constant decline in the share of individual control over the national income. In practically all OECD countries the inflation in claims combined with democracy has led to a socialisation of the economy, to a steady increase in the share of taxation and social security contributions and a fall in individual economic powers of control. This trend may be seen as being insidious, in so far as political majorities were found for each individual case – often differing from case to case – while it is unlikely that a majority would have accepted the final result of this continuing process.[23]

The reason for this becomes apparent when we observe the compromising attitude of most political constitutions in the West which give rise to a fatal, vicious circle of claims on the State. The socialisation trend, therefore, has something to do with the system of free elections rather than with the rule of law. Thus, although democracy may in principle be a sufficient condition for the market economy, the democratic system by no means guarantees less state, free, deregulated markets, lower taxes and the safeguarding of private ownership rights. Indeed, it clearly has a built-in self-destruction mechanism. The recognition that economic freedom will be increasingly restricted is by no means new – previously, Montesquieu and de Tocqueville[24] warned of the dangers of unlimited democracy, and in the last century the *Kathedersozialist* Adolph Wagner formulated his law on growing state activities.

The fatal expression 'justice' with its emotive attraction, vagueness and suitability for use as an argument for interventions against the market has proved particularly erosive in this context. It is one of the most important roots of a rampant social state which ultimately boils down to collective self-destruction. The belief that distributive justice can be attained without the need to lose any freedom or efficiency is widespread in all democratic societies.

We may approach the tension between democracy and market economy from yet another angle. Bernholz[25] poses the question as to whether a system of low taxes, a balanced budget and the financing of public services by means of user charges, as it exists in Hong Kong, could be attained in a democracy. His answer is negative. The rather surprising thesis, that a lack of democracy (in the sense of free elections) is precisely the condition which makes a market economy possible, or at least favours this kind of economic system, is the conclusion to this. The argument – that the colonial power of Great Britain is, after all, a democracy – loses the force of its conviction when we consider that the classic example of economic system reform – the currency reform and the foundation of a social market economy in Germany after the Second World War – would scarcely have been possible without the dictator-like power basis of a man like Ludwig Erhard. Thus it would appear that more democracy can in particular situations lead to less market economy, and less democracy can make more market economy possible.

THE TIME DIMENSION OF INTERDEPENDENCE

Up to now we have largely treated the interdependence of systems statically instead of dynamically. And yet the German currency reform is a particularly good example of the importance of the dynamic aspect of interdependence. Although the power which Erhard derived from the occupation forces was the clear prerequisite for the reform in the year 1948, democracy and the market economy certainly belonged together in the period which followed. Thus we would need to examine interdependences during the auspicious hours when fundamental reforms take place, as well as in the normal run of economic policies.

We touched on a further dynamic aspect of interdependence within the context of socialisation trends. Despite the fact that the market economy and democracy suit one another in a purely static sense, mechanisms exist which destroy the parallelism encountered at a particular moment in time. They may lead to a drifting apart of the political and economic systems. This 'reverse interdependence' would appear to exist between the market economy and democracy (or more precisely, the free election of rulers) in particular, but not between the planned economy and totalitarianism.

Finally, the length of the period under observation is also of relevance when considering the validity of interdependence of systems. The longer one sets the period of observation, the more one gains the impression that despite all limitations an interdependence of systems really does exist. Market economies may well survive over the short term without too much democracy, and yet over time economic freedom and private ownership would have a destructive effect on an authoritarian system, even more so on a totalitarian political system. In the reverse direction, socialisation trends in the economy are likely to undermine a free democratic system over time. Thus Hayek's thesis of the *Road to Serfdom* – and thus also the interdependence of systems – would appear to be valid only in the long term.

CONCLUSIONS

The assertion of 'interdependence of systems' does not gain any relevance until we define it precisely. But this also makes it more problematic. At any rate, there are many exceptions to interdependence in reality, and many limitations have to be made. And yet the thesis of interdependence may still claim a certain validity. It holds mainly in the long run and where the combinations are relatively extreme – whereas in reality we are confronted only with mixed forms. In addition, interdependence also has to take social aspects into account, not only economics and politics. Even if we set all these limitations interdependence still remains fairly loose. Finally, opposing forces exist – democracy, in particular – which undermine interdependence and work against it.

Notes

1. Compare Walter Eucken, *Die Grundlagen der Nationalökonomie*, 7th edn (Berlin/Göttingen/Heidelberg: Springer, 1959) and Walter Eucken, *Grundsätze der Wirtschaftspolitik*, shortened edn (Hamburg: Rowohlt, 1959).
2. Eucken, *Grundsätze*, p. 126.
3. Alexander Rüstow, *Rede und Antwort* (Ludwigsburg: Martin Hoch, 1963), p. 221.
4. Alfred Müller-Armack, 'Stil und Ordnung der sozialen Marktwirtschaft', in A. Müller-Armack, *Wirtschaftsordnung und Wirtschaftspolitik* (Berne: Haupt, 1976), p. 238.
5. Compare Walter Adolf Jöhr/Gerhard Schwarz, 'Wirtschaft und Politik II: Ursachen und Gestaltungsprobleme', in *Handwörterbuch der Wirtschaftswissenschaft* (Stuttgart/New York/Tübingen/Göttingen/Zürich: Fischer/Mohr/Vandenhoeck & Ruprecht, 1980), vol. 9, pp. 12 et seq, in particular p. 30.
6. Ota Sik, *Demokratische und sozialistische Plan- und Marktwirtschaft* (Zürich, Arche, 1971), p. 9.
7. Henner Kleinewefers, *Grundzüge einer verallgemeinerten Wirtschaftsordnungstheorie* (Tübingen: Mohr, 1988), p. 68.
8. Eucken, *Grundsätze*, p. 126.
9. This classification is based on a speech made by John Greenwood at the Mont Pelèrin Society Annual Conference 1988 in Tokyo and Kyoto and entitled, 'Freedom and Prosperity in the East and the West: The Equation with Capitalism and Socialism'.
10. Compare Gerhard Schwarz, 'Liberale Böe oder Brise: Wie dauerhaft ist Frankreichs wirtschaftspolitische Wende?', in *Aussenwirtschaft* (Grüsch: Ruegger) 36. Jg. Heft II, Diessenhofen 1983, S. 141 ff.

11. Compare *Gerhard* Schwarz, 'Far Eastern Lessons for the First and Third Worlds', in *Swiss Review of World Affairs* (Zürich: NZZ) vol. 38, no. 9, December 1988, pp. 22–3.
12. Milton and Rose Friedman, *Free to Choose* (New York: Harcourt Brace Jovanovich, 1980), p. 69.
13. Friedrich August von Hayek, *Der Weg zur Knechtschaft* (Munich: DTV, 1976).
14. Compare François Bilger, 'Frankreich vor der ordnungspolitischen Wende? Die wirtschaftspolitischen Wahlprogramme der französischen Parteien', in *Ordo* (Stuttgart/New York: Fischer, 1986) Band 37, S. 11.
15. Kleinewefers, *Grundzüge*, p. 68.
16. Compare Walter Adolf Jöhr, *Ist ein freiheitlicher Sozialismus möglich?* (Berne: Francke, 1948), p. 15.
17. Compare the dispute with Benedetto Croce, in Wilhelm Röpke, *Civitas Humana – Grundfragen der Gesellschafts- und Wirtschaftsreform*, 4th edn (Berne/Stuttgart: Haupt, 1979), pp. 50–1, 91–2.
18. Compare Greenwood, 'Freedom and Prosperity in the East and the West'.
19. On this differentiation compare Peter L. Berger, *The Capitalist Revolution* (New York: Wildwood House, 1986), pp. 83–4.
20. Compare Röpke, *Grundfragen*, p. 51, and Dan Usher, *The Economic Prerequisite of Democracy* (New York: Campus, 1981), p. 6.
21. Compare Joseph A. Schumpeter, *Capitalism, Socialism and Democracy* (New York: Harper, 1942).
22. Walter Adolf Jöhr, 'Wirtschaft und Politik I: Lehrgeschichtlicher Ueberblick', in *Handwörterbuch der Wirtschaftswissenschaft* (Stuttgart/New York/Tübingen/Göttingen/Zürich: Fischer/Mohr/Vandenhoeck & Ruprecht, 1980), vol. 9, p. 8.
23. Compare Gerhard Schwarz, 'Die schleichende Einengung von Freiräumen', in G. Schwarz, (ed.), *Wo Regeln bremsen – Deregulierung und Privatisierung im Vormarsch* (Zürich: NZZ, 1988), pp. 127 et seq.
24. Compare also Jean-Francois Revel, *So enden die Demokratien*, 4th edn (Munich/Zürich: Piper, 1986), S. 20 ff.
25. Compare Peter Bernholz, 'Political–Economic Systems as Preconditions for Freedom and Prosperity', paper presented at the Mont Pelèrin Society Annual Conference in Tokyo and Kyoto.

References

Berger, P.L. (1986) *The Capitalist Revolution* (New York: Wildwood House).

Bernholz, P. (1988) 'Political–Economic Systems as Preconditions for Freedom and Prosperity', paper presented at the Mont Pelèrin Society Annual Conference in Tokyo and Kyoto.

Bilger, F. (1986) Frankreich vor der ordnungspolitischen Wende? Die wirtschaftspolitischen Wahlprogramme der französischen Parteien', in *Ordo* (Stuttgart/New York: Fischer), Band 37, pp. 3 et seq.

Eucken, W. (1959) *Die Grundlagen der Nationalökonomie*, 7th edn (Berlin/Göttingen/Heidelberg: Springer).

Eucken, W. (1959) *Grundsätze der Wirtschaftspolitik*, shortened edn (Hamburg: Rowohlt).

Friedman, M. and R. Friedman (1980) *Free to Choose* (New York: Harcourt Brace Jovanovich).

Greenwood, J. (1988) 'Freedom and Prosperity in the East and the West: The Equation with Capitalism and Socialism', paper presented at the Mont Pèlerin Society Annual Conference in Tokyo and Kyoto.

Hayek, F.A. von (1976) *Der Weg zur Knechtschaft* (Munich: DTV).

Jöhr, W.A. (1948) *Ist ein freiheitlicher Sozialismus möglich?* (Berne: Francke).

Jöhr, W.A. (1980) 'Wirtschaft und Politik I: Lehrgeschichtlicher Ueberblick', in *Handwörterbuch der Wirtschaftswissenschaft* (Stuttgart/New York/Tübingen/Göttingen/Zürich: Fischer/Mohr/Vandenhoeck & Ruprecht), vol. 9, pp. 1 et seq.

Jöhr, W.A. and G. Schwarz (1980), 'Wirtschaft und Politik II: Ursachen und Gestaltungsprobleme', in *Handwörterbuch der Wirtschaftswissenschaften* (Stuttgart/New York/Tübingen/Göttingen/Zürich: Fischer/Mohr/Vandenhoeck & Ruprecht), vol. 9, pp. 12 et seq.

Kleinewefers, H. (1988) *Grundzüge einer verallgemeinerten Wirtschaftsordnungstheorie*, (Tübingen: Mohr).

Müller-Armack, A. (1976) 'Stil und Ordnung der sozialen Marktwirtschaft', in A. Müller-Armack, *Wirtschaftsordnung und Wirtschaftspolitik*, (Berne: Haupt).

Revel, J.-F. (1986), *So enden die Demokratien*, 4th edn (München/Zürich: Piper).

Röpke, W. (1979) *Civitas Humana – Grundfragen der Gesellschafts und Wirtschaftsreform*, 4th edn (Berne/Stuttgart: Haupt).

Rüstow, A. (1963) *Rede und Antwort* (Ludwigsburg: Martin Hoch).

Schumpeter, J.A. (1942) *Capitalism, Socialism and Democracy* (New York: Harper).

Schwarz, G. (1983) 'Liberale Böe oder Brise: Wie dauerhaft ist Frankreichs wirtschaftspolitische Wende?' in *Aussenwirtschaft* (Grüsch: Ruegger) 36. Jg. Heft II, Diessenhofen, pp. 141 et seq.

Schwarz, G. (1988) 'Die schleichende Einengung von Freiräumen', in G. Schwarz (ed.), *Wo Regeln bremsen – Deregulierung und Privatisierung im Vormarsch* (Zürich: NZZ), pp. 127 et seq.

Schwarz, G. (1988) 'Far Eastern Lessons for the First and Third Worlds', in *Swiss Review of World Affairs* (Zürich: NZZ), vol. 38, no. 9, December, pp. 22–3.

Sik, O. (1971) *Demokratische und sozialistische Plan- und Marktwirtschaft* (Zürich: Arche).

Usher, D. (1981) *The Economic Prerequisite of Democracy* (New York) p. 6.

4 Economics, Environment and the Faustian Imperative

Hans Christoph Binswanger, Malte Faber and Reiner Manstetten*

We want (a) to discuss new dimensions which should be taken up by economic theory and (b) to show how difficult it is to find a consensus and to develop a common approach to deal with economic and environmental problems. (c) Finally, we wish to take a fresh view on modern economies by interpreting Goethe's *Faust*.

For our representation we use typifications of an economist and an environmentalist which are in some respect one-sided. Both persons of our debate, though they often do not understand each other, may be present within one person, even within each of the authors. For this reason, no economist and no environmentalist should identify himself with the respective typification. In addition, we will introduce as *personae dramatis* a commentator, and later a writer.

COMMENTATOR: An economist's and an environmentalist's view differ so much in so many essential aspects that we cannot expect them to have a true dialogue. This will become apparent when comparing their answers to the question: what is economic activity?

Let us first hear the Economist about the subject of his science.

ECONOMIST: I will begin my statement with an often used definition of economics:

The economist studies the disposal of scarce means. He is interested in the way different degrees of scarcity of different goods

* We are grateful to Peter Michaelis, John Proops, Matthias Ruth, Armin Schmutzler and Gerhard Wagenhals for helpful comments.

give rise to different ratios of valuation between them, and he is interested in the way in which changes in conditions of scarcity, whether coming from changes in ends or changes in means – from the demand side or the supply side – affect these ratios. Economics is the science which studies human behaviour between ends and scarce means which have alternative uses. (Robbins, 1932, p. 15)

We see that by focusing one's attention on 'different ratios of valuation' between scarce goods dependent on 'different degrees of scarcity', Robbins emphasises the choice aspect, and thus determines human behaviour as a main corner-stone of economics. The human behaviour expresses itself as a relationship between two sides: ends and scarce means. The first side of this relationship refers to interests and wishes of individuals which are expressed in their preferences. The second side refers to material aspects of economics: primary factors of production such as land, natural resources and energy expressed in the form of labour. The transformation of these primary factors into secondary factors of production yields buildings, capital goods, etc. The information concerning the technology, the stocks of primary and capital goods, the preferences as well as the institutions are contained in the so-called boundary conditions of an economic problem. These boundary conditions contain also all natural data, in particular all stocks of resources and all necessary environmental parameters. In general, we assume that all the information of the boundary conditions is given. I shall comment on three characteristics of my approach.

(i) We economists mainly consider the relationship between human ends and scarce means but take these as given. If the boundary conditions are given we can prove with mathematical methods, i.e. with the approach of general equilibrium theory, that solutions to the allocation problem of scarce resources exist and that under certain assumptions these are even Pareto-optimal (Debreu, 1959). In simple words, we can offer a good, and in some sense even optimal, solution for the fulfilment of the wishes of individuals.

(ii) If the boundary conditions change then, by using methods of comparative statics, our main method of analysis, a new solution with the same characteristic as above, can be found relatively easily. However, comparative statics does not ask why and in which way these changes occur. As soon as the changes themselves are no longer regarded as given exogenously, but are also taken into the analysis, the tractability of such dynamic solutions of the allocation problem becomes intrinsically much more complicated, and even with advanced methods of mathematics it can often not be found. Furthermore, even if such a solution exists, the characteristics of being a good solution, such as Pareto-optimality and stability, cannot be expected in many cases. These results show that we have good reasons to leave the analysis of changes of the boundary conditions outside the realm of our analysis.

(iii) Although we mainly try to explain what is and not what should be, our analysis is based on value judgements. Important values are (cf. e.g. Bernholz and Breyer, 1984, pp. 21–5): (1) freedom, (2) justice, (3) security, (4) efficiency in production and consumption (Pareto-optimality). I believe that these values can best be achieved in a market-oriented system.

COMMENTATOR: How does our environmentalist perceive the question: what is an economic activity?

ENVIRONMENTALIST: The Economist's language is rather foreign to me. Since I am a layman you cannot expect me to deliver a professional answer. Instead I state certain criteria which a definition has to fulfil.

In contrast to the economist my point of departure is not the intentions and wishes of the individuals, but my interest in all kinds of life, of which human life is just one kind. Although I respect human life as an important factor and therefore also care for their living conditions, I am just as interested in nature, i.e. in the conservation of natural resources and the biosphere, the development of the numbers of species and plants, as well as of the quality of soil, water and air. All this is changed by economic activities. Therefore, I am mainly concerned with the consequences of economic activities for the environment at large. Hence, while the Economist takes the natural conditions, which he calls boundary conditions, as given, my main concern is the way in which these conditions are changed by economic activity. These neglected changes are often of an irreversible nature, as an analysis based on an entropy approach (Georgescu-Roegen, 1971) clearly shows.

COMMENTATOR: Having heard how the Economist and the Environmentalist view the economy, we now want to find out how each of them evaluates the states of both the national and the world-wide economies today.

ECONOMIST: Though I see certain deficiencies in the realisation of the values I mentioned above at a world-wide level, I generally believe that the industrialised countries have made considerable progress in the realisation of these aims and should, in principle, just continue the presently chosen path. In this way, one of the most important values, freedom, can best be secured and even widened; the very existence of freedom even contributes essentially to the other values. I see freedom as a prerequisite for the solution of environmental and resource problems, because it leaves space for individual creativity and the realisation of new ideas.

ENVIRONMENTALIST: My most important value is not individual freedom but the conservation of nature. However, the Economist does not seem to be concerned with the continuing extinction of species and plants and the destruction of habitats. I therefore doubt that he really believes security to be an important value. In my eyes, security exists only if it extends not only to human beings but to all species and plants. The way that economies are run at present reduces security. This holds not only for the species and plants, but also for the human species. And if this is the case, the other values of the economist become meaningless.

Furthermore, it is individual freedom that has led to the present deplorable state of the environment. For freedom, which allows one to pursue one's own interests, neither takes care of the living conditions of other species nor of future generations of humankind. I therefore question the whole market system. Hence, I even maintain that all people, and in particular the economists who contribute to the functioning of modern economies, are jointly responsible for the devastating consequences.

Many of us even go so far as to conclude that there has to be a radical reduction in the level of consumption, and perhaps also a drastic reduction of individual freedom (Hannon, 1985, p. 330). If, however, people learn to live in decentralised and self-sustaining communities, which are in harmony with nature, it may be possible that there is even more freedom (Seymour, 1980).

COMMENTATOR: Let me highlight the asymmetry between the two views. While the ends of the individuals are at the centre of the optimisation process for an economist, and nature is included in the boundary conditions, the salvation of nature is at the centre of the intentions and actions of an environmentalist, and natural needs (food, clothing, housing) and basic needs (such as health sanitary installations, education) are included in the boundary conditions.

(i) The difference in values between our two protagonists is also revealed in the perspectives of time which they employ. Since the boundary conditions often change, the Economist's method, comparative statics, only allows for a rather short-time horizon. This contrasts with the length of time horizon employed by environmentalists, which comprises the time-span of generations.

Hence the Economist is concerned with short-run restrictions while the Environmentalist is interested in long-run considerations. Irreversibilities are therefore little recognised by economists, a lacuna which was also noted by Samuelson (1983, p. 36): 'In theoretical economics there is no "irreversibility" concept which is one reason why Georgescu-Roegen (1971) is critical of conventional economics.' The occurrence of an irreversibility is a qualitative change in the boundary conditions (Faber, Niemes and Stephan, 1987). In addition, the full impact of this alteration can, in general, be comprehended only within a long time horizon. This explains why the Environmentalist is so much concerned with irreversibilities.

(ii) Our protagonists use different conceptualisations and have different kinds of knowledge.

The Economist, as a representative of one discipline, has precise concepts and elaborate methods. This enables him to develop an adequate solution with his box of tools once a problem is clearly formulated within his range of study. However, this approach has two major difficulties. (a) It occurs that problems within the range of economics, but which are difficult to incorporate into economic analysis, such as the long-run effects of economic activities on the environment, fall completely out of his sight or are regarded too difficult to analyse. As a prisoner of his own conceptualisation he may not understand at all where the problem has to be located. (b) Difficulties occur also with those problems for which his tools partly suffice, but partly do not. This is so because the economist is unable to formulate with the concepts of his own discipline the difference between those questions he is capable of analysing and those he is not; to this end he would need a meta-language. Hence he may tend to ignore important aspects of certain problems and offer only one-sided solutions. Environmental issues often belong to this kind of problem.

The Environmentalist cannot be attached uniquely to one particular discipline but he may be found eventually in all disciplines; not seldom does he mix colloquial language with scientific language. In general, such an approach does not enable him to develop clear solutions. Nevertheless, his questions and his answers offer helpful intuitive insights. His strength is to make others aware of important problems which do not occur within the range of one particular discipline.

We see that our protagonists have two different kinds of objects of study and speak two different languages. We have not yet seen how a translation may be achieved and how these two different objects of study might be integrated. We cannot expect that we can achieve this great task in our discussion. But it will be helpful to hear what each of them proposes as a means to solve the most urgent environmental problems.

ECONOMIST: I do not agree with the commentator's statement that our professional tools are not sufficient to solve environmental problems. These problems occur because of a combination of external effects and the problem of the supply of public goods. As Solow (1973, pp. 49–50) stated:

> Excessive pollution happens because of an important flaw in the price system. Factories, power plants, municipal sewers, drivers of cars, strip-miners of coal and deep-miners of coal and all sorts of generators of waste are allowed to dump the waste into the environment, into the atmosphere and into running water and the oceans, without paying the full cost of what they do. No wonder they do too much. So would you, and so would I. In fact, we actually do – directly as drivers of cars, indirectly as we buy some products at a price which is lower than it ought to be because the producer is not required to pay for using the environment to carry away his wastes, and even more indirectly as we buy things that are made with things that pollute the environment.

A solution to this important flaw in the price system is the introduction of market prices for environmental goods. If these prices can be determined appropriately by a state agency, the market system will deliver a Pareto-optimal solution.

This implies that as a new value the 'conservation of nature' has to be additionally considered. For this purpose the boundary conditions of the market economy have to be newly defined.

I insist, however, that freedom is the most important prerequisite for the solution of environmental problems; freedom gives space for individual creativity and the competition of the market will select the best clean technologies: 'If history offers any guide, then, in the developed part of the world at least, the accumulation of technological knowledge will probably make our great-grandchildren better off than we are, even if we make no great effort in that direction' (ibid., p. 42).

ENVIRONMENTALIST: (1) To give nature, e.g. a dying species, a price is as cynical as to give a price to human beings. (2) Why did it take such a long time for the economists to become aware of such an 'important flaw' in the price system and to react to it? (3) A price for water, for example, implies that it is possible to pollute water to a certain extent. Many environmentalists hold the following view: 'Barry Commoner and other ecological writers [have] emphasised the possibly serious, if unpredictable, hazards of *any* discharges' (Roberts, 1974, p. 21). Hence discharges should be avoided altogether. (4) History has provided ample evidence that the individualistic dynamics, which are given so much space by the market system, lead inherently to ecological damage.

Therefore, I conclude that even under optimal circumstances all the alterations proposed by the Economist can only lead to a partial repair of the ecological system; changes of these kinds do not guarantee that no fatal damage occurs. The price system is therefore in no way suitable for the solution of the environmental problem.

ECONOMIST: Your kind of criticism leads either to no solution at all or to puristic solutions which cannot be realised. Instead of taking up every point of your critique I shall describe the consequences of such a puristic solution. In 1972, the American Congress enacted a very ambitious water law, the Clean Water Act (CWA) of 1972. Roberts (1974, pp. 18–21) (cf. also Brown and Johnson, 1982, p. 949, fn 72) showed that the environmental lobby groups had the decisive influence on its drafting. The intention of the CWA was to prohibit every discharge of pollution by 1985 (Roberts, 1974, p. 11).

This aim was to be achieved in two stages: 'By July 1, 1977 everyone was to employ "the best practicable technology"; by July 1, 1983 this was to be upgraded to "the best technology achievable" as determined by the Administrator' (Roberts, 1972, p. 11). Brown and Johnson (1984, p. 952) characterise the Act as follows:

> First, it emphasises as its goal the total ban of discharges of wastes into public waters instead of applying cost-benefit principles which would proscribe only those dischargers of waste which are not cost-justified for a particular body of water, considering the alternative uses for those waters and their assimilative capacity. Second, the US system relies heavily on the threat of punishment, i.e. fines and/or imprisonment, rather than on economic incentives to induce industries, municipalities, and other waste dischargers to reduce the pollutants they discharge into public waters.

The latter argument was also emphasised by Roberts (1974, p. 12): 'One of the striking features of the law is its starkly anti-economic viewpoint. There is to be no case by case balancing of cost and benefits, no attempt at "fine tuning" the process of resource allocation . . . Technology alone will be the constraint.'

Thus 'a technical optimism was combined with an institutional pessimism' (ibid., p. 21). It expresses the environmentalists' hope to solve environmental problems with technical means. This led to a curious coincidence of the environmentalists' interests with those of the engineers and the heavy construction industry, because the CWA

> offered a whole new range of potential projects, which were in short supply in many areas where all the relevant rivers had long since been damned. The highway program was beginning to run down and the pressure for finding new things for that [the heavy construction] industry to build was obvious, especially in an election year. (ibid., p. 20)

Roberts (1974, p. 13; see also Brown and Johnson, 1984, p. 952) pointed out:

Thus there is no guarantee under the 1972 Act that economies of scale would be exhausted, that methods which act directly on the environment will be employed, that variations in the ecosystem will be responded to, that costs will be minimised or benefits maximised. Instead enforcement loopholes are to be tightened and all variety and flexibility squeezed out of the system.

An actual realisation of the enforcement of the no-discharge condition would have implied a far-reaching restructuring of the American economy with all those consequences experienced after the oil price shock in 1973, but on a much larger scale.

For all these reasons it turned out that it was impossible to enforce the no-discharge approach: 'It was not surprising that the 1977 Amendments of the FWPCA altered the emphasis of the federal program in the direction of the receiving water standards approach and away from the no-waste-discharge principle' (ibid). The water legislation in the USA during the seventies was a failure measured by the goals formulated in the CWA of 1972 (OECD, 1987, p. 54).

Thus it turned out that the complete success of the environmentalist lobby in the legislation was a pyrrhic victory, given their ultimate aim of no pollution of water. In contrast to the USA, the Federal Republic of Germany used market incentives, in the form of charges, in their water legislation in 1976. While in the USA the percentage of the waste water treatment plants on a biological or chemical basis increased from 44 per cent in 1976 to 53 per cent in 1980 and to 59 per cent in 1984, in the FRG it increased from 56.4 per cent in 1975 to 71.6 per cent in 1980 and to 79 per cent in 1983 (cf. OECD, 1987, pp. 53–4). Not only are the 59 per cent in 1984 in the USA a far cry away from the strived for 100 per cent in 1985, but the Waste Water Charge Law in the FRG has had, and still has, a much greater effect, since at the beginning of the 1990s the level will be around 90 per cent. This shows the superiority of economic incentives over attempts to regulate by standards.

COMMENTATOR: I see growing displeasure in the face of our Environmentalist. He is certainly eager to contradict the Economist. Since the writer, however, has listened silently up to now, I propose to ask him if he can mediate between the two parties.

WRITER: Hearing your differing viewpoints I see us all playing a drama. One might call it 'the drama of modern man and nature'. We, the actors in this drama, have some influence on how the play will end. But apparently, we do not know the roles we play in this drama, and although we all attempt to contribute to a happy outcome it might be that we end in tragedy.

It is for just this reason that we should try to understand which roles we play in this drama of modern man and nature before we decide how to behave and which actions to pursue. As I perceive it, Goethe dealt with these fundamental problems in a truly visionary way in his drama *Faust*. Faust is the prototype of modern man. He employs the forces and potentialities of nature to pursue his aim to find, using a phrase of Keynes (1930, p. 373), 'economic bliss'. Let me first point out some important traits of Faust and then explain their relevance to your arguments concerning the economy and the environment.

Not believing in God and eternal life, Faust suffers from a present that never offers real satisfaction; he longs to experience a moment in which he could say: 'Tarry . . . so fair you art!' Finding this moment would mean for Faust boundless fulfilment of all his wishes at once and therefore complete happiness and – by seemingly abandoning the course of time – he would feel like a god. But neither philosophy nor theology, neither love or the scientific dream of making an artificial man, nor the timeless beauty of art grant him this moment, although Faust in his striving does not only utilise all his own forces but also all those of hell, represented by Mephisto. Finally, however, it seems that Faust finds this moment with Mephisto's help, in a *vision which is based on economic and technical activity*.

Since this vision is of central importance for understanding the dynamics of modern economies, I shall describe it briefly. Faust, being half a prince and half an entrepreneur (paper money has been invented by Mephisto!), has drained and cultivated an infertile stretch of coast, and protected it against the sea by a complicated system of dykes. Only one marsh is left which threatens the new land. While calling for labourers to drain this marsh, Faust has the vision that he opens 'room for millions there' who will follow his way of life: fighting against an 'aimless' nature (symbolised by the sea with its tides) day by day, they will progressively change the earth into a paradise and live in liberty: 'For liberty, as life, alone deserveth/ He daily must conquer it'. This vision implies that mankind can be, that in a certain sense, the creator of his living space, in which the natural environment and the forces of nature are made more and more usable for human purposes. This creativity of modern man is based on technical and economic activity. On the one hand, this vision is fascinating: unlike all other periods, modern man seems to have the possibility of being the creator of his own world, of his own freedom and happiness, independent from the will and the plans of a transcendent god. The economy as a creation of mankind

> exercises a tremendous fascination. It is the fascination of infinite growth, of eternal progress. The economy thus gains the transcendental, i.e. across the border character, which the human beings sought in religion in earlier times. Not the belief, but economic activity opens man the outlook to infinity. (Binswanger, 1985, p. 61.)

A great part of modern thought is pervaded with this kind of fascination; thus for example Keynes (1963, p. 373) wrote:

> The pace at which we can reach our *destination* of economic *bliss* will be governed by four things – *our power* to control population, *our determination* to avoid wars and civil dissensions, and *our willingness* to entrust science to the direction of those matters which are properly the concern of science, and the rate of accumulation as fixed by the margin between our production and our consumption; of which the last will look easily after itself, given the first three. (Our emphasis)

I believe that it is just the dynamics of the Faustian kind of economic activity which determines the pace of the present development of the world economy. Science and its application, in the form of technical progress, allow for tremendous economic growth. In this view, nature in general, and the environment in particular, is reduced to factors of production to achieve this growth. Time in its limiting function seems to be erased; thus time is reduced to only one function, to the future as the space where economic growth takes place.

All of us who use electric light, who watch TV, work with a PC, drive cars, and believe in progress, take part in this Faustian dynamic economy, which offers new useful things day by day in order to make life more easy and comfortable and come a little bit closer to the realisation of paradise. But Goethe points clearly and emphatically to the problems which arise from the Faustian vision of a man-made economic world creating its own money and technology.

(a) Modern man loses his sense for nature. Seeing the wide and beautiful sea and the everlasting alternation of the tides, Faust exclaims: 'Pregnant with might, wave upon wave there reigneth, /Yet each retires, nor any end attaineth./ Me to despair it doth disquiet truly,/ This aimless might of elements unruly.' Nature in itself is considered as aimless, without any end; this view makes modern man despair, except if he acts like Faust: 'Here would I battle . . . '

(b) Modern man also loses all feelings for forms of human life which are embedded in the environment: Faust cannot bear the small hutch of the old couple, Philemon and Baucis, because they live in harmony with their environment; he is especially disturbed by the ringing of the bell at their chapel; the bell, as Mephisto remarks, 'In each event, or sad or merry all,/ Mingles from the first bath to burial,/ As life 'twixt ding and dong did seem/ A shadowy, forgotten dream.' The Faustian world as a picture of the modern economy is based on permanent growth.

(c) This vision of unstoppable progress lets modern man forget his mortality. While Faust, dreadfully blinded, believes that he is hearing the noise of the labourers working on a new ditch, a noise which initiates his great vision and therefore makes him feel completely satisfied, Mephisto comments: 'They talk – such news to me they gave – / Not of a groove, but of a grave.'

(d) The freedom which Faust strives for lies always in the future, never in the present. While Faust has the vision of the 'free people' the spectator recognises at the same time the presence of 'Lemures', which Mephisto characterises as: 'Patched up of sinew, bone and skin; / Nature but half appointed.' With this allusion Goethe hints to the one-sideness of labour in modern economies.

(e) But the entrepreneur cannot enjoy his freedom either. Even if 'Guilt', 'Want', and 'Need' are suppressed, 'Care through the key-hole slips stealthily in'. The present is always endangered by the uncertainty of the future, because of unpredictable market forces and the forces of nature.

(f) From where do the five problems I have mentioned arise? Goethe's answer may cause surprise. Life of modern man depends on a certain kind of magic, of which he is unable to free himself: 'Could I but form my path all magic banish,/ Bid every spell into oblivion vanish,/ And stand mere man before thee, Nature! Then/ 'Twere worth the while to be a man with men.'

ECONOMIST: I don't understand you. What does magic mean for modern men? Hasn't magic been substituted by science and technology in modern times? In my opinion the old magic dream has been by far surpassed by modern man. This has enabled humankind to gain security and welfare in four respects: (i) to protect themselves against natural disasters, (ii) to provide plenty of food, (iii) to protect themselves against diseases and (iv) to delegate human labour to machines.

WRITER: You are right, but modern man is only the master of those traits of nature which he has discovered in order to pursue his own ends. This is so because modern man asks only how the elements and their relationships can be explained and how they function. The questions, what the things are and what their essence is, are neglected, because they do not contribute to men's control. However, as Goethe believed, the essence of all things is derived from a 'world soul' and the treatment of all things should be in harmony with it. From this point of view it follows that neglecting this harmony leads not only to unexpected and unwanted, but even to disastrous, consequences. Since Faust does not consider this harmony in his economic activity, the devil may say: 'Lost are ye, lost in every manner!/ The elements are leagued beneath our banner,/ And all in nothing still must end.'

Modern man equals the 'Zauberlehrling' (magician's apprentice) of Goethe's ballad. He knows how the things function, but does not know why. Thus the Zauberlehrling is able to make the broom carry the water into the bath, but he is unable to stop it again, and therefore must confess: 'I called the ghosts but can't get rid of them!' I think that many environmental problems, as e.g. the Waldsterben (forest death), the ozone problem and the CO_2 problem, occur because modern man has the same attitude as the 'Zauberlehrling' and also ignores this harmony.

COMMENTATOR: Has this harmony ever existed? Has it been lost?

earlier times humankind considered this harmony as an ideal which it should strive for.

For modern man, however, God is dead; the hereafter is only an imginary product of human phantasies, wishes and hopes; the Earth and its life is not a divine creation, nor is there any more a harmony in itself, but an accidental result of natural laws which have been, or will be, discovered by science (Faber and Manstetten, 1988, pp. 101–4). This kind of attitude has led Faust, the prototype of modern man, to take the place of the creator. This in turn implied that life in this world had to take the place of eternity, and the present Earth the place of the Kingdom of God. However, man can only be creator if he is a man of action, driven by the longing to realise eternity in his own life, and shape and form the Kingdom on the Earth by his own will.

Since for modern man there does not exist a transcendental life, all promises of religion for the hereafter have already to be fulfilled in the present life. The example of Faust demonstrates that the religious striving to reach the Kingdom of God has been transferred into the restless dynamics of economic life. I believe that almost all of humankind is more or less seized by these dynamics.

ENVIRONMENTALIST: I object. This does not hold true for us. We are the ones who oppose this attitude.

WRITER: I maintain that just like most of the economists, most of you do not have a real understanding of the Faustian dynamics. Even those who have a certain hunch about it always believe it is the dynamics of the others, and not their own. Therefore, environmentalists who criticise Faustian activities do not realise that their own approach has Faustian traits. Some of them reject participation in the common search for solutions, because they maintain that first it is necessary to abolish the market system. But how will they proceed if this aim is realised? Will they not try to *create* thereafter a new world in the *same spirit* as Faust *created* his world? The other part of them, who make active contributions, do not escape this Faustian dynamics. For their proposals heavily depend on an implicit hope in technological solutions for environmental problems. They all have in common that they overvalue human possibilities and believe that man alone can determine the fate of the world, for better or worse.

Nevertheless, all of us, in particular both of you, Economist and Environmentalist, have to proceed further in your searches for new solutions. An essential part of this process will be to listen to each other.

COMMENTATOR: May I add that despite the differences in opinion we can presumably agree on one issue: even though nature cannot truly be priced, prices do regulate our economies. If this is so, then this price mechanism should be used as far as possible for the conservation of nature. But somehow I feel that this will only be a first step.

ECONOMIST, ENVIRONMENTALIST (Chorus):   Writer, do you have a solution?

WRITER: I do not have one. But I believe that an essential pre-requisite for a solution is to recognise what we do and what we really are and how deeply we are involved in the growth dynamics of the Faustian economy.

References

Bernholz, P. and F. Breyer (1984) *Grundlagen der Politischen Ökonomie* (Tübingen: Mohr (Paul Siebeck)).

Binswanger, H. C. (1972) 'Ökonomie und Ökologie –neue Dimensionen der Wirtschaftstheorie', *Schweizerische Zeitschrift für Volkswirtschaftslehre und Statistik*, Band 108: pp. 251–81.

Binswanger, H. C. (1985) *Geld und Magie: Deutung und Kritik der modernen Wirtschaft anhand von Goethes Faust* (Stuttgart: Edition Weitbrecht).

Brown, G.M. and R.W. Johnson (1982) 'Pollution Control by Effluent Charges: It Works in the Federal Republic of Germany, Why Not in the US?' *Natural Resources Journal*, vol. 22, pp. 929–66.

Debreu, G. (1959) *Theory of Value* (New York: John Wiley).

Faber, M., H. Niemes and G. Stephan (1987) *Entropy, Environment and Resources. An Essay in Physico-Economics.* (Berlin/Heidelberg/New York/London/Paris/Tokyo: Springer-Verlag).

Faber, M. and R. Manstetten (1988) 'Der Ursprung der Volkswirtschaftslehre als Bestimmung und Begrenzung ihrer Erkenntnisperspektive', *Schweizerische Zeitschrift für Volkswirtschaft und Statistik*, Heft 2, pp. 98–121.

Georgescu-Roegen, N. (1971) *The Entropy Law and the Economic Process* (Cambridge, Mass.: Harvard University Press).

Goethe, J.W. von (1908) *Faust*, transl. A. Latham (London: Dent; New York: E.P. Dutton).

Hannon, B. (1985) 'World Shogun', Communication, *Journal of Social Biol. Struct.*, vol. 8, pp. 329–41.

Keynes, J.M. (1930) 'Economic Possibilities for our Grandchildren', in J.M. Keynes, *Essays in Persuasion*, (New York: Norton), pp. 358–73.

OECD (1987) OECD Environmental Data, *Compendium 1987*, vol. 42 (Brussels).

Proops, J.L.R. (1988) 'Ecological Economics: Rationale and Problem Areas', Working Paper 88–9, University of Keele, accepted for publication in the Journal of Ecological Economics.

Robbins, L. (1932) *An Essay on the Nature and Significance of Economic Science* (London: Macmillan).

Roberts, M.J. (1974) *The Political Economy of the Clean Water Act of 1972: Why No One Listened to the Economists*, prepared for the OECD, mimeo. (Paris).

Samuelson, P.A. (1983) 'Rigorous Observational Positivism: Klein's Envelope Aggregation; Thermodynamics and Economic Isomorphism', in F.M. Adams and B.G. Hickmann (eds), *Global Econometrics: Essays in Honour of Lawrence R. Klein* (Cambridge, Mass.: MIT Press), pp. 1–38.

Seymour, J. (1980) *Friedliches Land – Grünes Leben* (Ravensburg: Otto Maier).

Solow, R.M. (1973) 'Is the End of the World at Hand?' *Challenge*, vol. 10, pp. 39–50.

5 Systems Reproduction in Interdisciplinary Perspective

Leonhard Bauer and Herbert Matis

ASSUMPTION: SOMETHING IS SET IN MOTION

By far the most dominant approach in the social sciences, particularly in economics, is a fundamentally ahistorically constructed theory of equilibrium, in which the actions of elements are conceived of as being voluntary. Apart from a reduction in the scope of the approach, resulting in momentary images being taken as the explanation, both of the whole and as a description and evaluation towards ends, the extensive loss of the historical dimension, the elimination of the parameter of time in the prevailing social sciences has resulted in the virtual disappearance of the analysis of economic and social development from theoretical discourse. Furthermore, this does not seem quite so strange when one considers Parson's maxim that the 'task of every scientific theory is to conceptually reduce what is changeable to what is constant',[1] a view which can be regarded as representative of the access to the mainstream. This prevailing approach in economics is reflected in the 'classical system theories in sociology'. The latter regard social change 'in the sense of a structural change as a disruption of a normally stable social equilibrium'.[2] Despite the wish, for example in economic theory, to regard such constructions as indispensable: 'as a standard with which the given state of the economic organism can be investigated and, where possible, evaluated',[3] and an ever greater emphasis on logical and highly formalised mathematical consistency, the ever-decreasing proximity to reality, as far as the provision of meaning and operationality is concerned, can no longer be overlooked. It is becoming increasingly clear that movement, change and dynamism are anything but a 'disruption of the equilibrium', a 'relatively unstable equilibrium'. Processes, conflicts and transformations cannot be forced into this Procrustean bed.

Increasingly, the view is gaining currency that instead of (viewing) 'society in a state of repose (which does not exist in reality), the change in socio-economic relations must be understood'.[4] In a world which seems to be characterised by planning changes, permanently overtaking each other and interrelated on so many levels that they produce almost incalculable, 'unplanned' changes, the choice of a constant, of something immutable, as a point of departure is surely an anachronism. A radical formulation of the approach of our thinking as an attempt to explain the 'real' must, therefore, lie in the concept of change. Is it not a surprise and a stimulus to considerations if we think we discover constants?

SOCIETY AS MOVEMENT (PRODUCTION): TWO MODELS

In the course of the production of theories, various different approaches have been developed to explain both 'society as a whole' and its division into parts. The basic supposition is that the problem to be solved is one of 'reproduction'. A theory of society which does not permit the relation of individual activities and fields to the social cycle is inadequate: such a theory views society not as a system but as an amalgam of differing structures and activities, linked by external relations.[5] If the related approaches are applied to explain the cycle of social reproduction, then two basic models emerge. These two have to be examined in relation to one another.

The first model is based on the problem of how the totality of society reproduces itself. Taking a continually changing 'basic structure' as its point of departure, the process of reproduction is understood as an expanding cycle. A typical example of such theories of reproduction[6] is the analysis of capitalism in the tradition of Marx and Engels. (Similar, although they cannot be accommodated in this schema of reproduction without some difficulty, are the theories of Quesnay, based on Harvey's concept of blood circulation, or possibly modelled on Richelieu's concept of tax circulation and Keynes' circular flow.)

For Marx, the basic structure of society is formed by the relationship between labour and capital. The understanding of this structural contradiction is to be found in the theory of labour value. According to Marx, the mode of production provides the basis of society. A legal and political 'superstructure' determines the corresponding forms of consciousness (thought, feeling, behaviour). If, during the development of the forces of production, the shaping of the forces of production should contradict the relations of production, then a process beginning with social tension and conflict, and leading to possible revolution would result: 'When the economic basis changes the entire monstrous superstructure [also] changes.'[7]

The dynamics of this social development is not independent of human consciousness, but social developments cannot be explained by it. This consciousness is much more the result of 'the contradictions of material life, of the existing conflict between social forces of production and relations of production'.[8]

The starting point for the second model is not a totality divided into parts to reveal a multiplicity of relations, rather it is based on a fundamental sociological (psychological) interpretation of the 'elements' of the system. By analogy with classical physics, the elements of a system of society provide the lead-in for the construction of a theory.[9] The starting points are either 'individuals' or their 'actions'. Mainly linked by mutual expectations, the relationships between active individuals function as relations. Thus society can be analysed as a general system of actions. The formulation of such theories of the systems of social action is associated with Luhmann, Parson and Weber.

Social processes as 'systems of action' are of a fundamentally open nature, and the direction of their development is not determined. Similarly, social processes, also understood as systems of reproduction, never follow exogenously given aims and purposes. This does not mean, however, that blind chance is allowed to rule. What was previously there, what emerges in the historical process, however, restricts a theoretically infinite number of possibilities of development to only a small ensemble. As a result of specific configurations, the way is opened for only a specific spectrum of potential development. Independent processes take shape within this framework, and the categories and forms of association of thinking which reflect the process are correspondingly influenced. Analyses dealing with long-term development are based on a postulate which regards socio-economic reality as a system with a particular inherent structure. This involves both structural and genetic aspects (element – individual). In order to incorporate given structures and developing processes in the analysis – i.e. the 'investigation of the structural laws which appear in this system, while at the same time taking its complementary character into consideration in order to analyse processes'[10] – the framework which is shaped by social–organisational factors must be included as an *additional dimension*, both as an assumption and as a possibility of development.[11] Social processes and the phenomenon of the transition from one system of society to another can be interpreted from both a dynamic system–theoretical point of view, and on the basis of mutual dependency, namely from a reproduction––theoretical point of view.[12] This clearly distinguishes the evolutionary from the 'revolutionary' changes and vice versa.

THE INTERPRETIVE POTENTIAL OF THE CONCEPT OF THE PARADIGM

The concept of a transition to a new scientific paradigm, developed on the basis of the history of the natural sciences by Thomas Kuhn, Paul Feyerabend, Imre Lakatos and other authors who, like Ludwig Fleck, have only recently been rediscovered, seems to contain a considerable general historical or at least heuristic potential as an interpretive model. The direction taken in the French tradition by Bachelard, Canguillem and Foucault can be viewed in a similar light. If this approach is applied then each element of the system can be seen to have a specific array of means at its disposal to influence and to solve problems. These are used to come to terms with experience and problems and, understandably enough, also with structural changes. Should this not succeed; if the powers made manifest in the changes prove, on the one hand, to be too strong and, on the other, too laden with conflict for the integration to be maintained, then, depending on the centrality of the area of action, a crisis in the system results. 'Then indeed we can speak of crisis . . . (a) crisis – whether it includes a revolution or paves the way for it – appears as a necessary process, which moves history forward and (at the same time) guarantees continuity'[13] – or at least can do so. The non-reproductability of political, social, meaning-providing as well as economic preconditions of a social system results from a very broadly conceived casuality, inherent in the conditions which determine decision-making. This is no way to be understood, however, as the teleological realisation of an 'inner principle' or 'essence' of a particular historical configuration.

A combination of the classical approaches of system-theory and reproduction theory in the sense of evolutionary-processual theories of development can thus be achieved. Such systems are not understood as something static and, at the same time, in a state of homeostatic equilibrium, rather they are conceived of as something dynamically and continually changing. The requirements of reproduction are conditions to be fulfilled, which do, of course, preform the scope of the elements or systems. As a result, one speaks of 'open systems', characterised by adaptation and resistance or, in operational terms, by assimilation and accommodation[14] of impulses from inside or outside the elements or systems. Inside and outside are not to be understood as a dichotomy, because systems determine themselves by defining their own boundaries.

THE UTILISATION OF PIAGET'S RESEARCH ON THE DEVELOPMENT OF INTELLIGENCE

This follows Piaget's genetic approach to psychology. Although this approach is individually conceived, it nevertheless possesses sufficient potential as a model to interpret social systems on account of the special nature of Piaget's thinking: the structures of knowledge with which he deals belong just as much to the individual in society or to a society of individuals as to the individual alone; man is a living organisation, which despite, or even because of, its immanent structure and self-regulation is *by no means autarkical.* For an essentially autonomous structure, the environment is neither an additional luxury, nor is it a dispensable element. The biological environment is the world which is strictly necessary. It is this world in and through which a biological organisation lives, and with which it interacts. If – as is the case with humans – social and cultural influences form part of the normal environment, then human *knowledge* can never develop in a humane way without the social and cultural environment.[15] This position only becomes clear in the generally individualised justification of our thinking, if one is explicitly reminded of the fact that man is a 'social being'.[16]

Piaget described intelligence as the totality of the coordinations of behaviour at certain stages of development. If one views intelligence in general (with attention to the fluid previous forms, etc.) then it corresponds to a 'biological organ', which regulates the exchange of behaviour of an organism with its environment. The behaviour of an organism (system) towards its environment is a particular way of functioning; starting with the internal organisation (also internal structure) form which was developed internally in confrontation with its external world, the adaptation of the organism finds its expression in behaviour. Adaptation can take only two different forms: Piaget describes as assimilation an organism's incorporation of environmental data in its internal organisation, i.e. the activity of conservation and retention. If, on the other hand, an organism adapts its internal organisation to the special conditions of the environment, then this is defined as accommodation, which is characterised as a changing activity in which, among other things, new concepts and operations are possible. In this accommodation, the patterns of behaviour of those acting is changed as a result of various learning processes (e.g. classification and logical operationalisation). This activity consists in using reality to test the effectiveness of the intellectual apparatus.

This act, which forms the basis for change, is described as a formal, reflective abstraction. According to Piaget, empirical knowledge does not develop additively, rather it develops along the lines of an increasingly constructive rationality. Combined with the extension of constructive rationality, an increasing decentralisation of the subject can be observed.[17] Assimilation is the necessary precondition for the movement away from an egocentric to a decentralised mode of observing. Piaget's specific way of thinking, his genetic epistemology, provides new insight, not only to the development of individuals, but also to the development of entire social systems.

Each society and system, therefore, not only reveals specific internal structures, but also functions in accordance with a particular set of rules. This is a result of the fact that, as stated above, individual and society are not to be understood as being mutually independent. (The questioning of the subject–object relationship elucidates the importance of the assumption upon which these considerations are based, as well as Marx's considerations on fetish character.) Social systems can be characterised by the fact that they possess a structure of values which permits consensus and which provides the symbolic legitimation of the particular structure of interaction and stratification of its member, i.e. it makes them morally acceptable. In concrete social systems there is a large number of divergent structures of value, although a certain amount of agreement is, of course, necessary. It is doubtful whether this agreement should take the form, for example, of a sufficiently large intersection of values (or norms), or whether there should be a 'family resemblance' (in the Wittgenstein sense). Within specific social conditions of production, there exists (or develops, or is forced) a movement towards agreement concerning necessary rules, expectations and moral concepts; 'every system of production structures expectations along the line of the least resistance, i.e. in conformity with its rules.[18] Even 'rational' behaviour can therefore not be regarded as absolute, rather as only being in a self-referential, socio-economic context. The internalisation of modes of behaviour which are acknowledged to be rational determines a relatively strict 'blocking out' of new 'rational' rules.[19] In the specific context of individuals and systems, this hinders the development of adequate structures of action. The present discussion between the apologists of economic growth and the ecologists can be understood from this perspective. The greater the degree of change in living conditions, e.g. because of economic and technological innovation, the more difficult the socio-institutional and cognitive adaptation to changed reality becomes. (The opposite might be a presentation of the problem which corresponds more to our basic position.)

We employ our knowledge, which is predominantly production oriented (technological),[20] as a framework for social, political and economic actions; it has specific, controllable aims and is interest-determined. Such knowledge can neither control, predict, nor reconstruct the multiplicity of interdependent and complex consequences which are associated with it.

As a result of the prevailing rules and goals which a particular society generates (e.g. safeguarding one's livelihood, redistribution, distributive or commutative justice, the principle of an income in accordance with status; economic growth, capital accumulation, the right of disposal of factors of production), there is at the same time an extremely specific preference, with regard to the selection of the material and non-material means, which are to be employed to achieve these goals. The aims conceived of, or the means, are determined according to the particular level of the systems (society, organisation and elements).

It seems, however, that because of the conditions of its genesis, each (open) socio-economic system has an inbuilt germ of crisis, i.e. its limits are mapped out. The factors governing its development, the underlying regulatory mechanism also define its limits. This occurs when the bases have been achieved as far as the provision of meaning and fulfilment of reproduction is concerned. Opposition to the system is to be most expected from those groups which cannot be fully integrated, which do not acknowledge the legitimacy of the system, and from whom cognitive dissonance is also to be expected.

An example may illustrate this point: the crisis of feudalism occurred as soon as there was no more land to be distributed, the population increased and the previous monopoly on power which the aristocracy enjoyed was broken by new techniques and technology for the production of armaments. The impulse for change came from commercial capital engaged in international trade, which was not bound to any specific location and which was the first to overcome the traditional restrictions of scholastic economic ethics. The emergence of economic relations based on money, the ever-lengthening chain of activity, the reduction of autonomous areas of production and the establishment of markets led to the dissolution of traditional socio-economic relations. The transformation into the capitalist, market economy system (metalevel) then followed, as did a simultaneous and contingent crisis in the previous social and political systems and the traditional world view which gave them their meaning and which held them together.

The capitalism which subsequently developed possessed a potential for integration, the extent of which has obviously often been underestimated – in this context the history of the European labour movement bears eloquent witness. This is also associated with the fact that a considerable possibility to shape structures within such systems of action exists and corresponds to the reproduction development. Problems regarding its expansion capability only become serious if the limit of its ability to reproduce is achieved (metasystem), or if the internal reproduction of meaning in newly formed systems reaches its limit.

Despite the contradictions and problems which arise, both in the system of action and on the level of reproduction, one can only speculate as to the future development of society. From the point of view of all historical reconstruction, one must rely on the development of the possibilities of human action (development of intelligence) and therefore on systems and vice versa.

Notes

1. T. Parsons, *Social Structures* (New York, London 1963), p. 258.
2. N. Elias, *Prozess der Zivilisation*, I (Frankfurt am Main, 1977), p. 8.
3. J.A. Schumpeter, *Konjunkturzyklen*, I (Göttingen, 1961), p. 10.
4. E.H. Carr, *Was ist Geschichte?* (Stuttgart, 1963), p. 64 ff.
5. H.J. Giegel, *System und Krise: Kritik der Luhmannschen Gesellschaftstheorie* (Frankfurt am Main, 1975), p. 18f.
6. J. Ritsert, *Probleme politisch-ökonomischer Theoriebildung* (Frankfurt am Main, 1973), p. 45 ff.
7. MEW, 13, Berlin, p. 9.
8. Ibid.
9. A critic on natural science as a standard, cf. L. Bauer and H. Matis, *Geburt der Neuzeit* (München, 1988).
10. A. Schaff, *Strukturalismus und Marxismus* (Wien, 1974), p. 218.
11. This point illustrates the criticism of many biological transfers into society.
12. Cf. U. Habermas, *Rekonstruktion des Historischen Materialismus* (Frankfurt am Main, 1976).
13. R. Vierhaus, *Problem historischer Krisen* (München, 1978), p. 319.
14. Cf. H.G. Furth,*Intelligenz und Erkennen* (Frankfurt am Main 1976), p. 362.
15. Ibid., p. 37f. Cf. N. Chomsky, *Regeln und Repräsentationen* (Frankfurt am Main, 1981).
16. This reference would hardly have been necessary between Aristotle and A. Smith (Cf. L. Bauer and H. Matis, *Geburt der Neuzeit* (München, 1988), p. 444 ff.) Cf. U. Holzkamp-Osterkamp, *Grundlagen I* (Frankfurt am Main, 1977).
17. K. Boulding, *The Impact of the Social Sciences* (New York, 1966), p. 4.
18. E.P. Thompson, *Plebejische Kultur* (Frankfurt am Main/Berlin/Wien, 1980), p. 317.
19. K. Gödel, 'Über formal unentscheidbare Sätze der Prinzipia Mathematica und verwandter Systeme', in *Monatsheft für Mathematik und Physik*, 38, 1931, p. 173 ff.
20. J. Habermas, *Erkenntnis und Interesse* (Frankfurt am Main, 1973), p. 68.

6 Why Some Reforms Succeed

Gerhard O. Mensch

SUMMARY

When the editors asked me for a contribution to the Festschrift for Ota Sik, they suggested that I use the Long Wave concept for deriving some fundamental thoughts that appear equally interesting to East and West. Assuming that Easterners and Westerners are equally interested in the conditions under which reform plans emerge and either succeed or fail, it seems reasonable, indeed, to try to relate cumulative causes over long stretches of time to both the emergence of new needs (and reform plans) and the emergence of (sufficient) conditions for their favourable socio-political reception in the respective country.

In evolutionary economics, a range of alternative patterns of events can be studied on the basis of new micro–macro theory. Kondratieff waves are one special case, my Metamorphosis Model is another one; one that permits gradual evolution (steady growth) at some periods and breakthroughs (rapid phase transitions) at other intervals of time. Metamorphosis is structural transformation combined with transformation in the order of things (wihout chaos, though). At the core is the theory of structural readiness for basic innovation (and for clusters of basic innovations tied in with previous mishaps and subsequent series of improvement innovations). Throughout breakthrough and rapid change, however, the notion of what is good and bad doesn't get lost. If it doesn't, reform plans that emerge at the right time have a high probability of succeeding.

Underlying long waves and other patterns of economic change are causal relationships representing either an equilibrium path or a chain of events that can be characterised as 'vicious' or 'virtuous' circles. Only in the latter case can reformers expect to succeed. Part of the struggle is demonstrating reform benefits at an early stage of the reform process (such as cuts in military spending in the 10 to 20 per cent order of magnitude). Another part of the struggle is to point fingers at forces that are part and parcel of the 'vicious circle' (such as state monopolies, and vested interests that do cost the public dearly if you think it through, or care to figure it out). Without being able to prove it scientifically, I conjecture that the ultimate sufficient condition for success of reform plans is that state-funded institutions of socio-economic research dare, when the time has come for breakthrough, formally to announce research programmes which promise to think through, and figure out, the disbenefits of doing business as usual.

DYNAMIC DISEQUILIBRIUM CHANGES IN EAST AND WEST

Precisely when George Bush took presidential office at the White House, Mikhail Gorbachev at the Kremlin announced plans to cut military spending by 14 per cent, and, specifically, expenditures for weapons by 19 per cent. People wonder if this is coincidence, prompted by financial necessities in the Soviet Union as anywhere, or a cooperative move aimed at balancing the budgets in both the Soviet Union and the United States, or maybe even a constructive step towards better global relations. Anyway, the world appears to be poised for an evolutionary leap. Economic reforms are under way in Eastern and Western countries, and international communities. Waves of financial innovations stimulate international capital flows, and reversals of such flows as technological innovations, notably in the information gathering and handling field, facilitate multinational transactions. The innovation pushes international market integration, which in turn pulls swarms of product and process innovations that generate structural change.

In China, for example, Deng Xiaoping's economic reform has reached an advanced stage. 'Today,' said Ota Sik recently in an interview commemorating 21 August 1968, 'in China the chances stand very good for consequent economic reforms' (*Süddeutsche Zeitung*, 22 August 1988). When a Chinese corporation floated stocks in 1988, this institutional capital market innovation in China made Deng 'the Hero of the Eastern World' in the *Wall Street Journal* (same day). Sceptics, on the other hand, think – or say that they think – that new stocks in China, and a new stock exchange in Hungary, first of all constitute another legalised means to privatise further value created by public enterprises which socialise both the risk of misreading the market and the cost of mismanagement and corruption. Reforms also induce the formulation of dissent, and of positive affirmations. Zhao Ziyang, the Secretary General of the Chinese Communist Party, insisted that new ways of financing need not and should not contribute to contribute to corruption, one of the three great evils in China, he said.

In the USA, Reaganomics as a Keynesian demand boosting policy in disguise is even more popular among American investors than Thatcherism is among British investors. Less government, less business tax, this was Reagan's bold and blunt message. At the White House reception for the US Small Business Report, on 29 October 1987, the President commented on the key performance figures of the US economy. Between 1983 and 1985 3 million new jobs had been created, 88 per cent of these by small businesses with less than twenty employees. On a per-employee basis, small firms contributed over twice as many 'first-of-type' innovations than large firms. 'I was asked some time ago what the difference is between a small business and a large business,' Reagan said, 'and I said, a large business is what a small one would be if the government would get out of the way (Laughter).' No mention at the reception and in the press release, of course, of the trade deficit and budget deficit that accompanied the innovation and job creation rate throughout the reign of President Reagan. As the US national debt reaches staggering proportions, readjustment is overdue; and people wonder if it will be managed as a gradual process, causing – or coinciding with – a gradual long wave (Kondratieff) downswing, or as a swift and brutal correction. Doesn't every leader worth called that commit his most radical acts, if he must, right at the beginning of his term in office?

In Sweden, the 1989 elected social democratic government of Carlsson and Feldt is introducing massive tax cuts to boost private investment in open markets, where 'open' denotes both open to new competition (innovation) and open to foreign competition (imports). In Switzerland, a complete overhaul of economic policies and regulations have been called for by the legislature – to make Swiss industry competitive 'on a level above average', the Bundesrat in Bern added with a hint at market integration in the European Community. Austrian Bundeskanzler Vranitzky, at the 1988 Prognos Forum in Basel, spoke of an 'Integrations-Schub' combined with an 'Innovations-Schub' that forces economic reform in Austria, notably in Austria's public enterprise conglomerate, which today is a huge complex of mismanagement and monopolistic practices – more so than it was fifty years ago, at a smaller scale, when it served Schumpeter to dwell on 'monopolistic practices' in his landmark book *Capitalism, Socialism, and Democracy*. Monopolistic practices are, as everyone can see, no less a problem in Eastern European countries.

Last, but not least, perestroika. Innovation elsewhere is a mirror for seeing more clearly the lack of it at home, or for seeing what little there is in perspective. Perestroika is a bundle of major radical and disruptive innovations. In comparison, innovations in Western countries are minor in scope (given a higher rate of change to begin with). And earlier innovations in the Soviet Union, few as there may have been during the Brezhnev era, also appear minor in comparison to planned innovations ahead. If, thereupon, the Brezhnev era deserves to be denoted an era of stagnation by Gorbachev, he is justified in proclaiming that 'the stagnation in the Soviet Union cannot be overcome by timid reforms'. Comparing 'perestroika' plans in 1988 with 'prestavba' plans of 1968 in Prague, Ota Sik observed that the Czech reform plan then did not go anywhere near as far as Soviet reform plans do today. Perestroika is nothing short of an economic revolution combined with social and political changes of giant proportions. Can the emerging branch of evolutionary economics, which has yet to pass the tests of validity under capitalist conditions, where the 'natural rate of microeconomic transformation' is relatively high, provide any useful insights into

— revolutionary changes in the USSR and other countries which in the past experienced low rates of microeconomic change, only,

— and radical reversals in the USA and other countries which in the past experienced low rates of macroeconomic adjustment to aggregate disequilibrium developments – unemployment, debt explosion, etc.

This question begs for more research, and for investment in the production of consequential knowledge of transformational management of large human systems. In the following, I shall surmise some hypotheses derived from evolution theory – as when addressing socio-economic topics.

PRINCIPLES, PROCESSES AND PATTERNS OF ECONOMIC EVOLUTION AND CO-EVOLUTION

In the social sciences, we have to cope with the fundamental fact that reality coexists with our ways of looking at both the reality and conceivable alternatives. Reform plans emerge upon reflection of both, and upon visualisation of an alternative based on past experiences, present information, and future expectations of wants and needs and the odds of their fulfilment. Reality evolves as reform plans coevolve within the corresponding awareness context. The chances for success, therefore, greatly depend on the presence of people who come, see, speak their mind and convince others. Or, who come, see, and conquer (Caesar).

The fundamental element of socio-economic evolution is an event. Events emerge and may or may not occur ($X=0,1$). One general theory of co-evolution is probability theory. It attaches to events the likelihood of occurrence (probability). Most events depend on others (preconditions). Conditional probabilities and transitional probabilities are used to define causality (interdependence) and driving, directing, and disciplining forces (processes). Processes, or webs and hierarchies of process (stochastic processes) organise events into patterns. Patterns are sets of events that are either perfectly ordered or partially ordered. Establishing a partial order means mobilising forces that are placing events in space, scheduling events in time, and creating the side-conditions for events to happen (preprogramming). Bayesian theory is a well-known branch of information sciences which serves to conceptualise emergence of new plans and new facts as a multistep information process under uncertainty about side-conditions.

Some special theories of emergence also exist. With Herman Wold, I have done work on non-linear interdependencies in multivariate networks of stochastic processes (*Nonlinear Extensions of Soft Modeling*). With Wolfgang Weidlich and Günter Haag I have applied Synergetics (mixed difference–differential equation systems) to economic evolution patterns such as business cycles, and phase transitions in structural shift and trend reversals, for example, in Phillips Loops and Okun Loops describing non-linear motions in inflation, unemployment, and capital utilisation ('The Schumpeter Clock'). At present, the family of scholars applying such non-linear, stochastic interaction models to economic patterns and econometric testing is rapidly expanding, and within the last two years, scholarly output in this line of theorising has sharply increased.

As a result, more and more complicated patterns of socio-economic evolution become known. If patterns are, again, ordered sets of events, simple patterns such as series, chains, and sequences become recognised as temporary subpatterns of larger patterns such as phase-specific cumulative processes, waves (with relatively few events most of the time and rushes at some intervals far and in between), and cycles (with trends, and trend reversals in regular succession). Moreover, circular patterns become visible, such as limit cycles in dynamical economic models, and spirals, which incorporate swarms of disruptive events (such as clusters of basic innovations) into dynamic development patterns. At the moment, the literature connects these notions of patterns with traditional notions of the driving forces and constraints, such as technology push, demand pull, financial burden, institutional inertia, social movement, political pressure, wage stickiness, interest rate fixation, and hysteresis in labour markets and capital markets. Much of this literature is in the tradition of Schumpeterian discontinuity theory, which now becomes operational as model-building skills, and econometric capabilities have emerged to a level that allows incorporating more and more of his vistas and conjectures.

CONTRARIAN TRADITIONS GUIDE THE TRANSITIONS

Innovations researchers have studied in detail the step-by-step process of emergence of new things, and the stage-to-stage diffusion of the new thoughts or things through populations. I conceived the notion of a basic innovation (as a triggering event of series of improvement innovations and ripple-effects in socio-economic contexts) and pseudo innovation (when the context becomes stale and technology settled-in) when working with Herman Freudenberger on the bunch of change processes that originated the Industrial Revolution in the Habsburg Empire, in and around Brno, now in Czechoslovakia (*From a Provincial Town to Industrial Region: The Political Economy of Social Innovation*, Göttingen, 1975). Table 6.1 shows the types of changes studied as series of events that extended from basic invention to basic innovation. In each case, the innovation process (emergence) took several decades until a successful version had emerged – side by side with supportive and facilitating side conditions which in turn emerged as processes of basic innovations. In Table 6.1, fourteen such co-evolutions have been listed and timed.

Table 6.1 Series of fundamental changes and their sequential emergence (co-evolution pattern)

New concept	Basic innovation	Basic invention	Years lead time	Tempo of Change
1. Institutionalisation of the mercantilist concept of development policy	1743	1653	90	1.11
2. Establishment of a development bank	1751	1686	65	1.54
3. State investment in textile industry	1762	1701	61	1.63
4. Build-up of viable textile manufacturing plant	1764	1715	49	2.04
5. Forcing labour into the textile industry	1762	1694	68	1.47
6. Technical training of textile workers	1765	1701	64	1.57
7. Restricting guild control over industry	1754	1672	82	1.21
8. Highway connection to Brünn	1740	1704	36	2.72
9. Establishment of central commerce administration	1746	1666	80	1.25
10. Procurement and dissemination of economic information	1754	1666	88	1.13
11. Introduction of a general protective tariff	1775	1737	38	2.63
12. Abolition of the monopolistic privileges for textile factories	1763	1672	91	1.08
13. Departure from rigid economic policy direction	1785	1747	38	2.63
14. Establishment of a market for domestically produced textiles	1769	1727	42	2.38

Source: H. Freudenberger and G. Mensch, *Von der Provinzstadt zur Industrieregion (Brünnstudie); Ein Beitrag zur Politökonomie der Sozialinnovation, dargestellt am Innovationsschub der Industriellen Revolution im Raume Brünn*, Göttingen, 1975.

Note that the sequence of basic innovation and the sequence of basic inventions are quite similar. If we apply rank regression analysis to these patterns, we find with a statistical significance of above .95 that the causal order of change if fairly stable and can be described as the Seniority Principle: mental configurations (innovative ideas and plans) precede the emergence of actionable concepts and new institutional arrangements and new technologies (innovation). In addition, the order of their joint occurrence is guided by the Seniority Principle applied to the coemergence of parallel processes. In short, old ideas govern new activities – atleast that was the historical pattern in the past. Even clusters of basic innovations obey the rule: traditions guide the transitions.

In the aggregate, much of this new insight is compatible with traditional long-wave notions (the Kondratieff cycle). It is understood that complicated transformation processes may in the aggregate reveal themselves as macroeconomic fluctuations of long duration. My Metamorphosis Model, given in Figure 6.1, depicts gradual and sudden changes and reversals, too. It is compatible with more complicated patterns, such as running inflations and breakdowns and breakthroughs of swarms of innovations. The pattern of coevolution then is, for example, a spiral or an open circle.

CONCLUSION

There exists, as everyone knows, 'virtuous' and 'vicious' circles. Reform plans succeed if they are an element of a virtuous circle and come at the proper time (proper means that enough people who count have come to regard current practice as 'vicious'). This message I derive from Karl Deutsch's work on what he calls 'the assembly line process of history', which he studied in extenso in the context of international integration and alliance formation in Western countries, taking account of élite attitudes, on the one hand, and significant world politics issues, on the other hand. Born in Czechoslovakia, he did this seminal work at the same time as reform plans were being drafted in that country, and published these landmark studies in 1967 when those reform plans were being implemented with the help and engagement of Ota Sik, whom we are now celebrating. I know of no better scholarly gesture to Ota Sik than including in the list of references only the two books of Karl Deutsch. They are fresh today, and instructive today, as if written today for our present concerns.

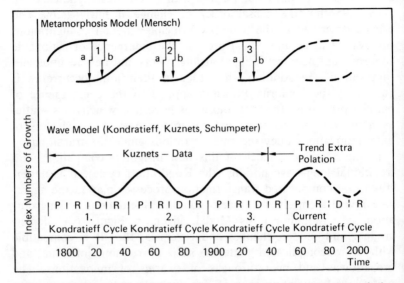

Figure 6.1   Wave model and metamorphosis model of economic evolution and transformation
Source: G.O. Mensch, *Stalemate in Technology – Innovations overcome the Depressions* (Cambridge, Mass.; Ballinger, 1979).

References

Deutsch, Karl W. (1967) *Arms Control and the Atlantic Alliance: Europe Faces Coming Policy Decisions* (New York: John Wiley).
Deutsch, Karl W. (1967) *France, Germany and the Western Alliance: Elite Attitudes, European Integration, and World Politics* (New York: Charles Scribner).

7 A Cognitive-evolutionary Theory of Economic Policy

Alfred Meier and Susanne Haury

INTRODUCTION

Economists often charge that politicians turn a deaf ear to their advice, whereas politicians find that economic analyses seldom provide them with workable guidelines. The cognitive-evolutionary approach is an outgrowth of this situation with improvement of the quality of economic consulting as its objective. It is intended as a contribution to the solution of communication problems between politician and economist. Because we believe that these problems arise largely from inadequate representation of the politician's actual situation in economic models, we stress the importance of uncertainty and power.[1]

POLITICO-ECONOMIC ACTORS IN AN UNCERTAIN WORLD

Economic actors' abilities to process information are limited. Individual behaviour, therefore, is not determined by 'objective' reality but by so-called interpretation systems. These systems consist of the actor's accumulated knowledge and values and are at least partly socially determined. Choice is exercised according to a limited, approximate and simplified model of the situation which makes complexity manageable. Kühne summarises this concept as follows: 'The rationality of the individual is bounded. In search of a satisfying solution he uses his abilities suboptimally, behaves partly irrationally and is influenced by socially conveyed ideas and the pressure to act in conformity with his environment' (Kühne, 1982, p. 4, our translation).

If a politico-economic actor conceives of a situation as equivocal, it is because the information received from his environment lacks practical content. His cognitive abilities do not permit him to attach sense to the situation or divergent, inconsistent interpretations do not provide a basis for action. Situations of equivocality give rise to the need for what we call collective interpretation, that is, a socially conveyed interpretation of the situation that provides a generally accepted basis for action. This collective interpretation permits one to define, name and explain the situation provisionally, to evaluate alternatives and to legitimise final action. The adoption of other actors' interpretations facilitates the construction of a collective interpretation, since democratic policy must be based on a majority, however thin.

Collective interpretation changes the equivocal situation to one of uncertainty, in which the hypotheses considered relevant are still incomplete, but the actor's conception of reality is now dense enough to build expectations. These expectations are influenced by collective interpretation, individual interpretation systems and the allocation of legal entitlements and resources. The actor finally selects a concrete alternative that is based on his expectations. Figure 7.1 illustrates this process.

The politico-economic system is based upon division of labour. The actors accumulate different experiences and values and therefore interpretation systems that are not consistent from the point of view of society as a whole. From these the actors deduce diverse aims and chains of causality. Conflicts emerge, if – as is usual in economic policy – this happens in a situation of scarce resources and interdependent behaviour. Let us assume that interdependencies and scarcities cannot be reduced and consensus is beyond reach. In this case the problem can only be solved by relying on power, if it is considered important enough and if the distribution of power is flat.[2] Power, therefore, can be socially essential, if it is necessary to form a majority or to establish a basis for collective action. But the use of power can also be accompanied by dysfunctional effects. Olson (1982) showed that special-interest organisations and collusions tend to reduce efficiency and aggregate income and make political life more divisive. But influence and power also decide which conception of reality provides the actual basis for collective action. If there is evidence for the existence of a problem and the problem does not become an item on the collective agenda, we may speak of dysfunctional effects of power. Measures against pollution that

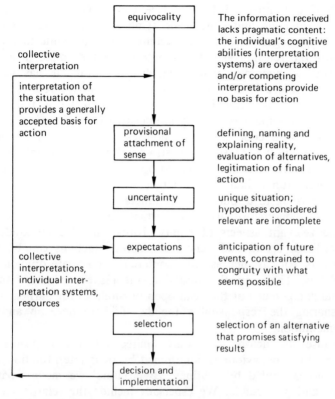

Figure 7.1   Individual behaviour under uncertainty

violate the interests of industry provide a possible example of this. Our highest priority for further research is a detailed analysis of the causes and consequences of the dysfunctional effects of power.

The ultimate goal of politico-economic action is to satisfy people by mitigating problems or emotionally deactivating them. From this point of view, economic policy might be conceived of as the management of popular conceptions of reality. This is possible by 'real' changes in the allocation of legal entitlements and resources as well as by influencing *symbolically* the actor-addressees' conceptions of reality and interpretation systems. Received economic theory provides an adequate analysis of 'real' welfare effects of changes in the allocation of resources, while it neglects the symbolic dimension or, in other words, the perception of politico-economic reality by the public.

Following Bennet (1980) and Edelman (1964) we distinguish between referring and condensing symbols. The former *refer* to the relevant segments of politico-economic reality, while the latter *condense* the relevant aspects normatively. For example, if a certain rate of unemployment is labelled 'natural', it has to be accepted – there is nothing politicians could do to reduce it. If unemployment is defined as 'cyclical', it will be a transitory phenomenon – there is nothing politicians should do, since time-lags may cause counter-cyclical policies to generate procyclical effects. Yet another possibility is 'structural' unemployment – there is perhaps nothing politicians could do, since it can be cured only in the long run (when we are all dead), while re-elections take place according to a much shorter timetable.

Politico-economic rituals are important mechanisms for condensing the relevant aspects of reality. Rituals involve all kinds of standardised, ceremonial behaviour. Three functions can be distinguished. Rituals such as press conferences elucidate opinions or complaints. They can also underline the respective actors' institutional competence or they can open possibilities for participation and sharing the responsibility for the ultimate decision and its implementation.

Because the actors have only limited information-processing abilities, their behaviour is determined by their interpretation systems and is guided by routines. By 'routine' we mean what is regular and predictable. We especially include the relatively constant dispositions and strategic heuristics that shape the politico-economic system's approach to the non-routine problems it faces (see Nelson and Winter, 1982, p. 15).

If a problem occurs, the first step will be to deduce rules of action from existing interpretation systems. If this approach is not successful, the actors look for new, more fruitful interpretations and solutions that may provide a basis for future action. In the first case, the politico-economic processes are shaped by the dominant interpretation systems, in the second by the institutionally provided rules that guide the search for new routines.

STRUCTURES AND PROCESSES IN ECONOMIC POLICY

Our basic model of the politico-economic process broadly corresponds to the circular models of received theory. However, it is set apart from these models by the emphasis we place on the importance of different conceptions of reality and on the influence of power.

Items on the collective agenda originate from a comparison between subjective perceptions of reality and the actors' interpretation systems. Individual behaviour and political action are not directly guided by economic indicators such as rates of inflation, growth or unemployment, but by individuals' perceptions stemming from their respective interpretation systems. The following example illustrates this thesis: In the second half of 1982 the rate of unemployment in Switzerland rose significantly and reached a level of 0.3 to 0.4 per cent. Expectations for recovery were generally pessimistic and the mass media exerted pressure on the authorities. In March 1983, the Swiss Parliament decided to implement an employment programme. However, in more recent years Switzerland has become so accustomed to a higher rate of unemployment (about 1.0 per cent) that it now attracts little political attention.

To be actually set on the collective agenda and finally overcome, these subjectively perceived discrepancies have to pass a number of hurdles. The origin of these hurdles is to be seen in institutional determinants as well as in the exertion of influence and power that are effective during all phases of the politico-economic process. We distinguish between (1) the emergence of a problem, (2) the definition of the problem, (3) the decision on action and, finally, (4) the implementation of the decision.

1 Emergence of a Problem

The subjectively perceived discrepancies have to develop a collective dynamism to become an item of popular opinion. This process is based upon the interaction between the public and the actors representing its respective interests, such as political parties, special-interest organisations, members of parliament, and the government, with the mass media. The latter may channel communication processes or may play an active role in setting items on the political agenda. Two different patterns are conceivable: the dynamism arises 'bottom-up', which corresponds to the democratic ideal. The demand for politico-economic problem-solving is articulated by the public. The second, so-called 'top-down' pattern seems to be more common. Important and powerful politico-economic actors take the initiative and launch an issue.

Three types of barriers are effective on this level: not all interests are equally organisable. Consumers, taxpayers, and the unemployed have neither selective incentives nor the small numbers
needed to organise. Influential actors may prevent other interest
groups from finding an adequate forum in which to articulate their
postulates; censorship is an example. Yet another possibility is the
exertion of what Galbraith (1983, pp. 39) calls conditioned power.
The latter is exercised by changing belief. The act of submission
is not recognised. Behaviour is conceived of as reflecting individual
conviction.

2 Definition of the Problem

The objective of this phase is to establish a base for action by
isolating the relevant aspects of reality and connecting them with
an explanation. Other interpretations and postulates are simultaneously excluded. While the individual performs this process of
attaching sense intuitively, it is part of the collective bargaining
process on the level of society as a whole. Following Dyllick
(1983) we distinguish five steps. The relevant reality has to be
defined by answering two questions: what is relevant? What can
be excluded? After that, the reality must be given a name. This
step not only permits more efficient communication, it may also
contain a strong normative element, as our distinction between
referring and condensing symbols has demonstrated. Building
chains of causality to explain reality is the next step. If the item
is considered 'business as usual', the solution will be based on
existing routines. If the problem challenges these routines significantly, they will have to be modified. All these steps are most
important and influence the actual outcomes of the politico-economic process, since the diagnosis guides the therapy. Possible alternatives of action must be evaluated. The expected contribution of
an alternative to the actual solution of the problem *and* its congruity with the dominant interpretation systems such as the 'principles of a free-market economy' guide this process. The legitimation of the action finally taken is the last step.

There are different possible filters or hurdles on this level: conditioned power influences the definition of the problem. The actors
concerned lack the competence to interpret the situation. The
challenges are defeated by appeals to dominant values and

interpretation systems. Authorities attach low priority to the postulate or the formal procedures applied render it ineffective.

3 Decision on Action

Different decision processes can be identified. If the objectives and chains of causality are more or less homogeneous, rules of thumb may be applied that proved to be fruitful in similar previous cases. This so-called bureaucratic decision process is based on the centralised application of generally accepted procedures. These standardised rules minimise the effort necessary to solve routine problems. The counterpart is the political decision process. Potential conflicts emerge if heterogeneous objectives and inconsistent chains of causality coincide with interdependencies and scarce resources. If the conflicts become acute they can be solved only by relying on power. Because of different interpretation systems there is no generally accepted criterion such as Pareto-efficiency to guarantee a rational decision. Those actors who are in command of more influence will have their way. Different procedures take place within political decision processes; centralised, hierarchical decisions, democratic votes, negotiations, or open disputes such as strikes are possibilities.

Figure 7.2 summarises these characteristics. Limited interests or participation possibilities, limited information-processing abilities, defeat in votes or compromises that have little in common with the original postulates are among the filters that are effective during this phase.

4 Implementation of the Decision

Received economic theory has little to say about this phase of the politico-economic process. Politico-economic decisions are mostly compromises. The parties involved rely upon different interpretation systems and make contrary claims. The legal rules that are the formal result of the politico-economic process open room for further manoeuvre. Their character is necessarily general so that they can be applied to a broad class of cases and adapted to future contingencies. This vagueness gives room for interpretation and therefore resurgent claims. We propose to model this phase as an interaction between the administration and the individuals they administer. Since the administration lacks information and

	Bureaucratic	Political
aims	more or less consistent	inconsistent
chains of causality	homogeneous	heterogeneous
distribution of power	centralised because of general acceptance of the rules applied	dispersal, changing groups and coalitions
decision procedures	rules of thumb, procedures originating from leading cases or tradition	formal and informal procedures
information processing	fixed procedures and rules	strategic use of information
result	mirrors the rules	mirrors the distribution of power
main characteristics	stability and predictability	conflicts and disputes with winners and losers

Figure 7.2   Characteristics of bureaucratic and political decision processes

the individuals exert influence or even deny collaboration, the outcome of this phase is yet again filtered.

Our arguments can be summarised as follows: politico-economic processes originate in a comparison between subjectively perceived reality and the individual interpretation systems. Their ultimate goal is to make perceived discrepancies disappear. To be solved, problems have to pass a number of hurdles created by institutional characteristics, influence and power. Politico-economic processes, therefore, can be seen as bottle-necks that filter the demand for problem solving. Two patterns are conceivable. The status quo may be defended successfully against challenges, or the challenges cause changes in the allocation of legal entitlements and resources as well as in the guiding of individual and collective interpretation systems. Figure 7.3 illustrates this circular sequence.

IMPLICATIONS FOR POLICY ADVISING

The adviser we have in mind is not the neutral expert of received neo-classical theory, but somebody who is part of the politico-economic process in the same way as all the other actors. He

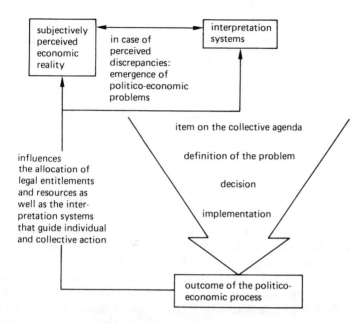

Figure 7.3   Basic model of politico-economic processes

pursues his own interests and must market his analyses and insights
in order to be successful.

Under good marketing we include the following functions: if his
analyses are actually to shape politico-economic structures and
processes, the economist must find influential protagonists. He
must know the institutional details of the politico-economic system
and be in command of realistic models of the behaviour and
influence of the relevant actors, namely voters, parliament, government, administration, mass media, households and firms. The
assumption of maximising behaviour appears to us as too abstract
and therefore we propose modelling the behaviour of the respective actors or groups of actors in greater detail by emphasising their
interpretation systems and interests (Meier and Mettler, 1988). But
most of all, the economic adviser has to be aware of the politician's actual demands and needs and must know where and in
what role economic knowledge can enter politico-economic
processes.

The traditional economist aims at finding empirically tested general laws or patterns and applies them to new phenomena. His
criteria of success are clear cut taxonomies, formal logic, empirical

testability and consistency with the guiding scientic paradigm. He interprets his findings primarily in the light of this paradigm and attaches secondary importance to common-sense interpretations. The economist chooses and systematically varies his abstract assumptions and often has long-term horizons for his research. The politician's situation tends to be the opposite. To offer fruitful advice, the economist therefore has to be aware of the latter's actual situation and needs: the politician wants to enforce or to prevent binding decisions that solve concrete problems. His criteria for success are generally accepted norms that are consistent with common sense and the dominant interpretation systems or ideologies. Legal norms, available time and the given power structure constrain his actions.

New economic knowledge will have difficulty entering the politico-economic process if the problem in question is considered 'business as usual'. If a problem challenges existing routines, economic knowledge will gain more authority since the actors lack information during all phases of the politico-economic process. We distinguish four functions of economic knowledge in politico-economic processes. (i) Economic insights such as forecasts, indicators or decision models may help to achieve politico-economic objectives. Received theory stresses this instrumental function exclusively. (ii) Politicians rely on economic expertise to legitimise their decisions. (iii) They struggle for influence and power and use economic knowledge strategically to increase their authority. (iv) Economists analyse questions of general social interest independently and outside the realm of daily politics. As exemplified by the work of Ota Sik, they enlighten politico-economic actors on the level of 'social consensus' (Frey, 1983, p. 261ff) by offering them advice on how existing structures and processes might be reformed.

Notes

1. This paper highlights the findings of a broader research project that is founded by the Swiss National Science Foundation. Meier and Mettler (1988) present the final report of the first, conceptual phase.
2. Under the term influence we subsume both authority and power. An individual accepts another's authority deliberately and consciously, because he has been convinced or rewarded. Power is exercised with-

out prior agreement and the individual to whom the power is addressed may be coerced against his will (Meier and Mettler, 1986, p. 43).

References

Bennett, W. Lance (1980) *Public Opinion in American Politics* (New York: Harcourt Brace Jovanovich).

Dyllick, Thomas (1983) 'Management als Sinnvermittlung', in *gdi-Impulse*, 1.Jg., pp. 1–12.

Edelman, Murray (1964) *The Symbolic Uses of Politics (Champaign, Ill.: Illinois University Press).*

Frey, Bruno S. *(1983) Democratic Economic Policy: A Theoretical Introduction* (Oxford: Martin Robertson).

Galbraith, John K. (1983) *The Anatomy of Power* (London: Corgi).

Kühne, Karl (1982) *Evolutionsökonomie: Grundlagen der Nationalökonomie und Realtheorie der Geldwirtschaft* (Stuttgart: Gustav Fischer Verlag).

Meier, Alfred and Daniel Mettler (1985) 'Auf der Suche nach einem neuen Paradigma der Wirtschaftspolitik', in *Kyklos*, vol. 38, pp. 171–99 (English summary).

Meier, Alfred and Daniel Mettler (1986) 'Einfluss und Macht in der Wirtschaftspolitik, in *Schweizerische Zeitschrift für Volkswirtschaft und Statistik*, 122. Jg., pp. 37–59 (English summary).

Meier, Alfred and Daniel Mettler (1988) *Wirtschaftspolitik: Kampf um Einfluss und Sinngebung. Grundzüge einer kognitiv-evolutionären Theorie der Wirtschaftspolitik* (Bern/Stuttgart: Haupt).

Nelson, Richard R. and Sidney G. Winter (1982) *An Evolutionary Theory of Economic Change* (Cambridge: Belknap Press).

Olson, Mancur (1982) *The Rise and Decline of Nations: Economic Growth, Stagflation and Social Rigidities* (New Haven/London: Yale University Press).

PART II

The Evolution of Market Systems: (1) Principal Aspects of Market Evolution

8 Evolution and Stagnation of Economic Systems

Ernst Heuss

In contrast to Marxism, based on the idea of evolution, the market economy is characterised by quite different factors. It received its early impetus from Adam Smith, a son of the Enlightenment and thus estranged from the idea of evolution. He emphasised self-regulation of the market, and it is therefore no coincidence that illustrations from the mechanical world as well as the concept of equilibrium are employed even today. These categories, however, are so far removed from evolution that there is no chance even to begin to construct an evolutionary concept. Thus it is not surprising that evolution has been approached from an entirely different side, namely from that of history. This development, as we all know, was so pronounced in the German language area, that in the nineteenth century national economics was for a while dominated by history.[1] Undoubtedly, history is concerned with developments, but also with the opposite, with regression. Both elements are part of man's history in general and thus also of economic and social history.

One is not surprised to note that political events were the major concern of historians. Only towards the end of the nineteenth century did a new point of view increasingly gain support. Economic factors and the closely related social changes which they brought about were now recognised as important and it was realised that they needed to be taken into consideration (Karl Lamprecht, German historian, 1856–1914).[2] It is, however, not enough merely to describe economic developments chronologically. It is also necessary to understand the phenomena taking into consideration intricate theoretical factors. To have accomplished this is the great achievement of Werner Sombart in his famous study, *Modern Capitalism* (1916). He succeeds in defining for us what we understand to be an economic system. From the historical development from precapitalism through early to high capitalism factors such as economic mentality (*Wirtschaftsgesinnung*), techni-

91

cal aspects, etc. have been distilled. We are not concerned here whether the terms of Sombart are applicable today, such as responding to need (*Bedarfsdeckungsprinzip*) as opposed to profit-seeking (*Erwerbsstreben*), or traditional thinking versus rational thinking. The same could be said about his concept of economic systems. Yet, all this in no way minimises his achievement which is to have been the first to have thought in terms of economic systems. Thus one might argue today that area considerations should be in the forefront, that is, that we should think in terms of a development from subsistence economy such as manorial economy (*Fronhofwirtschaft*) by way of numerous mixed forms to the present-day market economy. The latter, as we know, is characterised by the fact that firms in fact produce entirely for the market and not for their own consumption. Or, expressed differently, the father of the family as the manager of a closed domestic economy is replaced by the market as a coordinator of almost all human achievement. The fact that subsistence economy was still a dominant economic influence in the early nineteenth century[3] and therefore was in time close to the date of birth of Karl Marx, demonstrates that market economy in today's differentiated form is of much more recent origin.

The late twentieth century may well be the last moment when our planet is populated simultaneously by men living in the age of electronics and those still living in the Stone Age. This suggests that behind such change is a rather complex process that would appear to be historically unique and therefore far removed from anything distinctly related to an inner necessity.

For this reason alone one should exercise restraint in going back to biological developmental concepts, particularly as far as so-called natural selections in the Darwininan sense is concerned. If we take mutation into consideration there is a great difference. In biology, there are deviations from the known gene structure that are referred to as mutations, but the only ones to have any significance are those which are superior to the existing gene structure. For man this is different. If we use the term mutation here for economic developments, what is meant is man's capacity to imagine things which up to then have not existed in the environment. As we know, it is this faculty that allows man to think up new tools and to create them. It is this faculty also that permits man to create new forms of community life. Whether what is created in the mind of the individual can be diffused generally, that is to say, whether a diffusion of ideas takes place, depends largely on political structures and community organisation. Such a process of diffusion is by no means self-evident, because the most efficient innovations were not always accepted. History is full of the prevention of ideas,[4] in fact one might assume this to be the rule rather than the exception. In contrast to physical events, such as natural catastrophes, climatic changes, etc. which are quite beyond man's influence, we are dealing here with mutations endogenous to man. If new ideas are conceived here and if they are put into practice they will necessarily replace the traditional conceptions. That, however, is the great hindrance. The traditional is threatened and so are all, except for the inventor, who have been formed by the past and find their identity in that past. In the economic sector we are well acquainted with the measures taken to boycott the threat of the new. Although the introduction of basic human rights also brought the freedom of exercising a trade or craft (*Handels- und Gewerbefreiheit*), it did not take long to rouse the forces intent on limiting those rights. International protectionism (that is, the difficulty of access to the market caused by institutional barriers, for instance in form of so-called professional regulations) and national protectionism by way of tariffs and quota regulations since then are every day events. In textbook language, protective tariffs are referred to as faulty allocations and related welfare reduction. This is not an adequate way of describing the actual situation. What really happens is that stagnating or regressing industries block or hinder new ideas. Thereby diffusion is hampered and without it no evolution is possible. The individual's invention will be without impact on the economy. Only through diffusion does invention become a relevant factor that changes the economic structure of a nation and makes a national economy evolutionary.

DEVELOPMENT IN A MARKET ECONOMY AND IN A CENTRALLY PLANNED ECONOMY

For evident reasons the evolutionary design of the market economy is a well-known pattern in which both elements of evolution, namely the invention or the innovation and its diffusion, are clearly visible. The comparison with the idea of the division of powers seems quite natural. What in a political system is seen as the legislature has its counterpart in the inventor or in the enterprises which create the innovation and put it into effect economically. Moreover, the counterpart to the executive is competition. Demand, which accepts or rejects innovation, takes on the role of the arbiter or judge. As in the case of the separation of powers, there are three groups of persons which are independent of each other. Those who are negatively affected by the innovation do not decide whether or not it should be introduced; it is the demand factor which determines the decision. As we know, this is a hindrance to overcome and is responsible for the failure of many an invention. The fact that less than 2 per cent of patented inventions are successful is a clear indicator of this point.[5] Competition, as the executive, forces diffusion on the side of supply, the side of those who are negatively affected by the invention. They have to adjust to the innovation which has been adapted by the demand. The intensification of interwoven markets in the course of the nineteenth century, in this respect, has enormously increased the competitive pressure among the producers (decline of own consumption). When we are talking of an average profit on sales of 2 to 3 per cent, the adoption of innovations becomes a question of economic survival. Every competitor who has adopted the new production process or the new product exerts additional pressure on those who have not yet done so. Thus a continuous stream of innovations keeps the enterprises under constant pressure without any orders from the political hierarchy. Such sensitive reactions, however, are registered in a market economy only when changes have noticeable effects on sales or profits of a respective business enterprise. All other factors have no consequence on market economy calculations.[6]

In our consideration of evolution, the centrally planned economy is seen as the counterpart to the market economy. By this we mean not only the present socialist economies in Eastern Europe but all forms of economy which, by their legal systems, exclude an independent economic action by the individual – as used to be the case long ago under the guilds and the *Flurzwang* in the agrarian sector.[7] In this case, innovations and other changes in the production process can only be introduced by higher authorities, such as the duke or the king in the age of absolutism. Mercantilism, in Germany more properly called cameralism, is in fact governmental development policy. Such policy governed all sectors of the economy of a country, whereby agriculture was considered particularly important in German territories. If turnips, potatoes, flax and tobacco were to be cultivated, it was done by direction from above and not by the individual will of the farmers. It is not surprising, therefore, that such orders met with the resistance of those ordered, a resistance that expressed itself in ignorance, carelessness and disinterest.[8] The development of manufacturing locations was not handled any better since employees had to be pressed from the population and vagrants, beggars and orphans were put to work. Even if such manufacturing establishments were leased out and a new type of entrepreneur thus came about, nothing changed in principle. Privilege in the form of state monopoly saw to it that diffusion would not occur by way of competition. The trading companies organised for the overseas regions are a well-known example. Quite a different matter, however, were inventions of a military nature. In this case, one's own innovations do not affect members of one's own political community, the negative effect being felt by the enemy. Therefore, it does not come as a surprise that innovations in this sector are adopted independently of the economic system, a matter familiar to us since Heraclitus's famous dictum, 'war is the father of all things'.

While continental European mercantilism contains a whole gamut of differing components and is not governed by a continuous principle of order, the centrally planned economic systems of our century are quite a different matter. The latter, as expressions of a revolutionary act, were consciously planned in contrast to the market economy. The goal, however, is not only the realisation of socialist society, but rather also the development of the respective economies. Demonstrating the weakness of socialist economic systems in this way to the recipient of this book would be like carrying coal to Newcastle. However, we can register some economic progress under absolutism. In the Soviet Union, for example, some progress has taken place but it has nevertheless failed to approach the target of catching up with the free industrial nations.

In the 1920s when the well-known debate, started by Mises, about the allocation of production resources in a socialist planned economy was riding high, the central question was how far the free market price could be replaced by a new measure of scarcity for the allocation of resources. It is of some interest that the battle on both sides was carried out not with regard to evolutionary processes, but with a view to finding a position of equilibrium.

The question of how to create a climate for innovations and how pressure could be used to effect diffusion was seen at best as peripheral. Why should the socialist cadre look for innovations if these carried unrest and friction into a well-tested system and if, on top of this, such innovations would mean additional risk and unpredictability. Therefore, it is less the so-called optimal allocation than the waste of means of production that is responsible for the low productivity in the socialist countries. Such waste can always be registered when the resources do not produce what they could produce with their level of knowledge.

FROM EVOLUTION TO STAGNATION

As already pointed out, our globe is occupied by people of rather different levels of development. This reminds us that evolution is anything but self-evident and that there are constellations under which evolution or, by Western standards, only a modest evolution takes place. The two economic systems demonstrate two rather different forms of evolutionary processes within one human society. During the time of the Industrial Revolution, when people were less interwoven within the market and the market forces determining diffusion of technical progress did not encompass large sectors of economic life, the direction from above or rather form the ruling political power does not seem to have been entirely negative. As a rule, the area of the market was smaller than the territory concerned. On the other hand, the intensity and the speed with which our globe has been altered economically in the course of the last two centuries was made possible only by market economy processes. These technical advances in our century have been picked up by socialist countries and installed by order from above, but further development on its own, however, is seldom registered. This leads us to question the preconditions for evolutionary processes in society. Or, put differently, what causes the opposite of evolution, namely stagnation which is just as common among mankind.

In market economies one must keep in mind that the real impetus of technical progress emanates from a very small minority. Pioneers or pioneer businesses cast the stones into the water and cause ripples across the entire surface – in other words, they force this motion upon all other enterprises. Looking at it this way, it is not surprising if the majority becomes tired of this force and takes steps to stop those who continue to cause the ripples of unrest. This means that a counter-movement is set in motion which continues to spread. In this way the *ancien régime* has re-entered through the back door, particularly since the late nineteenth century. Even if the extent of this development varies from one economy to another, there is no doubt that economic life in the Western industrial nations has become increasingly dominated by restrictions and regulations, by social policies hindering employer and employee, and by lowering the diffusion processes on the one side while preserving regressive industries through subsidies on the other. Counter-moves are not impossible, such as the policy of competition in Western Europe following the Second World War, a counter-measure against total cartelisation of the economy. On the other hand, the writing of laws of an interventionist nature continues unabatedly and beginnings of deregulation are almost too small to be detected.[9] Thus, regulations tend to form a growing jungle increasingly paralysing the freedom of action of employer and employee. Technical progress can hardly escape this trend. Creativity and diffusion will be made difficult if the co-determination of those who are affected by progress is written into the law, as has been done in the German law of co-determination. Worded differently it means that economic separation of power is being successively emasculated and with it the process of innovation and diffusion.

In socialist societies, as in all human societies, a similar tension between the established and the pioneers can be registered. In a politicised economy, however, matters are attended to in different ways. In a modern diversified economy of millions of products, the design and execution of a plan is not as easy as in an undifferentiated economy of the pre-industrial world. The long way a message has to travel from those who give the directive to those who are to act on it diminishes all interest in operating accordingly. Disinterest increases correspondingly. Experiences of this nature have led to considerations of reform. The goal of such reformist ideas is to progress from centralisation to decentralisation of decisions and to replace mere instructed acceptance with direct responsibility. Such loosening or even destruction of the present organisational structures is synonymous with the destruction of present power positions, therefore producing quasi-automatically the resistance of the established. This is very similar indeed to the resistance of traditional enterprises who fear their market position threatened by innovators.

Both economic systems share the phenomenon of sclerosis: in the socialist system it is the sclerosis of bureaucracy; in the market economy it is the sclerosis of mutual assurance by association and law. The social factors underlying both are the same, which explains why situations supportive of the status quo are rather the norm in human society and why the turbulence of change is a rather rare occurrence. If the market economy as a concept is a product of the Enlightenment, then it should also be recalled that the driving force of the Enlightenment was not economic but intellectual. Freedom from intellectual restriction by state and church was the guiding concept of the seventeenth and eighteenth century. What one was not aware of was that basic economic rights (rights of freedom of trade and craft) open the way not only to an economic but also a social revolution. We might question whether economic basic rights would have been pursued with such verve if the consequences had been correctly anticipated. As things stand, the evolution in the market economy can be seen as the rather unintended side-effect of concepts of individual freedom.

Notes

1. Until the First World War economists belonged, with very few exceptions, to the Faculty of Philosophy in Germany and in Switzerland.
2. It is worth remembering that numerous economists have had their intellectual beginnings in the study of classical antiquity, as in the case of Karl Bücher, or Alexander Rüstow whose main activity developed after the Second World War.
3. It is well known that then the economic development in the northwestern part of Europe was more advanced than in central Europe. Nevertheless, concerning A. Smith's famous example of pin manufacture, one ought to remember that he emphasises something in his time that was still significant and no trivial matter.
4. The persecution of ideas especially of religious and political kind are well known in European history.
5. See K.V. Möllering, 'Die Alterserwartung deutscher Patente', *Zeitschrift für die gesamte Staatswissenschaft*, Heft 4, 1950.
6. Therefore, the main task of ecology is the transformation of external to internal private costs. In this case the pressure of private competition also reduces costs of this sort.

7. That means the obligation to use one's land in accordance to the communally decided crop rotation (especially common fallowing in the free-field system).

8. The story is told that farmers in Prussia were told to cultivate potatoes. When they discovered that the potato plants were inedible they burnt the potatoes. Afterwards they realised that the tuberous roots were fit to eat. Similar things happen at the present time in developing countries.

9. It will be an illusion to expect a change in this regard by the European Economic Community, because its policy of competition (see the actual draft of an amendment concerning the control of concentration) has to take into consideration the industrial policy that means the protection of branches of manufacture.

9 The Self-organisation of the Economy

Michael Hutter

The house is crazy, says a weary traveller to himself, and will not stand very long; but it is a chance if it falls tonight, and I will venture therefore to sleep in it tonight.

Adam Smith

SELF-ORGANISATION AND SELF-REPRODUCTION

Self-organisation of the economy is an old topic. But what is its nature? Is it akin to a valve which regulates a machine through a feedback loop, to the dynamic stability of a thermodynamic system, to the evolution of spontaneous order or to the self-reproduction of biological systems? In this chapter, I will introduce a particularly radical form of self-organisation. We will assume that the economy continues through a process of ongoing self-reproduction. Very much like a biological cell, the economy not only structures but generates the elements of which it consists. More precisely: the economy is defined as a network of elementary operations that recursively reproduces elementary operations.

I will briefly introduce the concept of self-referentiality and its application to an economy. Then we embark on a short exploration of our economy, using the sketch of the theory as our roadmap.

Recursive reproduction involves the logical condition of self-referentiality. Self-referentiality is the property of a system to constitute its own self. A system is a unity of interacting elements, distinguishing itself from its environment. The system is called self-referential if it is able to constitute its own elements (internal environment) and its own distinction between the self and its external environment (Foerster, 1981; Hofstadter, 1979; Bateson, 1979).

Life-forms are examples of self-referential systems: biological organisms produce their own elements in strict autonomy. At the same time, they are able to interact with what they perceive as their environment. Every single biological cell is such a self-referential or 'autopoietic' system (Varela, 1981).

Mental processes in humans are recognised as being self-referential since, roughly, the eighteenth century. The individual creates his or her own world through the distinction between the mind and everything outside it. Since Voltaire, Locke and Kant, the continuity of individual consciousness has become a common experience to modern observers. Traditional economic theories are still based on the discovery of mental self-reference.

Self-referential social systems, finally, are able to distinguish themselves from their environments through the use of at least one basic semantic distinction. That distinction defines the system's identity – its unity. The distinction itself – and here lies the technical difficulty of theory construction – cannot be reflected by the system which uses it because it appears in the semantic form of paradox (Luhmann, 1984; Hutter, 1989). The elementary operations of social systems are communication acts. The recursive application of communications to the results of former communications produces new communication. Social systems are exemplified in the performance of plays. Whether we are in them or whether we contribute to them, we always know the borderline between the words, movements and gestures of the play and its outside world. Every communication act within the play carries an invisible tag which says: 'This is play'. But the existence of the tag must not be mentioned. Otherwise, the play disappears or becomes part of a larger play. Some plays are as intricate as in classical theatre and opera. They generate reference to a complex and changing outside world. Some plays are as simple as children's plays, generating only reference to the immediate common environment of the interaction.

These remarks were intended to provide a rather intuitive understanding of what is meant by self-reproducing social systems, and to point immediately to the semantic difficulties involved in theory formulation. To make matters even more forbidding, we must keep in mind that the three types of self-referential systems evolve interdependently.

To summarise: (i) Social systems are self-referential. Their evolution is homologous to the evolution of biological and mental self-referential systems. (ii) Social systems consist of communication events. (iii) The observer of self-referential social systems contributes self-referentially to the system within or about which he or she communicates.

A theory of self-reproducing social systems is just emerging (Luhmann, 1984, 1986; Teubner, 1988). There have been several attempts, however, to apply it to economies (Luhmann, 1988; Baecker, 1988; Hutter, 1989).

OBSERVING THE ECONOMY

We now can approach the treasures of past economic research with a new set of questions: if an economy is a self-referential social system, we should find evidence of the following conditions:

1. Circularity plays a role in the description of economies.
2. There is a tenacious yet fruitless debate about some central distinguishing property of the system.
3. There is a debate about what constitutes the elementary operations of economies.

All three conditions are fulfilled.

'Circularity' is the organising principle of contemporary National Accounting Systems. The circle takes the form of a double circular flow of money incomes and goods. The monetary flow is exemplified through a money piece which changes hands until it returns to the initial point. But the circle never closes,it is only a metaphor. What we call 'circularity' is a process of transferring purchasing power again and again. The process is endless, because a payment is only accepted if a subsequent payment is expected. 'Money circulation means simply that it is possible to reproduce the ability to pay through payments. Circulation is autopoiesis: Reproduction of the elements of the system through the elements of the system' (Luhmann, 1988, p. 131; my translation).

The money flow is complemented by a flow of those goods and services which are 'exchanged' for payments. We simply choose, it is said, to look in the direction of the money flow because money is easier to add up. But if one chooses to look in the direction of the goods flow, one perceives nothing that corresponds to the chain of reproduction observed in the monetary flow. Goods and services are transformations of a physical, mental and social

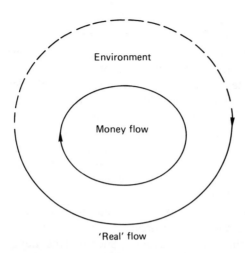

Figure 9.1 The flow of the economy

form for the purpose of their monetary evaluation. These transformations dissolve eventually and inevitably back into their
respective environments. The flow of the economy in first approxi-
mation consists of one closed and one open circle (Figure 9.1).

The monetary circle constitutes the identity of an economy. Its
closure means that only payments and nothing but payments can
reproduce new payments. It is the economy which initiates corresponding changes in the economy's environment. The acts of transformation are basically unlinked. We only observe a continuous
succession of such transformation events in the environment of
economies. They are triggered by the expectation that every payment generates a next payment, driving the economy like 'jet
propulsion' (Luhmann, 1988, p. 137).

We thus reach the somewhat surprising conclusion that the
money flow, far from being peripheral, is the central constitutive
activity of an economy. Money indeed matters, and the growth of
economies depends primarily on the evolution of those institutions
which are able to generate an adequate supply of money.[1]

Money is a medium of communication. But what determines
the use of the medium? Traditional theory traces the source either
to human suffering or to human pleasure. Self-referential social
theory traces it to a successful semantic paradox. Social systems
identify themselves through one basic semantic distinction. Since
the distinction cannot refer to itself, it appears as paradox: it is and

it is not identical with itself. One can easily spot such constitutive paradoxes. Around them, we find endless discussions which typically move in circles, unable to decide whether such concepts as 'justice', 'beauty' and 'truth' are of a subjective or an objective nature. In the case of economies such an age-old debate surrounds exchange value and use value. Value, then, is the basic semantic distinction of economies. Value is conceived and continuously generated within the process of economic communication. It is a property which develops frequently, but not always, in societies along with a sense of justice, truth and other self-referential properties. Around them, social systems in all their institutional complexity are able to evolve.[2]

We have yet to consider the elements of which a self-reproducing economy consists. According to the theory, the economy consists of communication events. Such events have only recently been recognised by theorists (Williamson, 1985). They are called transactions. Transactions are not exchanges because exchanges are one-time events. Transactions involve payment and an activity considered equal in value, intended to replace the inability to pay caused by the payment. Every transaction is part of the circular flow of money and part of the 'flow' of environment-related communication.[3] In terms of Figure 9.2:

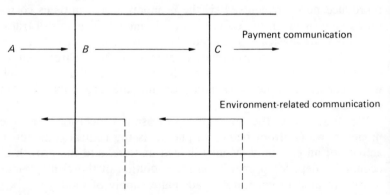

Figure 9.2   Transactions

The money which B receives from A for its activity is accepted because its acceptance by C is expected. Payment is given from one actor to the next just the way in which a child 'tags'another child in a street play. The act of transferring ability to pay generates a future counter-value in the environment of the transaction. The transaction is recursively linked to a subsequent transaction, which, in turn, is reproduced in the following transactions, and so on, endlessly.

WITHIN THE ECONOMY

In the previous section, we chose the position of an outside observer of the economy. We were unable to observe the inside of the economy because the theory of self-referential systems implies complete closure of the observed system. It is one of the most startling and consequential insights of this theory that we can't see the inside of what we have chosen as elements of observation. If we tried to do so, the elements would not be elements any more and we would saw off the branch of theory on which we are sitting. But there is a trick to overcome this methodological limitation: the observer can change position in time. He can move from an outside observation to an inside observation and back again (Foerster, 1981; Hutter, 1989).

Everyone knows what it means to act within an economy. But how can such an inside position be described? A self-referential social system constitutes its own semantic distinction between the self and its external environment. The previous section demonstrated that economies self-reproduce their value distinction, their medium of circularity and their elements. The economy, as the topic of our science-internal conversation, is a conversation or communication play observed by outside persons and inside persons. A visual two-dimensional representation shows that our focal system, the economy, looks like a torus rather than a closed surface (Figure 9.3).

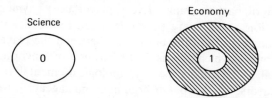

Figure 9.3 Observing the economy from the 'science position'

In the previous section, we observed the economy from position '0'; now we will observe it from position '1'. Within the context of a conversation based on the notion of value, a person in position '1' observes other persons as they act within the same environment (Figure 9.4).

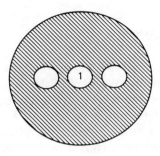

Figure 9.4   Observing the economy from the 'economy position'

The inside person perceives its economic environment in the same way an actor perceives a play. The play is called 'value reproduction', and the person knows how to play a part in it, depending on the actions and reactions of other players. The observation of the behaviour of other persons acting in the economy is a difficult and energy-consuming activity. Players structure their observations typically into subenvironments, distinguished by criteria we have yet to discuss. The perceptions of these subenvironments are called markets. Every market is characterised by a fluctuating set of prices, quoted in monetary units and corresponding to a specified transformation of the person's total environment (Luhmann, 1988).

Our present exploration will be limited to two basic issues: the nature of the players and the nature of economic environments called markets.

Every player is a past producer of payable value and a future consumer of payable value. Every player uses payments for self-reproduction, since every player is a self-referential system. The transactions constitute the borderline between the player's self and the economy – which now is in the position of 'environment'. Self-referential social theory permits biological, mental (human) and social players. To keep the argument manageable, we will limit the exploration to social players.[4] A handful of specialised social systems have evolved as economic players: corporations, associations and banks are the prominent institutional forms. As long as theorists tried to follow the emergence of value back to its source, they focused on the production of valued activities. Therefore, firms and their organisation of physical transformations received most of the attention. Little attention has been given to organisations which specialise in the maintenance of the monetary flow. Their role in the economy's self-reproduction is distinctly different from the role of firms, yet it is hardly explored. The organisation of human contributions through associations and unions has a long tradition in our economies. But they have had the most severe difficulties in adjusting to the economy's growth during the past century.

All the institutional forms mentioned see themselves as producers of value. Their perception, like ours, has been conditioned to follow the monetary flow rather than the flow of transformation from past into future environments. Only a few social actors seem to consider themselves primarily as future consumers of payable value. Therefore, even contemporary economies are still pushed by productive activities rather than pulled by consumptive activities.

It was stated above that markets are a player's perception of its economic subenvironments, perceived through their price sets. The criteria for distinguishing markets follow the three fundamental types of self-reproduction which were introduced in the first section: life-forms, minds and plays. This distinction corresponds to the economic theorist's distinction beween land, labour and capital. In consequence, it can be shown that the markets for land, labour and capital are the perceptions of economic players with respect to transformations in their biological, mental and social environments.

The biological environment contains life-forms. They can be harvested, sold and consumed. Once considered the only source of value, land has almost disappeared from the theorist's agenda, in spite of the fact that it was the theory of land rent which Marshall developed into the theory of price as we know it. Today, land must be seen as the entire physical space around us and life-forms are the entire spectrum of natural resources.

The mental environment contains minds. Minds operate (primarily?) in humans. They are economically coded as labour. It has always been recognised that labour is a special resource, if not the only source of value. Yet labour has been treated theoretically as just another physical factor of production. Human creativity did find occasional recognition. Following Schumpeter, contemporary theorists think of creativity as a property limited to special individuals called entrepreneurs. An extension of the creativity argument to all kinds of mental activity seems under way. Modern intelligent products depend much more on the cognitive inputs of inventors, programmers and designers than on physical resources. Research, education and communicative skills must be recognised as valuable factors of production and consumption (Hutter, 1987).

The social environment contains the economy and other social systems. One of them, the economy, has found our particular attention. Value can be gained from its performance as well as from the performance of other social systems. In the case of the economy, two perceptions are called capital markets, depending on the way the circular flow is perceived. Future self-reproduction means, in one direction of the circuit, continuity of payment and storability of money. In the other direction, it means continuity of production and consumption. In both cases, interest rates for financial and 'real' capital, respectively, indicate the present expectations of future value creations.[5] Modern economies have accumulated a vast and complex stock of credibility and trust which stabilises these rates. In the case of the other social environments, the argument is somewhat more difficult. The contribution of 'good government', of effective legal norms, of scientific inquiry and of aesthetic experiments is usually taken for granted. But the social organisation of production and consumption depends on the ability to generate and maintain these forms of capital as well. Although firms, banks, unions, associations and (to a lesser degree) households consider the economy as their focal social system, they still can participate in many other plays. Political, legal, scientific and aesthetic plays are sources of economic value, although they are not coded through price sets. If remnants of such plays do find their way into markets, as in the case of paintings, it typically remains unclear whether they are to be regarded as monetary or as 'real' capital.

We conclude: product markets, labour talent markets and markets for monetary, 'real' and other social capital are the environment interpretation patterns which have evolved. Price sets and interest rates guide the behaviour of self-interested self-producing actors, and they indicate how payments are distributed to actors involved in specific environment transformations.

OUTCOME AND OUTLOOK

Back in outer social space. A section ago, science was one of the environments usable as a source of economic value. Now it is, again, the observing social system. But now, more so than before, scientific observation can be perceived as one of several communication plays within a society, distinguished by its search for 'truth', rather than the economy's search for 'value'. If we give up the traditional idealistic goal of representing the economy through another social system's language, we can also fruitfully explore the direct interaction of science and economy. The economy produces the boundary with its internal environment, and it produces the boundary with its external environment. The external boundary is just as complex an affair as its counterpart. Self-referential systems always depend on close contacts with their environments, and they develop sensory channels. Social systems develop polycontextural persons able to translate between several systems' internal codes.[6] But this process of interaction between social subsystems belongs to another, wider phenomenon: the self-reproduction of societies.

Within the limitations of a few pages, I have outlined the basic features of our economy as it is perceived using a self-referential theory of social systems. The perspective is unfamiliar and, in consequence, all observations are tentative. But the rewards of further exploration are high. The theory promises heretofore impossible insights into the evolution of economies and their environments – including economic theories.

Notes

1. See, for example, Adam Smith (1970, p. 420) on the growth potential of paper money. Smith seems also to be well aware of the fictitious and thus basically uncertain nature of money. See the sentence in the epitaph, introduced in connection with a discussion of drawing and redrawing credit (ibid.).

2. Both 'scarcity' and 'cost' are consequences of the existence of an economic value play. Once a sense of economic value is established within a society, one can call the affected portions of the environment 'scarce', and one can call past exchanges, be they factual or imaginary, 'cost'.

3. Note that the sequence suggested differs from the one suggested by Marx: money is not transformed into goods and retransformed into

money. Both flows are simultaneous. Important, however, is Marx's recognition that productive activity reproduces the conditions of production (Sik, 1973).
4. To every one of these social persons, self-interest is attributable. Everyone is, at the same time, a conversation within which other persons constitute internal environments.
5. 'Interest indicates how high the price is which one pays or is paid in order to involve oneself within the autopoiesis of the economy into the incentives and risks of this autopoiesis' (Baecker, 1988; p. 294; my translation).
6. The extensive occurrence of such specialised 'conversation circles' has been shown for the interface between the pharmaceutical industry and patent law. See Hutter, 1989.

References

Baecker, D. (1988) *Information und Risiko in der Marktwirtschaft* (Frankfurt: Suhrkamp).

Bateson, G. (1979) *Mind and Nature: A Necessary Unity* (New York: Bantam).

Foerster, H. von (1981) *Observing Systems* (Seaside, Cal.: Intersystems).

Hofstadter, D. (1979) *Gödel, Escher, Bach: An Eternal Golden Braid* (New York: Basic Books).

Hutter, M. (1987) 'Music as a Source of Growth', in W. Hendon (ed.), *Economic Efficiency in the Performing Arts* (Akron: Association of Cultural Economics).

Hutter, M. (1989) *Die Produktion von Recht* (Tübingen: Mohr/Siebeck).

Luhmann, N. (1984) *Soziale Systeme* (Frankfurt: Suhrkamp).

Luhmann, N. (1986) 'The Autopoiesis of Social Systems', in F. Geyer and J. van der Zouwen (eds), *Sociocybernetic Paradoxes* (London: Sage).

Luhmann, N. (1988) *Die Wirtschaft der Gesellschaft* (Frankfurt: Suhrkamp).

Sik, O. (1973) *Argumente für den dritten Weg* (Hamburg: Hoffmann und Campe).

Smith, A. (1970) *The Wealth of Nations*, Books I–III (Harmondsworth: Penguin).

Teubner, G. (1988) 'Evolution of Autopoietic Law', in G. Teubner (ed.), *Autopoietic Law* (Berlin: De Gruyter).

Varela, F.J. (1981) *Principles of Biological Autonomy* (New York: North-Holland).

Williamson, O. (1985) *The Economic Institutions of Capitalism* (New York: Free Press).

10 Evolution and Innovation

Jochen Röpke

THE MEANING OF EVOLUTION

Our knowledge about evolutionary change is limited. Evolutionary economics is still in its infancy; indeed we are on thin theoretical ice in linking evolution and innovation.

If we are to reach a new level of understanding we must engage in quasi-scientific speculation in order to generate new theories, better able to explain the facts of economic life. Such new theories have been developed in recent years, and even if they do not yet possess a paradigmatic standing in the scientific community, they offer the chance to replace or substitute the mechanistic view of the world, the clockwork-modelling and equilibrium theorising, so prevalent even in those branches of economics that are specialising on the change and development of systems.

Our aim will be to provide a theoretical framework which can support the givens of mainstream economics – technology, motivation, institutions – as internally generated properties of a process of evolutionary change.

As recent advances in systems theory make clear, a fruitful alternative paradigm will probably take an evolutionary perspective which, ironically enough, brings us back to the founding fathers of economic science, the classical political economists, who have been characterised by a modern classical thinker as 'Darwinists before Darwin' (Hayek, 1973, p. 23). This is not only because of the well-known fact that Charles Darwin refined his idea of natural selection after a reading of British political economists (Hayek, 1988, pp. 24–5), but because their thinking about the economic world and many of their policy suggestions reflect a deeper understanding of 'evolutionary' processes.

The 'invisible hand' of Adam Smith, the first cybernetic thinker, can easily be rediscovered in the 'self-organising structures' of modern systems theory: the stability and order in the evolution of a system is the largely unintentional outcome of the dynamic interactions of individual actors. Self-organisation will be evolutionary when the behavioural results of the heterogeneous actors are tested and selected in a competitive environment and when the successful variations are retained and cumulated within the system (model of variation and selective retention).

In this sense, Campbell (1975, p. 1,104) defines evolution as 'a selective cumulation of skills, technologies, recipes, beliefs, customs, organizational structures, and the like, retained through purely social modes of transmission, rather than in the genes'.

Because a higher level of individual and personal competencies allows the discovering and exploration of new technological and product variations and paradigms, evolution can be seen as increasing the number of possible worlds or increasing the complexity of an economic system.

Who are the agents of variation in economic evolution? It is still unclear at which level evolutionary variation and selection operates and who are the units which evolve.

Very often variation ('mutation') is equated with innovation. But this view seems to be too simplistic. We would prefer to view as 'genetic' variation within socio-economic systems the changing 'property rights' of individuals, especially innovators, including socio-cultural norms and values. The units which evolve could therefore be individuals, organisations (firms), markets, nations, and even the earth (mankind). These property rights determine the degree of permission and of private appropriation of the benefits of innovation, and they help us to explain why not all conceivable variation is realised.

For other authors the 'social genes' are the behavioural 'routines' within firms (Nelson and Winter, 1982) or 'rules of conduct' (Hayek, 1979, p. 157).

ENTREPRENEURSHIP IN EVOLUTION

By focusing on innovative entrepreneurs of the Schumpeterian type we nevertheless have found the agents of economic evolution, even if their main action parameters – innovations – are not the mutations of economic life. Entrepreneurs drive the evolution of capitalism.

To clarify the theoretical and empirical link between innovation,

evolution, and entrepreneurship, we have to recognise entrepreneurial activity as a heterogeneous and multidimensional activity.

At one extreme, we find the routine entrepreneur (the 'Wirt'
in the language of Schumpeter) adaptively economising resources.
The routine entrepreneur operates within a well-defined domain
of business activity: existing products, markets (even if imperfect),
and production technology. A second type of entrepreneurial
activity is 'arbitrage' – the discovering (noticing) and exploitation
(removing) of profit opportunities resulting from buying/selling
spreads.

From an evolutionary point of view, routine and arbitrage entrepreneurship can be considered as 'marginal'. The first type tries
to maintain the economic *status quo* (the 'equilibrium'), whereas
arbitrage activity would result in establishing the equilibrium which
– after being reached – would make the arbitrageurs redundant.

Arbitrage can be considered a process of self-organising 'devol-
ution': bringing the economy back to equilibrium by feeding on
the profit opportunities created by an evolving system.

Who are the persons creating arbitrage opportunities? The main
sources of arbitrage are innovators in Schumpeter's sense, people
who, by creating new markets and technologies and destroying old
resource combinations, unintendedly provide arbitrageurs with new
profit opportunities. Without innovation arbitrage activity would
dry up, and without arbitrage routine business would not be
possible.

Can routine entrepreneurs, arbitrageurs and innovators coexist?
Can we have at the *same* time an economic system which is in
equilibrium, moving towards equilibrium and evolving? The answer
is yes and no, depending on the segment of the market we are
focusing on, how we draw the boundaries of a system, and the
time path we are considering.

Looking at the world economy, we can observe stagnating,
evolving and devolving regions, all at the same time. Focusing
on a national economy, we could observe evolving markets and
technologies, markets dominated by arbitrageurs, and even markets near equilibrium.

Schumpeter even seems to maintain that a developing economy
follows a time path (trajectory) consisting of innovation → arbitrage → equilibrium → innovation, all embedded in business cycles
of various lengths, stretching from a few years to half a century
(Kondratieff cycle). Because in an evolving economy innovative

variety will emerge between two equilibrium positions, the system will never reach the same position or old equilibrium again: 'what we are to consider is that kind of change arising from within the system which so displaces its equilibrium point that the new one cannot be reached from the old one by infinitesimal steps' (Schumpeter, 1934, p. 64).

Translated into the language of systems theory: self-organising systems that display evolution are characterised by intrinsic non-linearities and irreversibility. Innovations as non-linear activities can become self-amplifying and change the very environment (the selective mechanism) hitherto dictating innovative behaviour. Economic evolution then is a history of a system undergoing irrevocable changes 'in the economic process brought about by innovation, together with all their effects, and the responses to them by the economic system' (Schumpeter, 1939, p. 37).

It seems trivial enough to conclude that evolving systems can never be equilibrium systems (of the Walras–Arrow–Debreu type) – even if we may observe from time to time various segments and pockets of the market and therefore multiple equilibria which may clear in the Walrasian sense (and functioning as eternal falsifiers or proofs for those believing in equilibrium analysis).

It also seems difficult – and here we have to part company with Schumpeter – to reconcile evolution at a specific level of a system with a tendency to equilibrium, which does not rule out that at a sublevel of a system such tendencies may manifest themselves – depending among others on the success of the actors to isolate themselves – via property rights – from changes in their innovative environment.

Arbitrageurs work hard to achieve this, but in an evolving economy their achievements can be regarded as equivalent to those of Sisyphus.

Innovations not only drive the economy away from a stationary state, they keep the system away from it. An evolutionary regime operates beyond the equilibrium and it operates in fluctuations (for empirical studies see Kleinknecht, 1986; and Krelle, 1987). This perspective is carefully worked out in Schumpeter's cycle analysis, which – viewed from contemporary systems theory – is the most brilliant and visionary of Schumpeter's contributions to a theory of economic evolution: evolution occurs through a cyclical process. Cyclical fluctuations are the normal means by which capitalism develops and thereby evolves. Eliminating these fluctuations would kill off economic development.

Innovations present the main competitive challenge for firms in the market-place. Firms are able to survive and expand if they respond with innovative variety of their own making, given accommodative institutions and property rights that rule out, for example, the possibility of buying out your competitor instead of competing with him via innovation. Only innovative variety can destroy innovative variety (a variation of Ashby's law).

Innovative pressure stimulates a new round of innovative actions which prevents a motivational burning out of selective pressure – and therefore a move towards equilibrium; so long as the behavioural constraints of property rights and institutions do not outlaw innovative activity, with the result that the economy would approach a 'stationary state'.

Because innovating firms stimulate and motivate each other, there will be no tendency to zero profits and decreasing returns. The economy will generate from within innovative variety which keeps the system expanding and changing, generating structure and complexity. The real sources of change are in the system.

STABILITY IN EVOLUTION

Systems far from equilibrium, which evolve through fluctuations (cycles), nevertheless do express stability, but not necessarily any particular optimality. What characterises this stability of an evolving economy is changeability itself. Stability is created by the continuous adaptation and the innovative responses of the market participants. The system is stabilised by its own variations (Röpke, 1977, p. 43). Creative destruction has to be included in this picture. Innovations destroy old structures and resource combinations, but at the same time create new solutions, complexity and new structures.

A stable system of this kind can never be in equilibrium. From the view of equilibrium analysis evolutionary stability is, of course, 'unstable'. But without this kind of instability no creativity and innovation would be possible. The system would function (like a clockwork mechanism) but not evolve.

If we employ the rationality criteria of equilibrium economics, we would have to characterise an evolving economy as a system misallocating scarce resources or by the non-optimising behaviour of its elements. But optimal behaving or profit maximising firms could not survive for very long in the turbulent environment of an evolving economy. Because optimising under conditions of strong, unavoidable uncertainty (uncertainty not reducible by a probability calculus) is not possible, those firms that nevertheless try to do so, or those firms who cannot tolerate uncertainty and creativity, have by necessity to weed out innovative alternatives from their choice set, making them vulnerable to innovators and face extinction.

Firms working as neo-classical optimising machines lack the potential for absorbing uncertainty and producing uncertainty for others. They lack the capability to compete in an evolutionary regime. The economist's conception of behaviour as 'rational' maximising is, from an evolutionary perspective, woefully inadequate.

The way out of this dilemma has been for many firms – especially in the Anglo-Saxon world – to internalise (via mergers and the like) their more innovative competitors with the consequence of making not the 'fittest' but the 'fattest' able to survive and expand, to reduce the incentive for innovative learning and for investment in innovative capability, to lessen potential competition and generally to slow down economic evolution – which demonstrates the evolutionary importance of 'culturgens' or property rights in explaining the history and steering the future of an economic system.

We seem to face here a general problem – already spelled out clearly by Schumpeter (1950, p. 138; see also Allen, 1988, p. 107; Dosi, 1988a, pp. 130–2; Röpke, 1987): a system consisting of firms with optimal behaviour at each instant, maximising allocative efficiency, will underachieve compared to a system which 'misallocates' its resources at every instant, because a non-efficient allocative performance is a necessary condition for long-run evolutionary achievement. An economic system which is better off in terms of productivity and innovativeness will have to operate in conditions of (neo-classical) allocative inefficiency. Evolution requires allocation failure.

COEVOLUTION

In the course of the cross-stimulating innovative competitive challenges between firms, those who possess higher innovative capabilities may gain temporary competitive advantages over others. In evolution, the ability to innovate is what counts. Innovative competition provides a tremendous stimulation for increasing competencies to create and implement new knowledge and can therefore be characterised as a 'discovery process' (of the third order): in a discovery process of the first order as described by Hayek (1979, pp. 67–70) information travels via prices; in discovery of the second order (Schumpeter) new innovative knowledge is created and diffuses; and in the third order the competency to create and implement new knowledge (innovations) is increased.

This endogenous coevolution of innovative capabilities of minds and firms, together with selective environmental pressure and property rights is responsible for the cumulativeness of innovative capabilities, and also of the asymmetric competitive relationships between firms (and nations: Röpke, 1987). Firms achieving higher levels of innovative capabilities 'increase also their probability of maintaining or increasing their levels of competitiveness' (Dosi, 1988b, p. 1,161).

But there seem to exist inbuilt stabilisers (negative feedback loops) which prevent successful individuals, firms and nations becoming so capable and successful that the gap between these innovative leaders and their followers increases continually.

An expanding asymmetry of cumulative capabilities would in the end increase the difficulty of imitation and catching up. And this would tend to decrease the environmental pressure on the competitive leaders for increasing their innovative capability. Their motivation to achieve (McClelland, 1976) will weaken and organisational slack and non-innovative rent-seeking will use up more and more of their resources, with the consequence of decreasing the competency gap and easing imitation and catching up. The asymmetry is correcting in itself, and the motivation to innovate is reproduced and stabilised spontaneously within the system.

So far we have implicitly assumed that the social 'genes' (property rights), regulating innovative activity, remain unchanged during the course of innovation-caused fluctuations of the level of economic activity. But the right to act as an innovator, and the possibility for the appropriation of innovative rents, will tend to change because innovations themselves will change drastically the economic environment of other firms and resource owners. Those market actors who are especially faced with a wealth-decreasing fall-out from the 'creative destructors' (Schumpeter) will have an interest in changing the rules of the game against innovation or creative destruction, or in protecting 'old' (non-innovative) resource combinations. The very success of innovators tends to create opposition to them and changes the course of creative destruction and the pattern of evolution.

In a Hayekian world, governed by the rule of law and backed up by proper constitutional institutions, this would be impossible or difficult to achieve because rules of conduct protect only material domains and not market values (Hayek, 1976, p. 123).

But given the constitutional arrangements we find in the Western world, and the ambitions of political entrepreneurs catering for the votes of the distressed and the self-interest of voters and élites to use the power of government to alter the outcome of competitive markets, we can reasonably expect the imposition of constraints on the exercise of innovation which tends to inhibit it and could ultimately succeed in curbing innovative entrepreneurship altogether (Röpke, 1983; Baumol, 1983). If we try to endogenise the 'genetic' constraints of economic life, we cannot expect that innovative success breeds success. On the contrary, it is the success of entrepreneurship that stimulates change in the regulatory environment which tends to discourage innovational activity. (This argument, of course, is very similar to the Schumpeterian hypothesis that the very success of capitalism will tend to undermine the moral and institutional conditions on which its further evolution depends.)

The evolutionary outcome of the second feedback loop – innovations induce a change in the institutional constraints – is probably non-predictable; that does not mean that we would be unable to say how the property rights would have to change in order to provide stronger incentives to innovation. But whether such actions will be taken by the political system depends on conditions whose occurrence is difficult to predict, making the whole evolutionary process unpredictable – even if we possessed a good theory of 'genetic' change at the socio-economic level (i.e. a theory of change of property rights and institutions; see Witt, 1988). (We are discussing here a time horizon of decades and not of a few years.)

That is the theoretical price we have to pay for not deriving theorems from given motivational, institutional and technological assumptions, but making the self-organised change of these variables the core of evolutionary analysis.

References

Allen, P.M. (1988) 'Evolution, Innovation and Economics', in G. Dosi, C. Freeman, R. Nelson, G. Silverberg, L. Soete (eds), *Technical Change and Economic Theory* (London/New York: Pinter), pp. 95–119.

Baumol, W.J. (1983) 'Toward Operational Models of Entrepreneurship', in J. Ronen (ed.), *Entrepreneurship* (Lexington, Mass./Toronto: Lexington Books), pp. 29–49.

Campbell, D.T. (1975) 'On the Conflicts Between Biological and Social Evolution and Between Psychology and Moral Tradition', *American Psychologist*, vol. 30, pp. 1103–26.

Dosi, G. (1988a) 'Institutions and Markets in a Dynamic World', *The Manchester School*, vol. LVI, pp. 119–46.

Dosi, G. (1988b) 'Sources, Procedures, and Microeconomic Effects of Innovation', *Journal of Economic Literature*, vol. XXVI, pp. 1120–71.

Hayek, F.A. von (1973) *Law, Legislation and Liberty*, vol. 1: 'Rules and Order' (London: Routledge & Kegan Paul).

Hayek, F.A. von (1976) *Law, Legislation and Liberty*, vol. 2: 'The Mirage of Social Justice' (London: Routledge & Kegan Paul).

Hayek, F.A. von (1979) *Law, Legislation and Liberty*, vol. 3: 'The Political Order of a Free People' (London: Routledge & Kegan Paul).

Hayck, F. A. von (1988) *The Collected Works*, vol. 1: *The Fatal Conceit* (London: Routledge).

Kleinknecht, A. (1986) 'Long Waves, Depression and Innovation', *De Economist*, vol. 134, pp. 84–108.

Krelle, W. (1987) 'Long-Term Fluctuations of Technical Progress and Growth', *Journal of Institutional and Theoretical Economics*, vol. 141, pp. 379–401.

McClelland, D. (1976) *The Achieving Society*, new edn (New York: Irvington Publishers).

Nelson, R.R. and Winter, S.G. (1982) *An Evolutionary Theory of Economic Change* (Cambridge, Mass./London: Harvard University Press).

Röpke, J. (1977) *Die Strategie der Innovation* (Tübingen: Mohr/Siebeck).

Röpke, J. (1983) 'Handlungsrechte und wirtschaftliche Entwicklung' in A. Schüller (ed.), *Property Rights und ökonomische Theorie* (München: Franz Vahlen), pp. 111–44.

Röpke, J. (1987) 'Vierte industrielle Revolution und Dritte Welt: Entwicklungspotentiale zwischen schöpferischer Zerstörung, Rückindustrialisierung und Nachfolge', in The Society for International Development (Berlin chapter) SID (ed.), *Neue Technologien in Entwicklungs-*

ländern: Ein Beitrag zur Armutsbekämpfung oder Verfestigung technologischer Abhängigkeiten? (Berlin: ICT-Verlag), pp. 1–47.

Schumpeter, J.A. (1934) *The Theory of Economic Development* (Cambridge, Mass.: Harvard University Press).

Schumpeter, J.A. (1939) *Business Cycles* (New York: McGraw-Hill).

Schumpeter, J.A. (1956) *Kampitalismus, Sozialismus und Demokratie* (München: Francke Verlag).

Witt, U. (1988) 'Eine individualistische Theorie der Entwicklung ökonomischer Institutionen', in E. Boettcher, P. Herder-Dorneich and K.-E. Schenk (eds), *Jahrbuch für Neue Politische Ökonomie*, Band 7 (Tübingen: Mohr/Siebeck), pp. 72–95.

11 Waves in Long-term Economic Development

René Höltschi and Christian Rockstroh[1]

Among the long-term economic changes of Western industrialised nations one can readily discern between long periods of above average economic impetus with rapid growth and periods of little or no economic growth at all. In the attempt to explain this alternating behaviour a wide range of theories have evolved about the so-called 'long waves'. Most theories reach back to the initial ideas of Kondratieff (1926) who actually only became well known through the further developments in the work of Schumpeter (1961). Because of an overall faint development of world commerce in the late 1970s and early 1980s the long-wave theories have experienced a rebirth.[2] The majority of these theories describe four 'Kondratieff waves' since the onset of industrialisation, each wave having an approximate duration of fifty years. The fourth Kondratieff cycle started accordingly with the upward trend at the end of the Second World War. Today, we consider ourselves as being near the end of this cycle.

Nevertheless, the actual existence of such waves is very controversial. Often the long-wave theory appears too deterministic and also too mechanistic. This is because the Kondratieff cycles are described as general regularities – as more or less rigidly fixed patterns. Such an approach, of course, cannot account at all for the evolutionary character of economic growth, which is strongly affected by historical, technological, societal, and cultural forces. On the other hand, the empirical foundations which can be found in literature and which have been reconfirmed by our own research are explicit enough to discern patterns of long-term market fluctuations in the course of economic evolution.

Long-term fluctuations vary in duration; usually, they last a few decades. We call such a rise followed by a decline a 'growth wave' which contrasts with the much more deterministic concept of the 'long wave'.

In the course of our recent work (see Sik, Höltschi and Rockstroh, 1988) we studied one such wave in greater detail, pertaining to various Western industrialised countries: the United States, Germany, and Switzerland. In each of these three countries a certain growth wave, which started during the Second World War and is now ending, could easily be identified. We call it the 'post-war growth wave'. The insights hereby gained are strongly dependent on historical as well as geopolitical factors. They cannot be used directly for preindustrial countries or periods. Furthermore, their direct extrapolative use for countries with a markedly different economic as well as social structure (e.g. socialist countries) is also not possible. But despite these restrictions, there exist indications of wave patterns that will most likely repeat themselves, and also occur in a similar manner in other Western industrialised nations.

THE EMPIRICAL FRAMEWORK OF THE POST-WAR GROWTH WAVE

The rise and decline of the post-war growth wave can be illustrated when considering multiple economic indicators. The following hexagon (Figure 11.1) clearly shows the rising period from

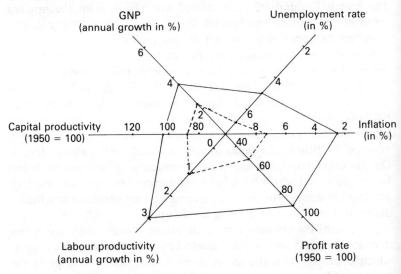

Figure 11.1   The hexagon of economic dynamism in the United States[3]

1950 to 1965 and the declining period from 1970 to 1985 in the United States.

The scales in the hexagon of the post-war growth wave are arranged in such a manner that the closer the values lie to the centre, the more 'negative' they become. The significance of the centre is: less growth, higher unemployment, etc. The outer circle contains values of the rising period between 1950 and 1965, the inner circle the one of the declining period between 1970 and 1985. During the first period, all values are more 'positive' (higher growth rates, lower rates of unemployment, etc.), and during the second one, more 'negative' (lower growth rates, higher rates of unemployment, etc.) values appear.

The indicators above clearly show the varying periods of the growth wave since 1950; however, they do not explain *why* the growth wave appeared in that way. In the following paragraphs, we shall introduce our own attempt at an explanation for growth waves.

AN EXPLANATORY MODEL FOR GROWTH WAVES

The nations' economic development can only be partially explained by economic consideration, since it is intricately connected to all other social processes. It is therefore necessary to consider it from a broad perspective, especially its interplay with the technological and socio-institutional developments.[4] All three elements – *technology*, *economy*, and *society* itself – have contributed in reciprocal action to the course and the final shaping of the post-war wave.

Technological Development

Technological development is the essence of any growth wave (see Mensch, 1975). Every such wave is coined by a so-called *technological paradigm*. Hereby, we mean the sum of new technologies and facilities that are used to overcome a wide range of technological problems. They can always be reduced to a few central key technologies and fundamental innovations (see Dosi, 1982).

The technological paradigm of the post-war wave came into existence because of the breakthrough of quite a few new technologies that enabled widespread applications as well as mass production. We are referring to electromechanics and electronics, petroleum products and the chemical industry, the combustion engine, which allowed us to develop various new forms of transportation, and the new manufacturing style invented by Ford. This particular technological paradigm of the post-war wave is currently being replaced by 'new technologies' such as microelectronics, biotechnologies and others.

Since a new technological paradigm requires time to mature, fundamental innovations are most commonly developed quite some time *before* the actual onset of the growth wave. It is only after their breakthrough on a large scale that they can become a determining force in technology and the economy, and the driving impetus of a new long-term growth period. The *motor car*, for example, was invented at the end of the nineteenth century, but it was not until the onset of inexpensive mass production in the 1930s, as well as after the Second World War, that it became a key industry.

Economic Development

Technological impetus stimulates *economic growth*: together with economic and institutional factors, a new technological paradigm can produce an extended period of economic growth. The overall advancement of technology makes an improvement possible in both the production and the use of capital, as well as in the use of labour. Besides the new key industries – in the case of the post-war wave, car manufacturing, for example – various other industries benefit from new technologies. On one hand, they are all stimulated by the increasing demand for the products of the new key industries, and on the other hand, they can utilise the new technological paradigm for their own purposes. In the post-war years, mass production and, consequently, mass consumption caused such a compound growth pattern for numerous industries.

In the course of a growth wave the productive possibilities of new technologies diminish more and more: growth itself begins to decrease until, finally, even *productivity diminishes*. In that manner, the production ceiling in our example was already reached during the 1960s: first of all, the initial demand by the population was satisfied; secondly, the consumers' requests shifted from mass-produced goods to more heterogeneous products. A further even more important factor was that the use of the technology could no longer yield an increase in production relative to the employed capital. Increasing amounts of capital became necessary for decreasing levels of output.

The relationship between output, labour input, and capital allocation worsens during the course of a growth wave. Economic growth and decline are very well reflected in the development of capital productivity, as seen in Table 11.1. After 1965 capital productivity deteriorated and its annual growth rates became markedly negative.

Table 11.1 Capital productivity in the United States, 1950–84

Year	1955	1960	1965	1970	1975	1980	1984	1950–65	1970–84
			1950 = 100					*annual growth in %*	
k^*	102.6	101.3	106.2	98.3	88.7	83.0	81.3	0.4	-1.4

* k = Capital productivity = GDP/Fixed capital
Source: Sik *et al.* (1988, p. 211).

During the declining phase key industries are still making great profits, even though with a much smaller profit rate. But they are now experiencing economic difficulties because they have to face the fact that investments in traditional technologies no longer yield higher profit rates. It also becomes evident that the now huge, rigid enterprises, working with traditional technologies and in old industries, fail to develop enough energy to invent and adopt fundamental new technologies. Satisfaction in innovation has markedly declined on the part of companies, even though the markets for products that were developed out of the prevailing technological paradigm are mostly exhausted. Technological advancements mostly occur as pseudo-innovations which create slightly different but hardly improved products.

Together with institutional factors, this situation causes tremendous changes as far as *returns of companies* are concerned: considering the national economy as a whole, it becomes evident that profit rates decrease drastically, i.e. the relationship between profits and capital input has worsened significantly (see Figure 11.2). On the other hand, because of the drastically declining capital productivity, *financial investments* for companies still making profits become increasingly rewarding. The immense demand for capital

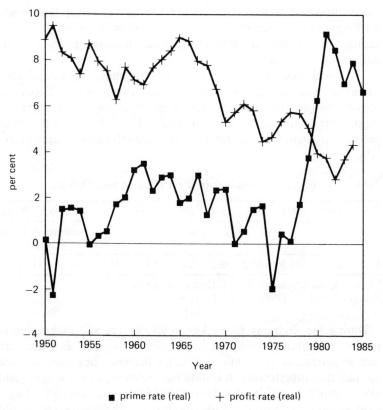

■ prime rate (real)　　+ profit rate (real)

Figure 11.2　Development of the profit rate and the prime rate, 1950–84, in the USA.
Source: Sik *et al.* (1988, p. 269).

by financially weakened companies (just like, in the case of the post-war wave, the monetary policies of Central Banks to fight inflation) lets interest rates soar until, ultimately, they exceed the profits of the economy as a whole. This means that financial investments become more rewarding than investments in new technologies, i.e. physical capital.

Social Development

The third intricate factor of a growth wave entails *socio-institutional development*. In the course of a growth wave, a *social paradigm* must evolve that is able to accommodate technological as well as economic developments. What we mean by that is the totality of political and legal organisations, the genius of the period, etc. that make up the environment from which an economic growth wave will develop.

Considering the rising phase of the specific post-war wave, it was only possible because society adjusted to technological and economic developments through close reciprocal action: mass production required and demanded a society of mass consumption which, for example, included a broad middle class or the employment of collective bargaining instead of a detrimental class struggle. The rising phase of this wave actually was the *Keynesian era* during which industrial societies strengthened the welfare state.

In the course of a growth wave, an increasing degree of *institutional immobility* can be observed (see Olson, 1982): enterprises, pressure groups, political parties, and institutions that are typical of a respective social paradigm, gain increasingly in members and influence. Hereby, they also become increasingly rigid and stationary. On all levels, one can see the so-called 'dinosaur-effect' (Mensch, 1975): the 'old' industries, but also the dominating pressure groups or political parties, have become huge, rigid organisations. Because of habits and constraints that have evolved over time and because of the influence of innumerable, their own as well as other interests, they tend to hold on frantically to what is already established and in existence. As a result, societies and nations begin to 'age': flexibility is replaced by rigidity. Society becomes more and more organised as well as regulated; cartels, concerns, and monopolies literally cement the status quo.

On the other hand, the technological and economic environment keeps on changing. It becomes increasingly difficult for the now rigid society to adapt to these changes. During the declining phase of the wave, a 'mismatch' develops between the technological and economic spheres and the social sphere which by itself contributes to the downward trend.

Towards the end of the 1960s, *institutional uproars* began to escalate because of the afore-mentioned reasons: in various areas, often unseemingly connected, there was a development of serious problems because the old, adapted systems incorrectly responded or did not react at all to the changed environment. So the Keynesian model and the welfare state increasingly met limits like the collapse of Bretton Woods, the oil crisis, and the first environmental problems. All these seem unique in appearance, though not in their causes and backgrounds since they are all very typical of a peak and the following declining trend of a growth wave.

It is not until society continues to evolve that technological innovations are finally supplemented by *social innovations*, and that a *good match* can develop on and between all three spheres, making a renewed economic rise possible. We therefore see that in order for new, improved socio-institutional structures to develop, the old ones need to be destroyed first. This process of *destruction followed by a new beginning* often happens very abruptly and can thereby entail great social conflicts.

In analysing a growth wave, it is imperative that one always considers the *reciprocity* between technological, economic and social developments. Even though we have considered the technological development to be the basis of a wave, it is precisely technology that is constantly influenced by economic and social forces. In this way, for example, the price increase of crude oil in the 1970s and the first half of the 1980s and the increasing ecological crisis have both led to the development of energy-conserving technologies, which, in future, may give room for a new growth wave.

Notes

1. The following chapter summarises some results of a research project under the promotion of Professor Ota Sik and the Swiss National Research Foundation. For more detailed elaboration see Sik, Höltschi and Rockstroh (1988).
2. For an overview of recent elaborations see Freeman (1984) and Vasko (1987).
3. Sources and Notes see Sik, Höltschi and Rockstroh (1988).
4. Compare as a fundamental approach Schumpeter (1935, 1961). Even today's experts on growth waves and long waves take this fundamental approach (see e.g. Dosi, 1986; Coombs and Kleinknecht, 1986; Perez, 1983).

References

Coombs, R. and A. Kleinknecht (1986) 'New Evidence on the Shift Toward Process Innovations During the Long Wave Upswing', in C. Freeman (ed.), *Design, Innovation and Long Cycles in Economic Development* (New York: St Martin's) pp. 78–103.

Dosi, G. (1982) 'Technological Paradigms and Technological Trajectories', *Research Policy*, vol. 11, no. 3, p. 147–62.

Dosi, G. (1986) 'Technology and Conditions of Macroeconomic Development', in C. Freeman (ed.), *Design, Innovation and Long Cycles in Economic Development*, (New York: St Martin's) pp. 60–77.

Freeman, C. (ed.) (1984) *Long Waves in the World Economy* (New York: St Martin's).

Kondratieff, N.D. (1926) 'Die langen Wellen der Konjunktur', *Archiv für Sozialwissenschaft und Sozialpolitik*, vol. 56; reprint: Autorenkollektiv, *Die langen Wellen der Konjunktur* (Berlin: Olle & Weter, 1972) pp. 133–69.

Mensch, G. (1975) *Das technologische Patt* (Frankfurt: Umschau-Verlag).

Olson, M. (1982) *The Rise and Decline of Nations* (Yale University Press).

Perez, C. (1983) 'Structural Change and Assimilation of New Technologies in the Economic and Social Systems', *Futures*, vol. 15, no. 5, pp. 357–75.

Schumpeter, J.A. (1935) *Theorie der wirtschaftlichen Entwicklung*, 4th edn (München/Leipzig: Duncker & Humblot).

Schumpeter, J.A. (1961) *Konjunkturzyklen*, vol. I (Göttingen: Vandenhoeck & Ruprecht).

Sik, O., R. Höltschi and C. Rockstroh (1988) *Wachstum und Krisen* (Berlin: Springer).

Vasko, T. (ed.) (1987) *The Long-Wave Debate* (Berlin: Springer).

PART II

The Evolution of Market Systems: (2) Reproduction, Institutions and Governmental Planning

12 Plan, Market and Banking

J. A. Kregel

FREE MARKETS, GOVERNMENT INTERVENTION AND PLANNING

The twentieth century has witnessed periodic revivals of discussion of the relation of the market mechanism to centralised economic planning. These discussions, usually restricted to pure theory, have concluded that there is no basic difference between 'market' and 'plan', because the central planner could always replicate the basic features of the Walrasian 'auctioneer' in the market mechanism, adjusting prices to eliminate excess demands.

In practice, things are not that simple, for the market has no auctioneer and seldom behaves as if it had one. The idea that the planner could reach the optimum efficiency of an idealised market system was based on a misconception of how capitalist economies operate; it is perhaps not surprising that most centrally planned economies not only failed to reach the theoretical ideal, they fell far short of the actual performance of most capitalist economies.

More insightful thinkers recognised that it was inappropriate to emulate a theoretical ideal which had never been experimented and which had no certainty of producing the results implied by theory. Although in practice there was no auctioneer, the market did not work in a vacuum; it is a highly controlled and regulated framework. As Lionel Robbins (1952) and Warren Samuels (1966) have extensively documented, the Classical economists, the architects of the free market system, emphasised the necessity of strong government action to set the boundaries within which the market mechanism could be allowed to function.

The real question in the discussion of market and plan was thus not which was more efficient in theory, but how they might be integrated to produce the most acceptable results in practice. This is a question that permeates Keynes's work. Keynes recognised that the unfettered market would eventually produce conditions which would lead to its own downfall, just as a fully planned system would eventually become impracticable. In Keynes's view, it is inappropriate for the State to displace the actions and choices of individuals. It is not the role of the State to take private investment decisions, but only to provide the general support to the level of overall demand necessary to ensure that private decisions might be taken efficiently. For Keynes:

> The most important Agenda of the State relate not to those activities which private individuals are already fulfilling, but to those functions which fall outside the sphere of the individual, to those decisions which are made by no one if the State does not make them. The important thing for government is not to do things which individuals are doing already, and to do them a little better or a little worse; but to do things which at present are not done at all. (Keynes, 1972, p. 291)

Now, one of the things that individuals do very poorly is to predict the future. Within the simple Walrasian model of the economy the market mechanism is usurped by the 'auctioneer', and time is abolished, so that the problem never arises. Many planners, trying to emulate the efficiency of the 'market' mechanism, were led into the belief that the plan could substitute for the unknown future.

But this was the very point at which Keynes located the breakdown of the market mechanism under the capitalist system. As Ota Sik recognised very clearly: 'The market mechanism by itself could never do away with the contradiction between direct decision-making concerning production in accord with present market demand and decision making preparing for future production to satisfy and create future demand' (Sik, 1967, p. 341).

For Keynes, money played a role in this breakdown of the traditional version of the market mechanism, not because of any intrinsic physical characteristic attached to money, but because it was the most certain link between the present and the future when individuals were paralysed by the inability to foresee what the future might bring. A crisis was always related to a flight to money as a store of value. The problem of planning for the future thus appeared to be inherently linked to the problems of money and finance. Again, most planners believed that once the plan had resolved future uncertainty, money and financial factors could be eliminated. One of the most impressive aspects of Ota Sik's reflections on the integration of market and plan was his recognition that this required the integration of production and financial planning.

Rather unexpectedly, over twenty years later, the debate on the role of the market in planned economies has been resumed today. Unfortunately, the present discussion seems to be plagued by earlier discussions, and appears to be centred on comparison between planning on the one hand, and the presumed performance of the idealised market mechanism of the timeless auctioneer on the other. As should now be eminently clear, free markets have never existed without active state intervention, so that the actual results of planning as it was applied in socialist economies versus the market mechanism is not the issue; what should be discussed is the way in which the State ensures that the operation of the free market produces coherent and acceptable outcomes. This was the problem that concerned the Classical economists as well as Keynes in the 1930s with respect to capitalist economies. Ota Sik recognised monetary and financial factors as being crucial to socialist economies as well. On the occasion of this celebration of his work, I would like to raise one particular aspect of this issue which may be of crucial importance to the role of the market mechanism within socialist economies.

FREE MARKETS AND GOVERNMENT INTERVENTION IN BANKING

There is one area in which central government control and the market have coexisted in capitalist economies: banking. This was even an area in which Adam Smith was willing to recognise the necessity of state control:

> To restrain private people, it may be said, from receiving in payment the promissory notes of a banker, for any sum whether great or small, when they are willing to receive them; or, to restrain a banker from issuing such notes, when all his neighbours are willing to accept them, is a manifest violation of natural liberty. But those exertions of the natural liberty of a few individuals, which might endanger the security of the whole society, are, and ought to be, restrained by the laws of all

governments; of the most free, as well as the most despotical. The obligation of building party walls, in order to prevent the communication of fire, is a violation of natural liberty, exactly of the same kind with the regulations of the banking trade. (Smith, 1976, p. 324)

Following Smith's admonition, the issue of bank notes in most capitalist systems is controlled either directly or indirectly by the State. However, this control does not extend to the entire means of payment. Creation of deposit liabilities (which are the modern equivalent of the 'promissory notes' referred to by Smith) is left to private banks. In most countries, this rather anomalous mix of government and private sector creation of means of payment was the result of historical accident, which became accepted practice. The Bank of England was created in order to help William III finance the war with France. In exchange for subscribing government debt of £1.2 million, the Tunnage Act of 1694 offered to a group of capitalists the right to call themselves the Board and Governors of the Bank of England and gave them the right to issue promissory bank notes. Within three years the Bank was unable to make cash payments on its notes, and was in continuous difficulty until the 1844 Peel Act which linked creation of notes to gold reserves and provided for the Bank's eventual monopoly of the note issue. Private bankers who issued private promissory notes found that their livelihood was threatened and responded by creating a new means of payment – the deposit subject to cheque. As long as bankers could guarantee that their liabilities would exchange at par with central bank notes, their private liabilities could act as substitute for central bank notes as a means of payment.

Thus, to this day, in most countries the basic M1 money supply is composed of public liabilities – the bank notes issued by the central bank, and a private component – the demand deposit liabilities of private bankers. History tells us why central control is needed. Just as the Bank of England in its early history, private banks also periodically underwent liquidity and solvency crises. Occasionally, the effects of these crises extended beyond the single banks and involved the entire financial system. It was at this point that the support of the private banks became the responsibility of the State, for their activity had economy-wide effects. The Great Slump of the 1930s was crucial in this respect, for most modern banking law dates from that time and attempts to legislate against its recurrence.

The problem of the control of the liability issue of private banks was met in different ways. In the United States, legislation gave the central bank control over the activities of private bankers in exchange for an effective guarantee by the central bank of private bank deposit liabilities. This guarantee was represented on the one hand by the implicit lender of last resort obligation of the central bank and through the creation of federal deposit insurance, nominally subscribed by the banks, but effectively underwritten by the federal government Treasury.

Aside from the difficulties the lender of last resort obligation created for the operation of monetary policy, there is a second criticism: moral hazard created by the deposit insurance scheme. If it is clear that insurance will support all liabilities of the private bank both depositors and other creditors, then there is no longer any effective market mechanism to sanction the risk-taking activity of private bankers. This market sanction normally occurs when riskier lending activities produce higher costs of borrowed funds, lower share prices and increased reliance on owners' equity. Losses are then borne directly by the risk-takers via write-downs (eventually bankruptcy) of owners' equity.

But, if reduction in equity jeopardises the ability of the bank to meet deposit liabilities, this will have an impact on the overall means of payment and thus on the stability of the financial system itself. To preserve the necessary means of payment and financial stability, the insurance fund must intervene to support the bank's liabilities. In the knowledge that its losses will be effectively sustained by the central bank, a private banker can undertake any degree of risk in its investment activities in the knowledge that any losses will be met by the insurance fund. This is equivalent to giving private bankers a one-way bet, they keep all gains and charge all losses to the public. In such conditions bankers will seek the highest returns on investment without reference to risk. This perverse effect of insurance can be seen in the operation of US Savings and Loan banks after they were granted increased freedoms in asset and liability portfolios in the 1982 Depository Institutions Act.

The basic argument to recommend elimination of deposit insurance is to restore the market mechanism as a sanction on excess risk-taking. But the government's decision to support Continental Illinois suggests that this is a false issue, for the full support of all but direct equity liabilities was motivated by the fact that it held more than 2000 correspondent accounts of smaller banks; for sixty-six of them their deposits represented more than 100 per cent of their capital (see Sprague, 1986, p. 155). Continental Illinois would not have been allowed to fail even in the absence of deposit insurance. As long as risk-taking activity is funded by means of payment liabilities, the sanctions of the market will be circumvented by the action of the central bank or the State. In the USA, this is leading to increased de facto nationalisation of thrifts nation-wide and of private banks in some regions.

In Europe, this problem is usually resolved by allowing universal banking which creates very large, risk diversified banks. It is clear that these banks will not be allowed to fail, even in the absence of specific support schemes. But, as the Herstatt experience suggests, it is now unlikely that failure of even smaller banks will be permitted, creating a similar moral hazard problem for regulators where the system is composed of a small number of large banks which cannot be allowed to fail, and a larger number of small banks which will no longer be allowed to fail.

An exception to this particular case is the Italian banking system, dominated by state controlled banks: three banks of national interest owned by IRI as a result of the bank crisis, and six public law banks, all under government ownership and control. Over half of deposit liabilities are thus de facto government liabilities subject to at least indirect government regulation. But this arrangement has a great cost in terms of the efficiency of the banks, which are about half as profitable as their European counterparts and suffer from the appointment of political activists rather than bankers to top positions. This has tended to affect the composition of their loan portfolios. Instead of the excess risk taken by US banks in order to maximise profit, in Italy this excess of risk is also without sanction, but taken in order to maximise political influence.

THE BANK DEPOSIT MARKET AND RECONSTRUCTION

If socialist enterprises are going to be more responsive to the market mechanism, these market sanctions must also be extended in terms of monetary loss and eventual bankruptcy. But the sanctions, and thus the losses, must be circumscribed to the individuals who are responsible for the errors, and not allowed to propagate into systemic effects. At the same time, individuals must not be sanctioned for systemic effects for which they have no responsibility. In a market-based economy these sanctions are usually enforced by the banking system which controls the efficiency of the economic system by means of allocating bank credit. But if this is to occur, the banks themselves must be subject to sanctions, i.e. to failure and bankruptcy. This has proved to be impossible because of their simultaneous role as providers of deposit liabilities which serve as means of payment. In short, it is not possible to support the means of payments function of banks' liabilities fully, and to have them act as allocators of resources and supervisors of credit.

This is the problem that socialist economies will have to face as they investigate the role of the State in the new market-based socialism. It will not be sufficient to follow any of the examples of the market economies. In early capitalism, private banking was considered to be strictly limited to providing transfers of funds. Lending was not considered respectable for a banker. The problems concerning the control and regulation of private banking discussed above are linked to a system in which private banks carry out both functions. To avoid this problem one might want to adopt a system which a number of European countries have attempted, but without much success: the use of the postal system as a payments or funds transfer system. Such a solution would leave the central bank responsible for the note issue, and would not require any support from private banks. The postal system would not make loans and thus would not have any risk exposure. Private banks could then sell participation in terms of bonds, shares or investment certificates. Following Adam Smith, it might make sense to impose legal restrictions on their use as a means of payment. The real problem is not to keep them from being exchanged, but to avoid the presumption that the central bank is responsible for their value. In this way the creation of the means of payment can be separated from the intermediation function of the banking and financial system, avoiding government subsidies to private bankers.

References

Keynes, J.M. (1972) *Essays in Persuasion*, volume IX of *The Collected Writings of John Maynard Keynes* (London: Macmillan).

Robbins, Lionel (1952) *The Theory of Economic Policy* (London: Macmillan).

Samuels, Warren (1966) *The Classical Theory of Economic Policy* (Cleveland, Ohio: World Publishing).

Smith, Adam (1976) *The Wealth of Nations*, Glasgow Centenary Edition (Oxford: Oxford University Press).

Sik, Ota (1967) *Plan and Market Under Socialism* (Prague: Academia).

Sprague, I.H. (1986) *Bailout: An Insider's Account of Bank Failures and Rescues* (New York: Basic Books).

13 The Market and the Classical Theory of Prices

Bertram Schefold

I

During the last decades, a tentative revival of the Classical theory of prices has been observed. It originated from diverse sources. The broad social outlook, the theoretical coherence and the political impetus of the Classical authors had never lost its fascination for economists but some distinctive traits of their analysis had been obscured by attempts to minimise the fundamental difference between the classical approach, based on the surplus principle, and the neo-classical one, based on the idea that supply and demand for factors of production, as governed by subjective preferences, regulate an equilibrium at full employment. Keynes had used the neo-classical theory of value and generalised the equilibrium concept to encompass labour unemployment. This led, in the age of growth theory, to a reconsideration of the classical processes of accumulation, as revived by Harrod and the followers of Keynes in Cambridge, who considered Classical paths of accumulation where the growth of capacity did not automatically adjust through the supply and demand mechanism to the growth of the labour supply and productivity.

In this context, a parallel reconsideration of the Classical theory of value became imperative. It is customary to associate the reconstruction of the Classical theory of prices mainly with the name of Sraffa, and in particular with his introduction to the Ricardo edition (Sraffa, 1951) and with his later *Production of Commodities by Means of Commodities* (Sraffa, 1960). But a number of other authors were groping for similar theories and models; von Neumann, Joan Robinson's *Accumulation of Capital* (Robinson, 1956), and Schwartz (1961) may be mentioned among others who were at least occasionally trying to formulate the equilibrium requirements for an economy with a uniform rate of profit, growing or in a stationary state, such that distribution and employment were not, or at least not exclusively, governed by supply and demand as understood in the neo-classical theory. Early activity analysis at times pointed in this direction (e.g. Koopmans, 1951). Morishima provided elegant mathematical reformulations on both sides: for Marx and Walras (Morishima, 1973; 1977).

The controversies on capital theory have tended to reduce the interest in the Classical approach in so far as the discovery that the production function cannot be constructed consistently from a sufficiently general disaggregated model was unwelcome. As a reaction, neo-classical economists have since tended to argue that the intertemporal neo-classical theory is not affected by the criticism, and their research has moved away from the theory of growth also for other reasons. But since it has recently been shown that the intertemporal equilibria converge to long-run equilibria with a uniform rate of profit if the time horizon is sufficiently long, the concern for the traditional concept of long-period equilibrium can be expected to revive, and with it the question of whether the neo-classical supply and demand mechanism is really capable of explaining distribution and employment in such a state (Schefold, 1989).

However, I should like here to pursue a different line of thought. A revival of Classical theory would be of very limited interest if it were confined to a formal reconstruction of the Classical theory of value and prices, as it originated in Smith and Ricardo. The connection between the Classical approach and the Keynesian theory is older than Sraffa's reformulation of the theory of long-period prices, and it was from the start directed at the solution of two problems: on the one hand, Keynes's focus on the theory of employment in the short run, with capacity given, did not square well with his inherited Marshallian theory of prices, based on rising marginal costs. For it is characteristic of a demand constrained economy that the level of prices does not explain the level of output of individual firms; unemployment usually means that there is excess capacity such that more could be sold at lower unit costs, if demand could be increased at the given price. This is the element of increasing returns in the short run which has been emphasised by Kaldor (1985). Keynes himself is known to have turned to a theory of administered prices in 1939, when it was shown that price setting was an established practice of firms.

Joan Robinson attempted to bridge the gap between the models of short-run price formation of firms, as inspired by empirical observation, and the theory of long-run normal prices – a precarious link, as she was to emphasise in her later years, when she more and more came to question the validity of long-period analyses of accumulation, including her own.

But, on the other hand, the investigation into the conditions of the long-run development of a capitalist economy undoubtedly concerned one of the most important questions in the discipline, not only on ground of the emphasis which has traditionally been placed upon it. We have recently witnessed a very lively debate about this old topic, under the heading of what the theory of employment should be in the long run, or shortly under the proposal 'to marry Sraffa and Keynes'. Of course, it is made clear that various difficulties obstruct the realisation of such a desirable relationship. It is all linked with the task of providing a reliable alternative to the neo-classical theory of distribution and employment. I regard it as quite legitimate ultimately to measure the value of the various debates by the success of this latter endeavour. The Kalecki-type 'post-Keynesian' theory of distribution is increasingly being challenged by a 'neo-Ricardian' one which focuses on the influence of the monetary rates of interest on the rate of profit. These themes were discussed intensively at the Sraffa conference in Florence, in 1985, the proceedings of which have, after much amending and, I hope, improvement, been published in 1989 by Krishna Bharadwaj and myself (Bharadwaj and Schefold, 1989).

Observers may ask: what does it all lead up to? Is this a new and rising theoretical paradigm or are these the last skirmishes of a decaying Cambridge school? And: what are the policy perspectives? Without hiding a certain optimism regarding the first question, I shall in this brief chapter focus on the second.

Good economic theory is primarily concerned with the analysis of causal relationships; it may be put to different uses; quick association of so-called economic paradigms with ideologies and associated policies are facile and should be avoided. It might be thought that the Classical approach lends itself to interventionist policies. The vision of the economy as a social producing system with a given structure of production seems to suggest, as in the case of the Leontief input–output system as a similar construction, that central planning would be easy once that structure is known.

The arbitrary variations of the rate of profit which are a familiar thought experiment in capital theory might suggest that income distribution could be changed at will. Both mistakes have been made.

But a different picture emerges if we remember that Classical theory originated with Classical liberalism. And the formal structure of the model or associated thought experiments must not be confused with the theory which explains, for instance, the process of competition between different technologies, the future development of which is largely unknown, hence difficult to plan, even in the firms where they originate. The conceptual variation of the rate of profit is no substitute for a causal theory of income distribution which explains, for instance, the interaction between growth, profitability and employment.

Yet it is true that the connection between the quantitative variables used in the theory on the one hand, and economic policy on the other, is viewed differently in the Classical and in the neoclassical approach. The political economy of neo-classical theory is by necessity concerned with market coordination failures which may be due to the structure of the economy (e.g. natural monopolies) or to misguided political intervention. The pure theory assumes technological conditions such that a state of full employment can be reached. Hence deviations and their corrections are the chief objects of policy. We have, as it were, the celestial bodies moving in perfect circular orbits, and observed discrepancies are explained in terms of epicycles as in the old Ptolemaic planetary system. Classical theory aims at a direct explanation of the planetary orbits as ellipses. Only the framework of the general theory at its most abstract level is of little specifity: the data are the given structure of production and the state of distribution; it is agreed that prices, wage rates and the rate of profit must be uniform as a long-run equilibrium condition, whatever the specific causes which may lead to temporary or permanent deviations.

By contrast, the forces which govern distribution and employment, as well as those operating on the choice of technique, are viewed from the start as shaped by specific historical and institutional conditions which may also be an expression of, and give rise to, political power relationships. For instance, the importance attributed to the datum of the real wage at a somehow historically given subsistence level in Ricardian times could not without substantial modification be applied today. In a fast-growing economy, the demand effect of the rising nominal wage which translates into rising real wages, may be more important for growth than would be the rise of rate of profit if the real wage could be made to stagnate. When Schumpeter observed the historically specific nature of the Ricardian theory, he was right. But he was wrong to speak about a Ricardian Vice and to attribute it also to Keynes (although Keynes's theory similarly contains historical and institutional elements), because some historical specifity is a virtue, while, on the other hand, not everything in Ricardo was historically specific. There are elements in classical thought which apply to a very long capitalist development and beyond.

The founders of the Classical school were celebrated for their objectivity which made it possible that a Ricardo advocated policies in favour of industry and the labouring classes which went against his own interests as a financier and landowner. For Ricardo, it turned out that reform meant in his days, paradoxically, a reduction of state intervention. But the theory also encompassed magnitudes which allowed to link the theory of economic development with the vision of a social transformation which accompanied the Industrial Revolution and its aftermath. There was not only the tie between social stratification and the economic functions of wage earners, entrepreneurs, landowners, etc., but also a theory of consumption which was linked with microeconomic *and* with macroeconomic considerations. The simplification of regarding the needs for the commodities entering the wage basket as essentially given, and the luxuries as volatile, being objects of expenditure out of rents and profits not saved, made it possible to visualise the rise of luxury consumption as one of the dynamical elements in the process of accumulation while the necessity to satisfy the elementary needs was stabilising.

In my main paper incorporated in Bharadwaj and Schefold (1989), I have tried (with others) to reformulate the theory of consumption and of the composition of output so as to leave room for the institutional influences. Similarly, the analysis of the work process and of the division of labour was in Classical theory not simply subsumed under the heading of technical progress but was also considered in its social aspects, and this, too, is being taken up today. The German and other historical schools developed the institutional aspect of the Classical heritage, supported by the broad historical movement within the humanities which flowered in the second half of the nineteenth century.

Neo-classical theory, in its attempt to isolate an abstract core of economic analysis, has made it a programme to leave the answering of these interesting traditional economic questions to neighbouring disciplines. While an increased division of labour among social scientists may further intellectual progress, it is to be regretted if, after the subdivision of the disciplines, the lack of an integration and of interdisciplinary approaches is not even felt. One of the reasons why the Classical approach is found attractive is that it provides a model for a more comprehensive understanding of the economic process and of economics. If Classical economics is to be revived, the social and institutional changes which the world has undergone must be reflected in the theory itself, not only in its data. It is an admittedly disturbing feature of present day Classical economics that the commitment to bring history into the picture occasionally does not get beyond abstract assertions and repetitions (with permutations) of the words 'historical', 'institutional' or 'social' conditions, although the proclaimed aim is, on the contrary, to be historically specific. I want to give examples, by considering three areas of economic policy in turn: at a microeconomic, macroeconomic and mesoeconomic level.

II

Modern Marxian economic thought often asserts that the main distinction between the capitalism of the nineteenth and that of the twentieth century is to be sought in the transition from competitive to monopoly capitalism, which has, it is alleged, once more been transformed through a vast increase in the intensity of state intervention. As a consequence, power relationships, especially regarding prices and distribution, would have come to play a dominating role. But, although the increased economic role of the State cannot be denied, a quite different picture emerges if we take account of the fact that, with the growth of at least some firms, there have not only been waves in the founding of new smaller firms but there has also been a growth in the size of markets so that competition may be said to be, if anything, more intense than it had been in the last century. In his article of 1926 (Sraffa, 1926), Sraffa had observed that oligopolistic structures exist not only among large firms but also among small ones which serve only a limited number of customers, with only a few customers actually migrating between firms unless price differentials become large.

There are thus reasons to doubt the image of an early capitalism characterised by near-perfect competition, as well as that of a late capitalism characterised by a kind of monopoly power of large firms. Clifton (1977) has argued that modern conglomerates are much better equipped than nineteenth-century firms to spot differences in profitability and to smooth such differences by a transfer of ownership and restructuring than the traditional firm of the nineteenth century managed by its owner. It is widely recognised that research and development are fostered most within wide oligopolies where large firms act as price leaders with a high productivity and compete, through cost-intensive research which lowers production cost and leads to the introduction of new products, with a fringe of smaller competitors which occasionally contribute new ideas and prevent the oligopoly from adopting too rigid pricing policies and from being technologically conservative through the formation of a cartel.

These findings have only relatively recently been incorporated in variants of the neo-classical theory (contestable markets), but they have always been part of the Classical in so far as the latter measures the intensity of competition not by the numbers of firms in a market but by the ease with which it may be entered, for that is the main consideration if profit differentials are to be explained.

This point of view allows at least a loose integration of increasing returns to scale. Neo-classical economists often find it difficult to comprehend Sraffa's assertion that no assumptions are made about returns to scale. And in fact, a neo-classical equilibrium with a large number of firms and increasing returns would not be stable at a given rate of profit because the firms would at once start to compete and, without some element of imperfect competition, there would be no clear limit before one firm supplied the entire market and competition had been turned into monopoly. In the Classical theory, the number of firms may be assumed to be small from the start and the threat of entry prevents the charging of prices much above average profitability, whereas the division of the market is seen as a question of market power which maintains profitability. Hence competition is present in the tendency towards a uniform rate of profit.

Even the administering of prices need not contradict the Classical concept, on the contrary: evidence has frequently been cited that prices are administered with a view towards obtaining an average satisfactory rate of return which would correspond to a subjective–normal rate of profit, to use Joan Robinson's expression, and the subjective concept of normality must be based on the experience with the objective possibilities in a particular trade and in neighbouring lines of production. It is true that such pricing theories, as developed, for instance, by Sylos-Labini and Roncaglia, are not very general; they aim at the explanation of the particular in the world of competition which is extremely varied. Kaldor emphasised the importance of cost differentials which contrast with a relative large uniformity of prices, confirming the thesis of price leadership as a further complication.

But, on the whole, an increased mobility of capital is plausible and supports the prices of production approach. The extent to which banks and financial capital operate as coordinators in the process (which seems to lend some stability to it, as used to be the case in Western Germany), or the degree to which the stock exchange plays an important role as in the Anglo-Saxon countries, varies geographically and over time. The capital market accelerates restructuring processes when the general conditions of accumulation undergo a major change but seems less effective for the raising of productivity in a steady process of accumulation. The stronger role of the banking sector on the Continent has sometimes been envied by Anglo-Saxon economists but the innovative potential of deregulation has been demonstrated to the world in the last decade, although at a social cost which was in places very considerable.

The conclusion is, at any rate, that the Classical theory affords less reason to advocate strong antitrust policies than does the conventional neo-classical theory. The history of West German antitrust policy had been characterised by an early programmatic commitment to enhance competition by favouring the survival of a multitude of small firms wherever feasible. But, in reality, the practice of the Social Market Economy has been to tolerate a process of concentration which was comparable to that in other countries, and the theory of economic policy has, slowly, adapted to this reality. There is ambivalence regarding the social aspects of the process of concentration, too. Managerial capitalism is not all bad.

The theory of distribution which would be compatible with this vision of economic development has undergone considerable changes. Kaldor first formulated his theory of distribution in terms of a full-employment economy, and when this unrealistic assumption was dropped, and when Kaldor came to admit that there are almost always considerable labour reserves either in the open or in the form of disguised unemployment in special sectors (he was concerned with backward segments of the services), the mechanism which explained the changes of distribution accompanying changes in the sphere of investment had to be modified. It was now thought that fluctuations in investment could be accommodated, and be financed, through corresponding changes of the share of savings, because capacity grows only at a certain rhythm, so that any acceleration of the growth process would be accompanied by a rise of money prices relative to money wages; the increased share of profits allowed to finance investment at unchanged propensities to save.

A more sophisticated variant of the theory was proposed by Eichner (1976). He observed that corporations are always faced with the choice between inside and outside finance. Internal financing can be mobilised by raising the prices of the firm, albeit at the expense of losing customers in the long run so that the rise in prices must be temporary. The firm can offset the estimated immediate increase against a future diminution of revenue, taking into account the increased eventual profit opportunities made possible through the internal financing of an investment project, and compare that to the possibility of external finance. A macroeconomic aggregation of this microeconomic model leads to the post-Keynesian result that an increase in investment activity allows the corporate sector to increase its savings: sustained growth thus becomes feasible and a post-Keynesian theory of distribution holds, without assuming full employment.

The rival view is that the corporate sector is more competitive and less able to fix prices than the post-Keynesian or Kaleckian theory suggests. Since firms usually provide for enough excess capacity to meet spurts of demand when equipment is planned, there is usually room to accelerate growth without necessarily hitting a bottle-neck, which would lead to price rises relative to money wages. In my view, the neo-Ricardian theory of distribution then makes sense if we think of a slowly growing economy with a strong financial sector. We may imagine that the prices firms charge are mainly governed by costs which include, apart from materials, wages and depreciation, an interest element as well as the profits of enterprise. If we assume the latter to be conventional (but this means to leave a very interesting variable unexplained), the variations in the rate of interest as engendered by the banking system (which in turn operates within a rather complicated network of national and international constraints) become the essential determinants of variations of the rate of profits.

Pivetti (1989) in Bharadwaj and Schefold (1989) has argued that the ratio of prices to money wages is thus essentially regulated by the rate of interest, leaving room for Keynesian employment policies which might, according to the other interpretation, earlier hit an inflation barrier. Pivetti does not accept the restrictions on his theory which I propose: outside finance and slow growth. He argues that competition will tend to reduce prices to costs, including the opportunity cost of outside finance plus profits from entrepreneurship, even if the resources for the growth of capital are generated within the firm and even if there is a high permanent level of effective demand. But he fails to specify the time periods within which the process of competition is thought to operate. Low interest rates may be compatible with high growth for long sustained periods, which are then characterised by high rates of profits so that large funds for internally financed growth are generated. The Keynesian and post-Keynesian view is that a lowering of interest rates raises capital prices and hence attracts investment. Against this, Pivetti argues correctly that lower interest will, if competition operates, also lower the costs of production so that investment need not have become more attractive in the long run because the proceeds of investment are reduced. As a matter of fact, it is clear from capital theory that a lower rate of profit need not imply a higher value of capital at a given level of employment. But, for considerable intermediate stretches of time, high profits, and a high rate of profit, may be associated with low monetary rates of interest and high growth. Thus, depending on circumstances, there may be truth both in the post-Keynesian and in the neo-Ricardian theory of income distribution; the former explaining more directly the element of pure entrepreneurial profit (outside interest payments given), the latter the interest cost element (assuming a conventional level of the profits of enterprise).

The post-Keynesian and the neo-Ricardian theory both exclude a direct influence of the wage bargain on the real, as opposed to the nominal, wage. If the price level is not free but constrained by foreign competition, this may hold if employers and the trade unions cooperate. My personal conclusion is that we can identify more influences on distribution than we have variables to be determined; we have, to use a term introduced by Einstein in his later works (Pais, 1982), 'supercausality', not a lack of causal mechanisms. A period of rapid economic growth with an important role of internal financing has been followed by one in which growth has been more sluggish, at least in Western European countries, and where the role of external financing is increasing. The economists who now regard the neo-Ricardian theory as convincing might have formed a different idea twenty years ago.

Whatever the conclusion about the theories of distribution, neither lends much support to assertions that the obstacles for increasing employment through increasing effective demand reside in constraints originating from *within* the private sector of the economy. If it is true that Keynesian demand management has proved to be much less effective than anticipated, this must then be due to failures of the state to execute the task assigned to it (and reasons to explain this failure are not far to seek), or to international constraints (which could be interpreted as coordination failures between states).

A similar sceptical conclusion will be reached if we consider economic policy at an intermediate mesoeconomic level. It seems rather obvious to me that the State intervenes a great deal – much more than politicians admit – in the structure of the economy through an extremely intricate system of taxes and subsidies which has grown large disorderly, which creates unequal advantages and which is not of any obvious rationality as far as the total of the interventions is concerned, however understandable any individual subsidy may be when it is first introduced. It appears as a drawback of the Classical approach that it does not afford a simple welfare norm such as Pareto-optimality to judge interventions. However, it is denied that the recourse to individual preferences could really be made operational. Instead, the traditional Classical approach had been to formulate development policies which are coherent from the point of view of an economic as well as from a social logic. The Sozialpolitik, as developed by the historical school, might be mentioned as an outstanding example, comparable to much older ideas like those of Adam Smith about education.

A modern analogue of such Classical visions of development

processes are the scenarios which are formulated to provide coherent images of where, e.g. future energy policy might lead to when the number of technical options is too large to admit a simple solution through optimisation according to a single criterion. While there is no strong logical connection between the scenario approach as a tool for formulating policies and the classical theories of accumulation, it seems to me that there are important methodological similarities which concern especially the attempt to formulate a few basic alternatives where a combinatorial approach of taking all feasible combinations into consideration would be bewildering. They are also similar in that the very construction, of a scenario or of a theory of growth, implies a belief that there is, after all, some characteristic unity and logic in long-run processes of development, despite surprising events which are endogenously engendered in the economic system. A major technological accident or a crisis at the stock exchange may have a permanent effect on a process of development but they fortunately do not happen all the time and they are, to some extent, avoidable.

There is one concept which links technology policy on the one hand and Classical analysis on the other: the idea that the technique which is given at any moment of time is in some sense 'socially necessary'. In the world of pure competition, this would be the dominating or least-cost technique but the technique actually adopted is shaped in many ways by institutions or factors, starting with technological norms, some of which are always historically given and can never all be changed at once. It is obvious that our future will largely be determined by technology which must be made compatible with the environment. Some control on the part of the State is unavoidable. The point is to couple it with social controls which must reside in the judgement of responsible citizens who are not just independent monads but live in an economy and society shaped by traditions which they constantly transform.

I have proposed to reintroduce the concept of 'economic style' to characterise a certain, to some extent precarious and contradictory, unity between the dynamics of an economy, the attitudes of individuals and the institutions which help to preserve it. In *Grenzen der Atomwirtschaft* (Meyer-Abich and Schefold, 1986), an attempt was made to design formal and informal controls which would help to sustain alternative paths of economic development, associated with alternative energy policies, through differences of the economic style. Whatever name is chosen, the task is to find solutions which will allow survival on a planet with a number of inhabitants which is growing at an alarming rate while new environmental problems are being discovered at a rate which is even more disquieting. Perhaps this concern is not that dissimilar from the one of Ota Sik who has become so prominent in his relentless search for *A Third Way* – a quest which we all cannot but admire.

References

Bharadwaj, K. and B. Schefold (eds) (1989) *Essays on Piero Sraffa: Critical Perspectives on the Revival of Classical Theory* (London: Unwin Hyman).

Clifton, J.A. (1977) 'Competition and the Evolution of the Capitalist Mode of Production', *Cambridge Journal of Economics*, vol. 1, no. 2, pp. 137–51.

Eichner, A.S. (1976) *The Megacorp & Oligopoly* (Cambridge: Cambridge University Press).

Kaldor, N. (1985) *Economics Without Equilibrium* (Armonk: M.E. Sharp).

Koopmans, T.C. (ed.) (1951) *Activity Analysis of Production and Allocation* (New York: John Wiley).

Meyer-Abich, K.M. and B. Schefold (1986) *Die Grenzen der Atomwirtschaft*, 4th edn (München: Beck Verlag).

Morishima, M. (1973) *Marx's Economics* (Cambridge: Cambridge University Press).

Morishima, M. (1977) *Walras' Economics: A Pure Theory of Capital and Money* (Cambridge: Cambridge University Press).

Pais, A. (1982) *Subtle is the Lord: The Science and the Life of Albert Einstein* (Oxford: Oxford University Press).

Pivetti, M. (1989) 'On the Monetary Explanation of Distribution', in Bharadwaj and Schefold, *Essays on Piero Sraffa*.

Robinson, J. (1956) *The Accumulation of Capital* (London: Macmillan).

Schefold, B. (1989) 'Comment on P. A. Samuelson, in Bharadwaj and Schefold, *Essays on Piero Sraffa*.

Schwartz, J. T. (1961) *Lectures on the Mathematical Method in Analytical Economics* (New York: Gordon & Breach).

Sraffa, P. (1926) 'The Laws of Returns under Competitive Conditions', *The Economic Journal*, vol. 36, December, pp. 535–50.

Sraffa, P. (1951) 'Introduction', in P. Sraffa (ed. with the collaboration of M. H. Dobb), *The Works and Correspondence of David Ricardo* (Cambridge: Cambridge University Press) vol. 1 (1951–1973), pp. xiii–lxii.

Sraffa, P. (1960) *Production of Commodities by Means of Commodities*, (Cambridge: Cambridge University Press).

14 Some Thoughts on Plan and Market

Alec Nove

'To combine plan and marfket is like being a little bit pregnant', wrote a (female) Soviet economist. This view is wrong, but is to be found both among the adepts of the Chicago school and among Marxist dogmatists. Indeed, the latter have good textual evidence to support their ideological interpretation. Recently, the Soviet professor, A. Sergeyev, put the point well:

> It is known that Marx and Engels held that socialism and commodity production were not only contradictory but also incompatible. Lenin adopted the same position. Even today no one would have the theoretical effrontery (*naglost'*) to claim that Lenin was the founder of the theory of commodity production under socialism. Was the theory of Marx, Engels, Lenin about socialism then incorrect?[1]

In 1988, the (well-justified) rehabilitation of Bukharin tempted some Soviet commentators to make of him a prophet of market socialism, but to do this is incorrect: Bukharin did strongly support the market under NEP, but, in common with the vast majority of other Marxists, believed that when socialism was achieved markets would wither away.

It is not my purpose in this paper to rehearse yet again the arguments about the need for markets under 'feasible socialism', since I have done so at length in my book of that name. The same basic points were made by Radoslav Selucky[2] and by Ota Sik himself. I will concentrate instead on two debates, taking place in isolation the one from the other: where should the dividing line between plan and market be in a reformed Soviet or East European socialist economy, and what is right or wrong with the unrestrained worship of the 'individualist' market on the part of Mrs Thatcher's right-wing think-tanks? There is in fact emerging an unconscious theoretical overlap within the two debates: in

Moscow, in January 1988, I encountered young economists whom I described (to their faces) as 'Muscovite Friedmanists'. In Poland, there is a vocal minority of ultra-free-marketeers, described as such by the philosopher Andrzej Walicki.[3] In Hungary, there is Tibor Liska and his ideas on entrepreneurial free-market socialism.

So, how to tackle these issues? First, let us assume without further argument that there exist spheres in economic life in which market relations should predominate. Thus if workers are paid in money, they should be free to spend it, in markets, in shops (which would be owned by the State, or be leased, or be cooperative, or private), and through backward linkages the production and wholesaling of consumers' goods and of the inputs they require should operate on market principles, providing clear material incentives for the satisfaction of user demand for marketed goods and services. At the other extreme, let us assume that 'market' ideologists accept the need for some sort of safety net (the poor should not be left to die in the street), state financing of at least basic education, road-building, garbage removal, plus measures to prevent or to penalise pollution. This still leaves a very large 'grey' area. Let us try to enter it.

Let us begin with *macrobalance*. General equilibrium theories examine a world in which unregulated coordination occurs exclusively through the market. In Western theories there is an uneasy division between 'macro' and 'micro', and a sizeable literature discusses the relationship between the two, the 'microfoundations' (if any) of macroeconomics. It has long been noted that the sort of problems which worried Keynes, i.e. major imbalances and market failures, could not arise in a world of general equilibrium and prereconciled choices. Recent developments of the theory of so-called rational expectations (or the 'new Classical economics') has built a bridge between the two, but it is based on assumptions – about knowledge of the future – so breathtakingly unrealistic that one needs a sociological theory to explain the fact that such doctrines are taken seriously; and they *are* taken seriously.

Is the economy self-balancing? Can crises, cycles, inflation, large-scale unemployment, be avoided without conscious state action? (Of course, incorrect state action can also help to bring these troubles about.) The definition of equilibrium by the 'new Classicals' is such that any actual situation must conform to it: if people are not working, this must be their personal preference. Markets (including labour markets) clear by definition – unless artificial obstacles prevent this. Remove the obstacles and all will be for the best in all possible worlds.

Axel Leijonhuvhud, reflecting Keynesian concerns, contrasts the idea of a ship which rocks to and fro in a rough sea but always returns to an equilibrium position, with one whose cargo shifts, which prevents its return to equilibrium without conscious action by captain and crew. Also that too great a list to port or to starboard could lead to catastrophe. He might have added that even a self-righting ship is nowadays equipped with stabilisers, to prevent the passengers from feeling ill!

The 'self-righting' theroy is at its weakest when one considers the reality of *investment*: criteria, procedures, decisions, financing. This has a link with the question of labour markets that should 'clear', and with capital–labour substitutions where unemployment exists as a major problem. After a short theoretical excursion I shall illustrate the point with recent British experience.

Orthodox microeconomic theory is very inadequate when dealing with investment, while macro theories deal only with aggregates, and so do not examine why investment decisions are made (though Keynes himself, with his references to uncertain expectations and the 'casino', did point to gaps in theory). The key to these gaps – if I may mix metaphors – is to be found in the work of the Oxford economist G.B. Richardson.[4] Let me summarise his argument.

Let us take the standard model of perfect competition, as the supposed *optimum optimorum*. To invest in expanding productive capacity requires the would-be investor to have information about future costs and prices.

> Presumably firms are supposed to equate future marginal costs with future prices. But how is the producer to predict future prices, depending as they do on the demands of the consumer and the supply plans of all his competitors? . . . If the future price of a good were known to be higher than the current cost of making it, then a profit opportunity may be said to exist; but if there are an unlimited number of firms able to respond to the opportunity, no individual firm will know what to do. A profit opportunity available to everyone is in fact available to none at all.[5]

To put the point in another way: suppose even that we know the price *and* the costs of production in five years' time to be $x and $y respectively, and all the competitors know it, and the model excludes collusion (under-the-table exchange of information about production and investment plans); then no basis exists for action. Indeed, we can in such circumstances *not know* the price to be $x, since the price itself is a function of competitors' response to the expectation that this *will* be the price, thus altering it! This is the exact equivalent of assuming that a horse will win a race at odds of 10–1. If many knew it would win, the odds would not be 10–1.

So even under normal conditions, with stable exchange rates and modest interest rates, the uncertainty engendered by the competitive process itself could inhibit investment, and investment creates workplaces and is required if unemployment is to fall. The existence of unemployment does not of itself provide a stimulus to invest, sufficient to overcome the uncertainty barrier. True, unemployment could lead to a fall in real wages and so to substitution of labour for capital at the margin. However, theory greatly exaggerates the actual opportunities for such substitution. There is not in real life an infinite set of technological alternatives of varying capital–labour intensity, and empirical studies show no support for the view that firms choose a more labour-intensive variant if they expect wages to be (say) 10 per cent lower.

Investment occurs because of so-called *imperfections*: imperfect knowledge (one firm knows, or thinks it knows, what others do not), temporary monopoly, collusion, long-term tie-ups with large customers, prior arrangements with providers of complementary inputs, state-sponsored coordination (e.g. what MITI does in Japan), and other departures from the so-called *optimum optimorum*, which is thus not optimal at all. One must also consider state-financed or state-sponsored investments in infrastructure, which in most countries can be seen to yield substantial external economies, a point well understood by Adam Smith (but not by the ultra-*laissez-faire* think-tank to which Mrs Thatcher listens, and which absurdly bears the name of the Adam Smith Institute).

A more active 'macro' role is required even if monetarist theories were accepted, for British experience shows that for control over private credit (and so over the money supply) one needs stronger weapons than just the interest rate. And if one inherits structural imbalances, with a tendency to underinvestment and low savings, plus regional distortions and high unemployment, the functioning of the market mechanism does not result in automatic correction of the imbalances. Indeed, regional distortions tend to be self-reinforcing, as the example of many countries, from Mexico to Yugoslavia, bears witness. Also capital markets tend to have a short-term view, especially when there is a high interest rate and uncertainty as to exchange rates and world market prospects. Yet someone must be concerned as to what could happen if North Sea oil runs out, say in ten to fifteen years' time. British coal might then be highly necessary – yet the very notion of an energy policy is 'planning' and ideologically suspect. Who but the State should feel responsible for the longer term?

Indeed, the British economy's present crisis illustrates vividly the 'non-self-righting' hypothesis. There is a record balance of payments deficit, due to a boom in demand which Britain's own productive capacity, much reduced in the 'deflation' of 1979–82, is incapable of meeting. Since direct control over credit, or a rise in taxes, is excluded by ideology, the only available 'weapon' is a sharp rise in interest rates. But this has a double negative effect: by attracting short-term funds to London it maintains a high exchange rate, rendering British goods less competitive, *and* it discourages borrowing for investment, thus inhibiting the expansion of productive capacity. (Statistics showing a rise in imports of 'investment goods' are misleading, since they include such things as the large rise in imports of lorries and buses, of cash registers for supermarkets, etc.)

It is sometimes asserted by *laissez-faire* ideologists that South Korea is a brilliant example of the success of free markets. Success, certainly, but – here is a quotation from a recent report from the (US) National Bureau of Economic Research.[6] This refers to

> an active, interventionist government policy that was credible, consistent, and coherent. Investment to promote exports received top priority, and the economy was led through a fundamental industrial restructuring. Korea instituted a series of five-year plans (beginning in 1962) that determined the level of investment necessary for a desired level of growth, and singled out sectors to be stimulated, focusing especially on exports. The close link between government and business in Korea made this strategy work.

> Government savings were positive in every year since 1962,

and the country's savings rate rose from 14% in 1965 to over 34% in 1986. With the exception of the late 1970s, Korea followed a consistent, credible exchange rate policy over this period, maintaining a competitive, sometimes undervalued, real exchange rate with low variance. Real depreciations often were accompanied by real wage *increases*, because labour productivity was increasing.

Finally, tax preferences and interest rate subsidies helped domestic industries after 1965. Also, import restrictions increased substantially during the 1970s. Almost all Korean imports are raw materials, intermediate products, or capital goods. Consumer products represent less than 5% of Korean imports.

If this is *laissez-faire*, then Ota Sik is an Eskimo . . .

What of the role of planning and/or state intervention in the 'micro' sphere? Of course, there are 'public goods', though here there can be legitimate arguments as to where the dividing line comes. While all but extreme fanatics accept (say) that a public authority should provide street lighting, there are disagreements over the role of the state in health, education, and in most countries there is both public and private provision, in varying proportions.

There is also an important 'hybrid': publicly financed provision *through* privately operated markets. Thus it is possible to envisage the state 'paying' patients or parents in the form of vouchers, which are 'spent' in purchasing privately provided medical and educational services. Similarly, while the city could be responsible for garbage collection, the actual collection could be undertaken either by municipal employees or by private subcontractors. Or a bus to take children to school could belong to the education authority or be hired from a private operator. There are advantages and disadvantages in these situations which we will not discuss here. The point is that they are all based on the public authority's responsibility that the services be financed.

Let me pass to problems relating to infrastructure, and also 'natural monopolies'. The one generates important externalities, the other raises problems linked with the absence of competition, which is an essential ingredient in any 'market' solution. Such questions must arise in East and West, in 'feasible socialism' and in modern capitalism. In every West European country except

Britain it is understood that railways and urban transport networks should be subsidised, since the positive externalities are important: congestion is reduced, property values enhanced, the beneficiaries include those who do not use public transport (as can be seen by the paralysis that occurs when there is a strike on the Paris Metro, for instance). Mrs Thatcher's advisers, however, oppose subsidies, and oppose any limitations on competition, while recent laws actually *forbid* British municipalities from operating a transport system! Even in America, *every* city known to me operates an urban transport network as an integrated public monopoly. The British extremist ideologists would not only privatise DC Transit (the Washington network), they would disintegrate it, considering each bus route and metro line as if it were a separate firm and forbidding 'cross-subsidisation'. The British law actually does outlaw cross-subsidisation in urban transport, even though *any* network which makes any kind of standard charge *must* cross-subsidise (every route, every bus, every segment of line, *cannot* yield the same financial results, cannot have the same costs and revenues!).

Only ideology stands in the way of understanding that a country benefits from having some kind of transport plan, national or local, with a public authority being directly concerned, as is the case in almost every West European country – though of course many providers of transport services are private.

'Natural monopolies' such as water supply, electricity, gas, the post office, present a choice between public and private monopolies, and both require supervision to avoid exploitation of monopoly position and the maintenance of standards. Competing parallel electricity wires or water pipes are clearly irrational. In these instances *laissez-faire* is plainly inadequate. In America, the Interstate Commerce Commission was an example of a regulating body concerned with privately owned public utilities. In Britain, even before privatisation some economists urged the application of 'commercial' criteria by nationalised monopolies, apparently unaware that profits can be enhanced by lowering standards, tolerating queues, delaying repairs and other forms of worsening quality. These considerations do not apply to nationalised enterprises operating in a competitive environment: the firm of Renault, which was nationalised, has and should have, the same operational criteria as any private firm, as I pointed out in a book written long ago.[7] Similarly, profit-oriented efficiency criteria should apply to those Soviet enterprises (state and cooperative) which are in the competitive sphere, but 'natural monopolies' exist there too and need a different approach.

British experience shows the dangers of excessive 'methodological individualism', which sees the whole as no more than the sum of its parts ('There is no such thing as society,' said Mrs Thatcher, presumably under the temporary influence of one of her ideological-extremist advisers.) Such an outlook blinds one to the importance of interrelationsips, complementarities, indivisibilities, the frequently contradictory interests of the part and the whole, be this whole a firm, a region, or any network or system. This can lead to foolish forms of fragmentation, affecting (in recent years) London, school districts, transport, electricity, and more recently even arms production.

In Soviet theory and practice, the individual was too often disregarded in the name of some larger whole, and it is salutary to be reminded that human satisfaction is indeed the sum of the satisfaction and welfare of millions of individuals and families, that to sacrifice them for some 'total good' is dangerous. But this can go too far. The interests of the whole are often distinct from the sum total of the interests of the parts, if the latter are separately evaluated. A moment's thought can surely produce dozens of examples. The first battalion of the Grenadier Guards is not *only* the officers and men composing it. Nor is the Chicago Symphony Orchestra just the sum total of the musicians, each of whom pursue his own interest. It is not true of any hierarchically organised unit such as a firm; its hierarchical structure is due in large part to the need for conscious coordination, to ensure that the parts *do* relate coherently to the interests of the whole. Or take the question of town planning: suppose there is an architectural ensemble, like the famous Georgian terraces in Bath. The ensemble is, in a physical sense, the sum total of the fifty houses composing it. Yet public authority rightly will forbid the owner of one of the fifty houses to demolish it or alter its appearance without permission, because of the effect it could have on the other forty-nine, on the totality, which is in a sense more than the sum of its parts.

The underlying theoretical conceptions of the 'individualists' are fragmentationist in another sense: they silently assume the divisibility of each set of economic acts and decisions into a virtually infinite number of transactions, each of them profitable as such. (It is this concentration on the *transaction* as the basic unit of analysis that is the weakness of the otherwise very valuable book by O. Williamson: *Markets and Hierarchies*, 1983.) As I have written on several occasions before, *margins are frequently hierarchical*, i.e. should be seen in contexts. Which, *pace* Williamson, is an important reason for the existence of hierarchies in private and public sectors alike. This should be obvious but is hardly ever stated.

Now back to the real world. I will quote two examples: in Britain, like many other countries, we have an interconnected national electricity grid, with publicly owned power stations 'feeding' it, and the undertaking also sells the electricity to the customers. The 'fragmentationist' ideologists have persuaded a credulous government not only to privatise but to break up the generating monopoly, 'to create competition'. Even they do not advocate destroying the interconnected grid, but in their model there will be competing power stations selling electricity to it – while the final customer still faces a monopoly supplier, since even the ideologists can see the waste in having competing wires running to each house, factory and office. But what they do not see is that no one will be *responsible* for ensuring the provision of *reserve capacity* which is needed to deal with peak loads and climatic abnormalities. The point is that reserve capacity seldom pays as such, *and* that investments in generating stations require to be based on information about future aggregate needs, which the Central Electricity Generating Board could at least try to acquire. The ideologists point to the fact that it did on occasion get its sums wrong, which is true, but it in no way follows that no such calculation is necessary, if the needed investments are to be made. So it is quite probable that within ten years it will suddenly be discovered that power cuts have to be imposed on very cold days.

No more is the reserve team of a professional football club profitable as such. The *responsible* management covers the loss because the first team, like the electricity supply, requires reserves. It is this, not 'transaction costs', which cause the reserve team to exist, this along with the uncertainties of real life.

The word 'responsibility' has been underlined because it is a concept totally absent from the textbooks. Just as they fail to mention the fact (which should be obvious) that what appears to be most rational to do depends in some degree on the area of responsibility of the decision-maker. This is as true in the private as in the public sector. The distinction in this context between private and public arises when one contemplates the level at which responsibility should rest, and the considerations which must inform the decision-maker. Thus the questions concerning what happens to the British economy if North Sea oil runs out (or the price collapses), the transport needs of the London conurbation, or the need for reserve capacity for arms production, would seem to be public sector responsibilities. The ideologists do not even make an exception for arms production: *Royal* Ordnance factories were sold off in 1988, and the private firm which bought them closed down half of them and sold the sites for profit. Clearly it should have been the ministry, not this firm, which should be responsible for deciding whether or not this capacity was surplus to requirements!

Space precludes further analysis. The only point to make in conclusion is to underline the evident need to avoid ideological extremism, now much more common on the right than on the left, and to appreciate the important role which both planning *and* the market should have in a modern industrial society.

Notes

1. A Sergeyev, *Voprosy ekonomiki*, no. 7, 1988, p. 40.
2. R. Selucky, *Marxism, Socialism, Freedom* (London: Macmillan, 1979).
3. A. Walicki, *Critical Review*, vol. 2, no. 1, 1987.
4. G.B. Richardson, *Information and Investment* (Oxford University Press, 1960).
5. Ibid.
6. National Bureau of Economic Research, *NBER Digest*, October, 1988.
7. A. Nove, *Efficiency Criteria for Nationalized Industries* (London, 1973).

15 An Institutionalist View of the Evolution of Economic Systems

Marc R. Tool[1]

In appreciation of Ota Sik's distinguished career-long concern with the evolution of economic systems. I wish, in this chapter briefly to sketch fundamental theoretical characteristics of institutional economics and, in this context, to develop the institutionalist argument that the problem solving process accounts for the evolution of economic systems.[2]

Most are aware that institutional economics began in the United States with Thorstein Veblen's writings in the late 1890s. In this century, a distinctive and comprehensive institutionalist literature has evolved that incorporates this Veblenian legacy, among others. In the last thirty years, in particular, this literature has become more extensive, sharply focused and tightly integrated.[3]

THE INSTITUTIONALIST PERSPECTIVE

In this section, I review general premises and tenets of the institutionalist perspective that support analysis of the evolution of economic systems. Here, such a review can only be indicative, not definitive.

The purpose of institutionalist analysis is to provide an evidentially grounded, causal account of processual reality. The social *process* in all its complexity is the object of inquiry. This social process is evolutionary and developmental, not necessarily cyclical, episodic or epochal. Two continuing and interrelated functions or categories of activity dominate this process: the economic process of social provisioning – the generation and distribution of goods and services – and the political process of determining and administering social policy. The institutionalist focus is always on emergent political economy.

165

In all cultures, institutions organise behaviour in pursuit of differing facets of these interdependent economic and political functions. *Institutions* are defined as socially prescribed patterns of correlated human behaviour and attitudes. However obscure the origins, all institutions are formed by human choice; they are, in principle, amenable to revision. Institutions reflect the acquired value structure of the society.[4] They represent historically successive determinations of what ought to be the controlling patterns of behaviour.

Socially correlated patterns of behaviour are internalised by individuals and become habitual. Institutions, then, are made up of habits but they are not determined by habits. Being constituted of habits, institutions are often resistent to change. Rules, codes, customs, and attitudes, once established and embedded as habits, define expected behaviour and are presumed to be continuing. However, when expectations are unfulfilled, questions of how come? or why so? arise. As people reflect on the consequences produced by existing institutional structure, they are prompted to appraise habitual behaviour. They come to see a difference between what is and what ought to be. Those with discretion in the community may decide that ineffectual or destructive consequences from the performance of existing institutional forms should be corrected through institutional adjustment.

To give meaning or content to 'ineffectual' or 'destructive' consequences – even to distinguish between 'what is' and 'what ought to be' – requires the use of normative criteria of judgement. As economic systems evolve through problem solving, the character of the institutional adjustments that comprise that evolution is specified by the criteria of appraisal chosen and employed.

But in explaining the evolution of economic systems, institutions can not themselves serve credibly as criteria for choosing institutions. To propose the existing structure of 'what is' as the determiner or criterion of 'what ought to be' is to reaffirm the status quo and, in effect, to deny the existence of real economic problems. Obviously, pertinent structural change cannot be effectively conceived and implemented until *after* the actual institutional malfunctions have been identified and understood.

Similarly, *a priori* patterns for economic systems – for example, the ideological models of capitalism, socialism, communism – cannot serve as criteria; they appear rather as utopian designs. Their *basic* system character is given; their distinguishing institutional components are not amenable to revision. They are, at best, of only remote or accidental relevance to the continuing real world task of making choices among institutional options. The current, single-minded insistence that 'reform' be conceived as a return to free market allocation, as exhibited in the Reagan and Thatcher administrations in the 1980s, is an example of this illusory quest. The normative use of the competitive market model is inadmissible and irrelevant precisely because it will not permit the identification or resolution of actual problems of institutional malfunctioning.[5]

The *modification* of institutional structures – institutional adjustment – is the process through which any community solves its economic and political problems. Problem solving is accomplished by revamping the problematic elements of prevailing institutions to bring them into congruity with what the expanding fund of reliable knowledge indicates is feasible and desirable. The evolution of any economic system is punctuated with institutional modifications initiated as corrections for what is perceived to be impairment, misdirection, or sabotage of the economic process.

The institutionalist view of human agency places discretionary persons in the role of initiators of evolutionary change. Human 'nature' is an emergent product of continuing and complex interactions between genetically equipped human organisms and their physical and cultural environment. This genetic inheritance permits the development of lingual facility, cognitive capability, and social interdependence. But specific behaviours, beliefs, motivations, and attitudes are acquired through cultural conditioning. 'All socially relevant behavior is learned and is, for the most part, habitual.'[6] Culture imposes attitudinal, and behavioural configurations on genetically endowed but educable beings. That educability permits subsequent critique and revision of cultural impositions. People are capable of developing the capacity to perceive means–consequence connections implied in such assessments. This developmental potentiality is the institutionalist referent for *rationality*. (There is no reliance here on maximising assumptions.) Men and women, to the extent permitted or encouraged by cultural constraints, choose among available options, and in their choosing they change both themselves and the cultural context of their own modes of living and livelihood. This indicates, then, that a credible explanation of the evolution of economic systems cannot deny human agency. No 'law of motion' of society, geographic or psychological determinism, or sequential stages theory of history will suffice. The evolution of economic systems is primarily a function of the exercise of human will. The questions of whose will governs and what purposes are to be served is the domain of inquiry in the political process.

The institutionalist mode of inquiry is addressed to an understanding of causality; prediction is of secondary interest. Inquiry originates with the appearance of doubt about the adequacy of received explanations or of expected behaviour; it seeks, through evidentially grounded and logically coherent analysis, to restore congruity of understanding and experience. The provisional outcomes of such inquiry are instrumentally warranted elements of reliable knowledge. Inquiry, so conceived, will explain the evolution of economic systems.

Moreover, since choices must be made at every stage of inquiry, and since such choices logically require criteria of choice, value judgements are endemic in all social inquiry. Inquiry is value-laden. The inquiry mode of institutionalists, then, is both positive in its pursuit of the causal determinants of *what is* going on, and normative in its explicit consideration of *what ought to be* done to define and resolve problems. The conventional dichotomy divorcing the positive and the normative is wholly rejected. Institutionalist inquiry into the problem solving process that explains the evolution of economic systems must, then, be evaluative as well as analytical.[7]

THE EVOLUTION OF ECONOMIC SYSTEMS

It is now possible directly to address what is meant by 'the evolution of economic systems'. How can their evolution be explained? Can the character of evolution be guided? Provisional answers are provided by the institutionalist theory of social change:[8]

An *economic system* is the structural composition of the myriad interrelated institutions through which people organise and correlate behaviour to carry on a host of social activities that sustain and enhance the life processes of the community. Among these are: the production of food and fibre, the determination of exchange ratios, the distribution of income, the generation and dissemination of knowledge, the education of the young, and the like.[9] The generation and delivery of such products and services requires specified institutional arrangements. The extant economic system reflects continuance of the cultural heritage, past judgements of public and private discretionary agents, and complexities and constraints imposed by external powers and circumstance.

In any modern economic system, the institutional structure is constantly being transformed. Its emergent character does not reflect an autogenetic quest for equilibrium, or accommodation to a law of succession of 'modes of production and exchange'. Institutionalists see the economic system as a product of deliberative, discretionary actions that are in principle knowable and reflect value judgement assessments. They customarily initiate inquiry in social value theory through consideration of the Veblenian dichotomy.

This dichotomy appears in one form or another in all Veblen's writings.[10] A representative formulation appears in his *Leisure Class*: 'Institutions . . . may be roughly distinguished into two classes or categories, according as they serve one or the other of two divergent purposes of economic life[:] . . . acquisition or production . . . pecuniary or industrial [activity] . . . [an] invidious or non-invidious economic interest.'[11] The version that is especially significant in this context is the distinction between ceremonial and technological behaviour and institutions.[12]

In a paper that significantly refines and extends this dichotomy, Paul Dale Bush has recently written: 'The institutional structure of any society incorporates two systems of value: the ceremonial and the instrumental, each of which has its own logic and method of validation. While these two value systems are inherently incompatible, they are intertwined within the institutional structure through a complex set of relationships.'[13] The distinction between these two value systems is a central construct in the institutionalist's explanation of the evolution of economic systems. Bush continues: 'Ceremonial values correlate behavior within the institution by providing the standards of judgment for invidious distinctions, which prescribe status, differential privileges, and master–servant relationships, and warrant the exercise of power by one social class over another.' In contrast: 'Instrumental values correlate behavior by providing the standards of judgment by which tools and skills are employed in the application of evidentially warranted knowledge to the problem-solving processes of the community.'[14]

Note that *both* sorts of value judgements are reflected in the institutional structure although their relative importance will vary with time and circumstance. Behaviour thus may be wholly ceremonial, wholly instrumental, or, more likely, may contain elements of each mode. Either behavioural mode may incorporate elements of the other, but the value traits are discrete and dichotomous. Examples of wholly ceremonial behaviour would include fascist use of coercive power or parental child abuse. Examples of wholly instrumental behaviour would include appeals to reason in political deliberation or teaching lingual skills to a handicapped child. Examples of behaviour reflecting both modes would include defence of democratic institutions (preservation of tradition and providing genuine choice) or the insistence that children obey school rules (exercise of unilateral authority and provision of safe environment). Ceremonial behaviour will be correlated by a ceremonial value as in the invidious use of coercive power. Instrumental behaviour will be correlated by an instrumental value as in the furtherance of political freedom and of effectual reflective communication. Where a ceremonial value correlates both ceremonial and instrumental behaviour, Bush argues that 'ceremonial encapsulation' of instrumental behaviour occurs.[15] An example would be fascist control of the instrumental flow of real income. Available knowledge and technology must be rendered 'ceremonially adequate'. With encapsulation, ceremonial considerations will dominate instrumental considerations.

Some measure of 'ceremonial dominance' will be found in all cultures. Ceremonial dominance defines the degree of permissiveness a culture provides for instrumental behaviour and judgement. An 'index of ceremonial dominance', then, would indicate the extent to which a culture will permit its *available* instrumentally warranted knowledge to be utilised in the correlation of behaviour. It follows that the higher the index of ceremonial dominance, the more retarded is the evolution of an economic system.

For an economic system to evolve progressively, the levels of ceremonial dominance must be reduced by the substitution of instrumental patterns of behaviour for ceremonial patterns of behaviour. An economic problem exists when, for example, significant impairments or terminations in the flow of real income, and/or its inequitable distribution, occur, that is, where unemployment, poverty, discrimination, and/or stagnation demonstrably prevail. The institutionalist approach is to discover, through empirical research and theoretical analysis, the levels and character of ceremonial dominance that generate these conditions and to seek ways of enhancing the magnitude and instances of instrumental correlation of behaviour through the formulation and implementation of institutional modifications.

The dynamic element in the evolution of economic systems is the growth of reliable (instrumentally warranted) knowledge and its application as technology to the productive process. Although it overstates the case to say that gunpowder destroyed feudalism and that the steam engine gave us capitalism, each such innovation did modify the community's knowledge fund and technological applications, stimulate fresh consideration of the adequacy of existing institutions, and encourage reflection on new options of coordination. While the attribution of causal potency for evolutionary change to class conflict, great men, entrepreneurial spirit, or 'innate' greed, may provide intellectual strategies of limited usefulness, none has sufficient explanatory capacity to warrant acceptance.

This technological continuum has cultural origins. As Bush explains: 'Technology for Veblen was a process that arose out of the human proclivity for workmanship and the exercise of intellectual curiosity. It was embodied in the tool-skill nexus of problem-solving activities. The essence of technological change, therefore, was the change in the 'prevalent habits of thought' associated with a given state of the arts and sciences.'[16] All the evidence appears to confirm that 'technological innovation is developmental in the sense of being cumulative, combinatorial, and accelerating in character'.[17] Given its cumulative attribute, the fund of knowledge that acts as a support to technology is unidirectionally expansive and irreversible. The interdependence and mutual promotion of tools, skills and ideas expands the knowledge fund. Such growth is the source of the emergence and identification of problems as people, with knowledge, perceive a difference between what is and what might be. It is, at the same time, the primary resource on which thoughtful people draw in efforts to resolve problems.

The community's fund of knowledge, then, 'is either "encapsulated" within ceremonial patterns or "embodied" within instrumental patterns of behavior'. But it is the community's index of ceremonial dominance that determines the extent to which the knowledge fund, the source and sanction for instrumental behaviour, is made available for problem solving purposes. With ceremonial dominance, only that part of the knowledge fund that can be reconciled with the existing ceremonial value structure will be implemented in instrumental behaviour. Instrumental knowledge is encapsulated and made to serve invidiously grounded power systems and their status demands.[18] To the extent that such conditions prevail, the evolution of economic systems is sabotaged and misdirected to serve ceremonial or invidious purposes. The imposition of the test of ceremonial adequacy overrides instrumental valuing.

When the index of ceremonial dominance, then, is high enough to permit ceremonial encapsulation of important elements of the knowledge fund, instrumentally warranted patterns of behaviour may be *replaced* by ceremonial or invidious patterns of behaviour. Where this occurs, there is *regressive* social and economic change. When, however, with a given stock of knowledge, instrumental patterns of behaviour displace ceremonial or invidious patters of behaviour *progressive* institutional change occurs. Problem solving occurs only with progressive change. The *character* of the evolution of an economic system is reflected, then, in the distinction between progressive and regressive change and hinges on the degree of ceremonial dominance that prevails.

The *rate* of progressive change is determined largely by three considerations:[19] The first concerns the availability of knowledge. Unless the culture permits and encourages the growth of reliable knowledge, including a willingness to borrow and/or exchange information and techniques with other cultures, so that adequate understanding of the actual determinants of problems can be acquired, progressive change will be severely constricted. The stock and sophistication of the knowledge fund, however acquired, defines the scope and character of investigations of problematic conditions. A paucity of knowledge will limit progressive evolution.

The second concerns the ability of a community to absorb and adapt to new knowledge and technology. Changes in habits of thought and behaviour specified or required to shift from ceremonial to instrumental values and behaviours are always difficult. Unless extensive efforts are made to inform the relevant communities of what changes are contemplated, why they are thought necessary, what the implications of the changes are (that is, how adequately will people be able to function under the new prescriptions), and to secure the prior approval or acquiescence of those affected, the change will be resisted, sometimes vehemently. A tops-down imposition of rule changes will often slow or prevent progressive evolution.

The third limitation concerns the timing and extent of change. Change initiated must be, in so far as possible, 'minimally disloca-tive'. While any change is dislocative in some measure, successful instrumental change must be limited to that which can be demon-strated to be essential for problem resolution. Other facets of the economy, not perceived to be problematic through invidious impairment, should not be disturbed, if possible. Accordingly, massive, convulsive economy-wide changes usually fail to reduce ceremonial dominance because they are excessively dislocative.

In sum, the institutionalist theory of social change, sustained by fundamental tenets of institutionalist thought, introduces non-traditional and pertinent tools of inquiry, identifies the dynamic element in the transformation of economies, provides a causal explanation of how and why the evolution of economic systems occurs, and offers credible principles for the normative assessment of economic change. Given such understanding, the policy agenda for the discretionary management of the progressive evolution of an economic system can be fashioned with both confidence and humanity.

Notes

1. The author is Professor Emeritus of Economics, California State University, Sacramento, and Editor of *The Journal of Economic Issues*. He wishes especially to thank Paul Dale Bush for most helpful comments on an earlier draft of this paper. The usual caveats apply.
2. Note especially that the Veblen–Dewey–Commons–Ayres-based insti-tutional economics addressed here is *fundamentally* incommensurate with contemporary, neo-classically based 'New Institutionalism', public choice analysis, and the neo-Austrian perspective.
3. For a recent and comprehensive presentation of this perspective, see Marc R. Tool (ed.) *Evolutionary Economics, Vol. I: Foundations of Institutional Thought, and Evolutionary Economics; Vol. II: Insti-tutional Theory and Policy* (New York: M.E. Sharpe, 1988).
4. Paul Dale Bush, 'The Theory of Institutional Change', in *Evolution-ary Economics*, vol. I, n.s., p. 128.
5. Marc R. Tool, *Essays in Social Value Theory: A Neoinstitutionalist Contribution* (Armonk, NY: M.E. Sharpe, 1986), pp. 104–25.
6. Bush, 'Theory of Institutional Change', p. 127.

7. Marc R. Tool, *The Discretionary Economy: A Normative Theory of Political Economy* (Boulder, Col.: Westview Press, 1985), pp. 274–336.
8. See Bush, 'The Theory of Institutional Change'; also his 'On the Concept of Ceremonial Encapsulation', *Review of Institutional Thought*, vol. 3 (December, 1986), pp. 25–45.
9. Tool, *Discretionary Economy*, pp. 105–37.
10. Tool, *Essays*, pp. 34–7.
11. Thorstein Veblen, *The Theory of the Leisure Class* (New York: Modern Library, 1934), p. 208.
12. Thorstein Veblen, *Imperial Germany and the Industrial Revolution* (New York: Augustus M. Kelley, 1964), passim.
13. Bush, 'Theory of Institutional Change', p. 129.
14. Ibid., p. 130.
15. Ibid., p. 134.
16. Ibid., p. 137.
17. Ibid.
18. For a consideration of 'past-binding', 'future-binding', and ' "Lysenko" type' forms of 'ceremonial encapsulation', see Bush, 'Theory of Institutional Change', pp. 142–9.
19. Bush, 'Theory of Institutional Change', pp. 155–7; Tool, *Discretionary Economy*, pp. 172–6.

PART III

Evolution of Planning Systems: (1) General Evolution of Planning Systems

16 Socialist Experience and Ota Sik's *Third Way*

Jiří Kosta

The first post-war publications of Ota Sik were influenced by the traditional Marxist doctrines of the Stalin era, although at that time some independent ideas emerged (Sik, 1953, 1955a, 1955b). However, before long, his work was characterised by critical accents. Already in 1957, he questioned the dogma according to which only the party knows the objective interests of all workers and only its policies can meet these needs. Every highly centralised planning system, Sik says, burdens the decision-makers with unconquerable information problems, which make an effective *ex ante* planning questionable from the onset. The existing conflicts in group interests and the information problem indicate that a decentralisation of the centrally controlled economic system is just as important as a stronger use of material incentives (Sik, 1957).

In an article written in 1958, but which could not be published before 1964 due to censorship, Sik explained why 'commodity-money relations' are necessary not only between different owners (state-owned enterprises versus cooperatives, public enterprises versus private households), but also between different state-owned companies. In continuity with a thesis expressed one year earlier, he strongly emphasised that the temporary and transient lack of information and perception should not be seen as the sole cause of increasing disproportions and decreasing efficiency; there are also, he said, unavoidable systemic contradictions between the particular interests of different enterprises among themselves, as well as between the partial interests of companies on the one hand and society on the other. According to Sik, these contradictory interests are due to the character of work (the existing distribution of jobs, long working day, physical exertion, mental stress, etc.), as well as to the persisting shortages of consumer goods (Sik, 1957, pp. 269–305).

Sik's book, *Economics, Interests, Politics*, published in 1962 but written during the years 1959–61, is to be interpreted as an answer

177

to Stalin's dogmas, which continued to influence economic policies. In this work, the author describes economic laws as an expression of specific material interests and the repetitive behaviour of social groups. Not all Stalin's theses interpreted as 'objective laws of socialism', were 'objectively necessary'. In particular, Sik criticised the concept of 'socialist property', i.e. state property considered by Stalin as a basic essential of a socialist economic system. Here, reform ideas emerge which criticise Stalin's 'etatist' position in contrast to the autonomous needs and interests of individuals and groups.

Among the party leaders, the attitude towards Sik, who had been the director of the Economic Institute of the Czechoslovak Academy of Sciences since 1962, was controversial. This can be seen in the fact that, from time to time, his comments were criticised or even censored. The latter occurred with the above mentioned study from 1958, as well as with an article written in 1963 which for months lay in the editorial office of the party newspaper *Rudé právo*, before it was finally released for publication. In this essay, the author opposed the thesis that the spreading economic crisis in Czechoslovakia was caused by 'too much decentralisation'. He pointed out that not the modest decentralisation, introduced in 1958, was responsible for the systemic weaknesses, but rather its half-heartedness. In addition, he described and explained the most significant defects of the system: the waste of resources, the lack of adaptation to demand and the enterprises' resistance to innovate. Sik also recommended the path that should be followed if these deficiencies were to be eliminated. According to him, it was imperative to utilise 'commodity-money relations' (Sik, 1964).

Considering the crisis of the early 1960s which threatened the political stability of the regime, the otherwise orthodox party leadership under Novotný appointed Sik as head of a commission which was to develop a concept for a comprehensive economic reform. Giving a theoretical basis to his ideas, Sik wrote a book in which he integrated earlier unpublished texts. In this work, he analysed more profoundly than before the old system's functional weaknesses and their causes and outlined the basic characteristics of his plan/market model (Sik, 1964). The book reappeared in a somewhat modified and extended form, in particular supplemented by an empirical analysis of Czechoslovakia's economic performance in the past: it was published in 1967 under the title *Plan and*

Market under Socialism, and is seen as the basic theoretical foundation of a market-oriented reform in a Soviet-type economy. We should not fail to mention the most important Prague reform documents from 1964–8, which were approved under Sik's leadership and were carried out as subsequent measures (Kosta, 1978, pp. 133–6). The economic reform concept, which assumed its definitive form in the Prague Spring of 1968, can be presented here only in brief. It describes four main characteristics: (i) delegation of property rights to work collectives, (ii) transition to indicative planning and its restriction to global macroeconomic data, (iii) indirect regulation through economic policies, (iv) the use of market mechanisms at the microeconomic level. Thus, a democratic plan/market model was conceived in which socialistic values were to be respected (ibid., pp. 136–47).

After the violent ending of the democratisation attempts in Czechoslovakia by the invasion by Warsaw Pact troops (August 1968), Sik emigrated to Switzerland. As a vice prime minister, which he was named in 1968, he was one of the first leading reformers to be dismissed directly after the Soviet invasion (Sik, 1988, pp. 287–8). Faithful to his efforts up until now, for Ota Sik an economy can only remain effective if it views the economic and political spheres as a whole. Even stronger than before – probably due to his negative experiences with both 'real socialism' and Western capitalism – since 1969 his work has been directed towards finding a third way for a humane society based on an effective economic system. His theoretical knowledge as well as his empirical evidence, now expanded through his move to the West, motivate him more than ever to search for alternatives which question traditions, prejudices and taboos.

In his book *The Third Way: The Marxist–Leninist Theory and Modern Industrial Society* (1972), Sik analyses in detail the 'entire Marxist–Leninist theory, as the basis of communism' (p. 13). He focuses on Marx's concept of commodity and value and on his accumulation and crisis theory; he deals with Marxist schools of thought, in particular with Lenin's economic and political notions, and, last but not least, with further alternative conceptions. With a differentiated attitude towards the works of Karl Marx, he accepts his materialistic view of history, the humane elements contained in his writings, and also parts of his theories on value and reproduction. Marx's rejection of market mechanisms, however, his 'Law of the Increasing Misery of the Working Class' and his explanation of crises, etc., are considered exaggerated or dismissed as incorrect. Lenin's theoretical writings are criticised sharply. In Lenin's work, Sik says, Marx's thoughts on man's emancipation are neglected and some features can already be recognised which finally lead to Stalinism. More thoroughly than ever before, the author now investigates the weaknesses of the economic system in developed capitalist countries, analysing particularly the inflationary tendencies. In an article published somewhat later, he shortly summarises the theses expressed in detail in his book. Three key sentences may serve to clarify his argument:

> Modern inflation is the result of the fight among giant interest monopolies for the macro-distribution of the national income under the conditions of a highly industrialised consumers' society. Huge employers' associations, monopolistic unions and the modern state are the actors in this fight . . . Thus, more is invested than is saved and relatively little is saved because too much is consumed. (Sik, 1974, p. 38).

This argumentation pattern, namely the macroeconomic disequilibrium caused by the distribution conflict, will accompany Sik's later analyses of capitalism (see below), as well as the author's resulting recommendations: the involvement of the worker as a participating co-owner in the development of the enterprise's investments – in other words, awakening the interest of the employees not only in their wages but also in their company's future.

In the mid-1970s, before having intensified his economic analysis of capitalist market economies (he turns to this task more than ten years later), Sik dedicates himself once more to societies with a Soviet-type communism. He is aware that his earlier criticism of the economic system is insufficient. Without illuminating the political power structures, the performance weaknesses of the central planning system cannot be fully explained. Thus, the politically involved economist writes a book on *The Communist Power System* (Sik, 1976). According to Sik, the structure of the system is characterised not only by false theories but also by the actual interests of the functionary bureaucracy. Thus, the principle of the 'leading role of the Party' means that the party apparatus controls all areas of social life, such as the economic and cultural acitivites, and even the intimate sphere of the citizens. The basic instruments for wielding power are the selection of cadres, repression and corruption, and last but not least the ideological monopoly of the bureaucracy. It is obvious that in this manner the motivations and initiatives of the rank and file become paralysed.

At the end of the 1970s, the time has come: Ota Sik is in a position to present a well-contemplated and thoroughly conceived alternative system which could eliminate the grave defects of both the existing ones. In his *Humane Industrial Democracy* (1979), which he published later in a shortened form as *An Economic System of the Future* (1985), the author presents human needs and interests as the decisive determinant of 'capitalism' as well as of 'real socialism'. In both systems, the 'economic interests . . . and among these . . . the income interests are the most intensive' (p. 118). This behaviour, Sik argues, results from the persisting short-ages of goods and the dissatisfying nature of work. Western capitalism, he says, is characterised by the contradiction between wage and profit interests (p. 14) and Eastern communism by the 'contra-diction of interests between the leading . . . bureaucracy and the population, which is deprived of all decision-making power' (p. 131).

From this diagnosis, the author arrives at his third way, which should succeed in conquering the conflict of interests which has existed in societies up until now. The focal points characterising this alternative are: participation of people in the economic decisions as well as in the profits made (chapter 5); the planning of a macroeconomic income distribution (chapter 7); the utilisation of a regulated market mechanism (chapter 8).

Participation means changing the established property rights. In public companies, so-called 'co-worker associations' (*Mitarbeiterge-sellschaften*) should enable the formation of an undividable collec-tive capital, the 'neutralised capital', through a step-by-step assign-ment of profit shares. In medium-sized companies, it is assumed that there will be both private and neutralised capital; in smaller companies, only private property will be retained. A democratis-ation of the decision-making process would have to accompany the gradual change in the form of ownership, aimed at a combi-nation of the principles of industrial democracy and of managerial competence. The profit should be used not only to neutralise capital, but also to pay percentage bonuses to the employees.

Macroeconomic distribution planning should fulfil two tasks: first, a well-balanced growth is to be guaranteed (today, more than ever, inflationary tendencies resulting from excess demand should be avoided). This has to be done through a regulated distribution of wages (i.e. the wage rates) and profits (i.e. the profit rate), because only then can a balance between consumption and investments be achieved. Second, with the help of a macroeconomic plan, the development of the infrastructure is to be regulated (education, medical aid, social networks, transportation and communication, environmental protection).

The necessity of utilising the *market mechanism* (its unfavourable effects should be limited through economic policies) is strongly stressed due to the negative experiences with Soviet-type command planning. Sik places particular emphasis on the main conditions for a functioning market economy. In his opinion, these prerequisites include: (i) the existence of a buyer's market, which is characterised by a slight excess supply; (ii) a competitive situation which counteracts monopolistic tendencies; (iii) profit incentives according to the enterprise's performance; (iv) equilibrium prices which induce demand-oriented decisions; (v) free entry to the market, and (vi) the possible shutdown of unprofitable companies (while ensuring social needs of the workers are met).

Considering the power structures established in the two existing systems, which are based on vested interests, the theorist of the third way is aware that politically his model faces major obstacles (chapter 9). In the West, thanks to democratically ruled societies, one would have to find a majority, which, however, would be difficult enough in itself. But the path to communist ruled countries would be even rockier, if one were to attempt to reach this goal.

While the social economic analysis of Eastern systems and the resulting concept of his humane economic democracy was the focal point of Ota Sik's works in the 1960s and 1970s, his writings in the present decade are dominated by theoretical investigations of capitalistic market economies and his critical reflections on their interpretation in economic theory. The limited framework of this chapter allows only a cursory overview of his most important statements which he presented in his latest interesting works in the years 1983–8, (Sik, 1983, 1986, 1987, 1988).

According to Sik, the main defect, intrinsic to market capitalism, is the periodic occurrence of cycles – the up and down of boom and recession. A recurring element in his critical statements on capitalism (as mentioned above) is the conflict between wage and profit interests, expressed in the disequilibrium between consumption and investments. In two regards, however, Sik's writings from the 1980s go far beyond that of his earlier studies (Sik, 1972, 1974). On the one hand, his cycle explanation of wages and profits, or consumption and investments, is enriched through a number of additional variables and their interrelations within the growth process: income and capital productivity, profit and interest rates, loans and profits, to name only a few of them. Sik also investigates why in earlier periods a macroeconomic demand gap existed (in this regard there are some rough similarities to Keynes), while in the recent past an excess demand appears, resulting in inflationary pressures. On the other hand (and this is yet another significant contribution by Sik and his Swiss colleagues in researching capitalistic cycles), the theoretical hypotheses are tested empirically (the data relate to the Federal Republic of Germany, the United States and Switzerland).

The insight into the backgrounds of socio-economic processes led Sik to the realisation as to how interest conflicts, which were thought to be unbridgeable, could be overcome. For Sik, it is not a question of either the labour theory of value or that of marginal utility; he emphasises instead the existence of rational elements in both theories which complement one another and form a whole. Similarly, for him there is no question of either market mechanism or central planning: rather he exposes the possibilities and advantages of their mutual supplementation on today's level of industrial development. Instead of either alternative, profit motivation or an economic activity which is foreign to profit incentives, he shows when and how profit orientation is meaningful, or under which circumstances it can cause damage to a society. Finally, he researches why the social contradictions of wage and profit interests are increasingly becoming a hindrance to further development and how this conflict could be overcome while still maintaining profit motivations in general.

While in traditional economic theories man is seen merely as *homo oeconomicus*, and while the analysis of economic processes is based on this axiom, Sik has analysed in all his work the nature and relationship of man's economic and non-economic interests and searches for ways of satisfying them together. For him, this alternative question does not arise: either private business and with it an alienation of the working mass, or removal of this alienation by eliminating private entrepreneur initiatives; rather he searches and finds forms of economic activity which enable socially

useful entrepreneurial activities while overcoming the capital alienation of the population. The prerequisite for this, in his view, is
a synthesis of an effective, individually responsible management
and of an increased workers' participation in the decision-making
process.

In this way, based on his theoretically founded analyses, Ota
Sik can formulate his comprehensive alternative of an effective
economic system in a humane society: his theory of a third way.

References

Kosta, Jiří (1979) 'Ota Sik – der Theoretiker einer alternativen Wirtschaft', in U. Gärtner and J. Kosta (eds), *Wirtschaft und Gesellschaft –
Kritik und Alternativen* (Berlin), pp. 17–28.

Kosta, Jiří (1978) *Abriss der sozialökonomischen Entwicklung der
Tschechoslowakei 1945–1977*, edition suhrkamp (Frankfurt/M.).

Sik, Ota (1953) *O některých ekonomických zákonech* (On Some Economic
Laws) (Prague).

Sik, Ota (1955a) *Socialistická hospodářská soustava a charakter ekonomických zákonu této soustavy* (The Socialist Economic System and the
Nature of its Laws) (Prague).

Sik, Ota (1955b) *Zákon plánovitého, proporcionálního rozvoje národního
hospodářství* (The Law of Planned, Proportional Development of the
National Economy) (Prague).

Sik, Ota (1957) *Teoretické zdůvodnění zásad nového systému plánování,
financování a řízení prumyslu* (Theoretical Foundation of the Principles
of Planning, Financing and Managing the Industry), mimeo (Prague).

Sik, Ota (1962) *Ekonomika, zájmy, politika* (Economy, Interests, Politics)
(Prague).

Sik, Ota (1964) *K problematice socialistických zbožních vztahů* (On Problems of Socialist Commodity Relations) (Prague).

Sik, Ota (1967) *Plan and Market under Socialism* (English translation)
(New York).

Sik, Ota (1972) *Der dritte Weg. Die marxistisch-leninistische Theorie der
modernen Industriegesellschaft* (Hamburg); Engl. edn, *The Third Way*
(New York, 1976).

Sik, Ota (1974) 'Kampf der Monopole', *Die Zeit*, no. 23, 31 May.

Sik, Ota (1976) *Das kommunistische Machtsystem* (Hamburg); Engl. edn,
The Communist Power System (New York: Praeger, 1981).

Sik, Ota (1979) *Humane Wirtschaftsdemokratie. Ein dritter Weg* (Hamburg); Engl. edn, *For a Humane Economic Democracy* (New York:
Praeger, 1985).

Sik, Ota (1983) 'Zwei Wirtschaftskrisen in der Bundesrepublik Deutschland', *Jahrbücher für Nationalökonomie und Statistik*, vol. 198/1
(Stuttgart), pp. 385–408.

Sik, Ota (1985) *Ein Wirtschaftssystem der Zukunft* (Berlin/Heidelberg/New York/Tokyo).

Sik, Ota (1986) 'Zur Problematik kurzfristiger Zyklen', *Jahrbücher für Nationalökonomie und Statistik*, vol. 201, no. 1, pp. 32–53.

Sik, Ota (1987) *Wirtschaftssysteme. Vergleiche-Theorie-Kritik* (Berlin/Heidelberg/New York/Tokyo).

Sik, Ota, René Höltschi and Christian Rockstroh (1988) *Wachstum und Krisen* (Berlin/Heidelberg/New York/Tokyo).

17 Socialism as a Socio-economic System

Branko Horvat

THE ETATIST INTERLUDE

European societies had been developing capitalist institutions for a couple of centuries before – in the first half of the last century – the term *capitalism* appeared. Thus, the term simply denoted the socio-economic system that already existed. At about the same time the term *socialism* was also introduced. But it denoted a system which did not exist, which was yet to be created. Of all known social systems, socialism is the only one that exists as *a project*, not as a fact. A project can be accomplished in different ways or fail to be accomplished at all.

It is, of course, possible to call an already existing system 'socialist'. For instance, East European countries call their social system *real socialism*. That should imply socialism as it actually exists as different from an ideal or utopian socialism. In this way, capitalism and socialism both refer to the actually existing systems and they can be compared.

The procedure is logically consistent, but is a source of great confusion. First of all, 'socialism as a project' and 'real socialism' differ not only as an ideal type compared with an empirical fact but represent two entirely different species. Secondly, 'real socialism' evolved from 'project socialism' which implies that either the project was wrong and unworkable or the evolution went astray, or both. Thirdly, socialism is supposed to be a socially and economically superior system and that justified socialist revolutions and, in general, the struggle for socialism. However, 'real socialism' turned out to be a politically and economically inferior system and today finds itself in a deep crisis. I propose to clear up this confusion by using two different terms, *socialism* for 'project-socialism' and its empirical realisation and *etatism* for 'real socialism'. As it will become clear in a moment, socialism and etatism are two different social systems.

Socialism as a project is simply a movement triggered by the failures of bourgeois revolutions. So much so that the theoreticians of the movement, like Lenin and Trotski, envisaged two phases of the great revolution in the lagging behind countries like Russia, the bourgeois-democratic and the socialist ones. In order to simplify the exposition, I shall treat as paradigmatic the French bourgeois revolution of 1789 and the Russian October Revolution of 1917.

French revolutionaries fought for a just society under a triple banner of *liberté*, *éqalité* and *fraternité*. The immediately emerging society was far from just. It took more than a century of development of political liberties before anything like a politically democratic state evolved. Equality was established only before the courts. Otherwise, one kind of social inequality – based on inherited status – was simply replaced by another kind – based on inherited wealth. Class differentiation and exploitation changed in form but otherwise continued. Under such circumstances fraternity simply disappeared from the list of political slogans. Egoistic competition generated a phenomenon which Marx, under Hegel's influence, described as alienation.

Many people were disappointed. Soon individual prophets, next small groups and finally entire movements appeared working towards eliminating social evils. Socialism as a project was born. And here is where our story begins.

Socialists wanted to eliminate class exploitation. That implied also curbing the repressive functions of the State ('the withering away of the State') which was seen as a guardian of the interests of the ruling class. There can hardly be a quarrel about the humanistic values of the two goals, and they are certainly consistent. One could perhaps question their realism. However, if a free classless society is envisaged as a gradual process and not as a state established at once, the two goals also appear as realistic. The real problem emerges with the selection of means. Here the nineteenth-century socialists – and many of their twentieth-century successors – turned out to be dangerously simple minded.

Since a *capitalist* market generates great differences in wealth and unemployment cycles, it ought to be replaced by *administrative* planning. Great private wealth means great private power and also means hiring and exploiting the labour of workers. Thus, private capital must be nationalised and *private* ownership replaced by *state* ownership. These ideas have been more or less generally shared but Russian Bolsheviks added something of their own. Russia was a backward country and needed strong guidance for it to catch up. Therefore, there was the need of a vanguard party. As capitalism was not well developed, there was ample opportunity for its further development which meant a constant danger of capitalist restoration. Thus the vanguard party had to assume a monopoly of political power to prevent such a restoration. Until recently, one-party systems have been a distinguishing characteristic of 'real socialism'.

It is not difficult to see that the conclusions derived represent a collection of non sequiturs. Market need not be capitalist and planning need not be administrative. In fact administrative planning is economically inefficient and politically repressive. Private and state ownerships are not the only options. State ownership is no guarantee against class exploitation. A vanguard party, which has political monopoly, will perhaps prevent capitalist restoration, but will not necessarily lead society towards socialism. Indeed, it is most likely that it will remodel society to serve its own class interests.

If we define liberal capitalism as a social system based on private ownership, market economy and the division of political power, 'real socialism' appears as a system based on state ownership, administrative planning and the unity of political power. It is thus capitalism turned upside down. Since the State is the only employer and the party the only political ruler, the party state is the moving force of the system – hence the appellation *etatism*.

Clearly, by definition an etatist society cannot be free. In fact the concentration of power reaches a theoretically possible extreme because economic monopoly is merged with political monopoly. Since the rulers are not controlled, either economically or politically, the class division between the rulers and the ruled is also pushed to an extreme. Class exploitation changes the form but otherwise continues unabated.

No doubt, etatism is as different from socialism as it could be – although it started from more or less the same socialist project. Wrong means produced unwanted results. It is an idle speculation to pose the question of how much the results could have been changed if a good social theory were applied. It is sufficient to note that the results are not surprising and could have been – and partly were – predicted.

And yet for quite a while etatism worked satisfactorily. The unity of power made possible a fast mobilisation of resources, administrative planning made for full employment, and the rate of growth was high. The inherited socialist ideology was responsible for a great concern for material well-being of the working strata. The education, the life expectancy and other social indicators were appreciably higher than in the comparable capitalist countries.[1] This, together with full employment and the reduction of social distance between manual and mental labour,[2] provided the legitimacy for the system. But the system could operate satisfactorily only as long as society was simple enough and the main task involved catching up. Once the process of industrialisation was more or less completed, which is true for all European countries (with the exception of Albania), the development potential of etatism was exhausted. A fact that was quite precisely predicted.[3,4] For a developed country, like Czechoslovakia, etatism was inappropriate right from the beginning and could be reimposed only by outside intervention. Etatism's monolithic structure is incompatible with the complexities of modern society. Economic expansion slowed down, the efficiency of investment dropped dangerously low, even social indicators deteriorated. One country after another encountered structural crisis. Here is where the original socialist project assumes an extraordinary importance again.

THE SOCIALIST PROJECT

Etatism is not necessarily the first or administrative phase of socialism. There is neither a need to pass through that phase nor is there a certainty that after it socialism will follow. In fact etatism, by claiming to be *real* socialism, thoroughly discredited socialism. It is, therefore, advisable to treat etatism as an outcome of coincidence and interaction of two different historical facts: mounting social tensions in the countries lagging behind and the socialist ideology of just society. Uneven economic development created great differences among countries and social tensions in those lagging behind were intensified to extremes; the resulting need for radical reforms implied also the need for catching up and the available socialist ideology served both purposes quite well. Etatism is thus a transitional developmental stage in which the pace of development was speeded up and economy and society were modernised. Once that was accomplished, etatism exhausted its development potential and is bound to disintegrate.

The socialist project remains unaffected by the historical vagaries of etatism, except in the sense that we now have empirical proof – theoretically known from the beginning – that certain strategies cannot possibly establish socialism. Let us now examine the socialist project more fully.

A series of bourgeois and anti-capitalist revolutions in the last two centuries have dramatically showed a quest for a more equitable society. Now, society wil be equitable if the individuals are treated as equal in their fundamental social roles as producers, consumers and citizens. Equality in production means an equal access to social capital. That implies producers' self-management and social ownership (in the social, not legal sense; legal titles to ownership may be anything[5]).

Distributional equality implies distribution according to work (corrected for person-creating goods like education and health which have to be distributed according to needs; clearly, also those who cannot contribute work should be treated on a different basis). Equality in political life implies political self-government, i.e. radical democracy.

If the members of a society are to be equal, all concentrations of power must be eliminated. The two main sources of power are economic and political. Capitalism begins with economic power which in turns leads to the achievement of political power for its dominant class. Etatism usually reverses the procedure. In socialism, social ownership, a competitive market and the economic policy of the government, the latter eliminating monopoly gains and (to a certain extent through planning) windfall gains and losses, destroy possible concentrations of economic power. Since permanently organised parties imply a concentration of political power – a sort of political monopoly, duopoly or oligopoly – the socialist political system implies political pluralism without parties. Universal education and modern information technology make that possible. I do not have space to elaborate this controversial point more fully and would like to direct the reader to my *Political Economy of Socialism*.[6]

If socialism is to be defined structurally in the same way as the other two systems previously, we may say that socialism is based on social ownership, a planned market and radical political pluralism. Alternatively, we may say that socialism implies radical political democracy complemented by economic democracy and distribution according to work.

Is such an ideal-type socialism workable? Or will it produce another etatist-type deformation? Many ingredients of our socialist project already exist in real life. Thus, one could argue that developmental tendencies provide empirical proof for its workability. I shall not follow this line of argument because, as is the case with empirical analysis generally, it would require too much space. Let me instead provide a brief theoretical argument concerning the economic component of the system.

In the design of a social system – as opposed to that of a machine – the system should be left 'open'. A machine is a fully deterministic system; a social system is not. It can learn and so it must be left open to incorporate any useful new knowledge – though avoiding transformation of its own structure. In this way, the system becomes self-correcting. This is a fundamental requirement for a realistic social system design. Bearing that in mind, we may argue as follows.

A meaningful self-management of producers means full autonomy of the enterprise which is the basic economic unit. The autonomy in the decision-making implies that enterprises will use available first-hand information to solve problems on the spot. Social property and national economic planning imply that all available macroeconomic information will be accessible to economic decision-makers. Thus a socialist economy is an *information*-efficient economy. Next, entrepreneurial independence and distribution according to work generate individual and collective initiative and hard work. Therefore, a socialist economy is a *motivation*-efficient economy. Self-management eliminates class conflict at the production place and so *reduces losses* due to social conflict. Full employment and social provision of person-building goods (education, health, social services) maximise the use of human resources and in this sense provide for *resource* efficiency. Finally, the market provides *allocational* efficiency and planning leads to *growth* efficiency. In sum, a socialist economy is an economically superior economic system.

If a social system is desirable on ethical grounds – the quest for equity – and if it is potentially economically superior, it must be workable.

Notes

1. B. Horvat, 'Welfare of the Common Man in Various Countries', *World Development*, June 1974, pp. 29–39.
2. B. Horvat, *The Political Economy of Socialism* (Armonk, NY: Sharpe, 1982), pp. 74–6.
3. B. Horvat, 'The Relation Between the Rate of Growth and the Level of Development', *The Journal of Development Studies*, 1974, pp. 382–94.
4. S. Crnković-Pozaić, 'The Relationship Between the Level of Development and the Rate of Growth: Some Empirical Evidence', *Economic Analysis and Workers' Management*, 1985, pp. 29–63.
5. B. Horvat, 'Social Ownership', in V. Rus and R. Russel (eds), *The International Handbook of Participation in Organizations*, vol. II, (Oxford: Oxford University Press, forthcoming).
6. Horvat, *The Political Economy of Socialism*, pp. 283–327.

18 On the Reformability of the Soviet-type Economic Systems

Leszek Balcerowicz

There is now a general agreement that the Soviet-type economic system (STES) displays great resistance to change: most of its attempted reforms have been rejected and practically none of them has produced – while it lasted – a radical increase in overall economic efficiency. One way of conceptualising the reasons for these failures is to say that the reforms did not reach a required 'critical mass' or – in other words – that they did not pass a necessary 'threshold'. This conveys the idea that one cannot depart from the STES by accumulating successive partial changes. For while the next such changes are envisaged, the previous ones remain ineffective or are simply discarded outright. Thus the main problem is that the reform of the STES is largely indivisible.

The present chapter takes up this idea of indivisibility, beginning with a discussion of the structure of the STES. In what follows I will focus on the reform in the socialist sector outside agriculture, thus disregarding the question of to what extent it is possible to improve the economic performance under the STES by allowing the private sector to grow, and whether the 'Chinese way', i.e. first reforming agriculture and then tackling the rest of the economy, has a general applicability.

THE 'CONSTRUCTIONAL LOGIC' OF THE SOVIET-TYPE ECONOMIC SYSTEM

This logic is manifested in the fact that the STES has certain basic characteristics which give rise to a number of derivative features. The distinction between these groups of traits is not based on their importance for economic performance, but that by definition the basic features generate, *regardless of the will of the economic actors*, the derivative features, not the other way round. The basic features themselves are interrelated, i.e. some of them are more important in shaping the STES than others.

One can distinguish four basic characteristics:

(1) The most essential basic feature is the command-rationing mechanism (CRM), i.e. the planning targets, administrative allocation of inputs, and the material balances which are meant to harmonise the first two instruments. All this is expressed in a comprehensive and relatively detailed central plan broken down during interlevel bargaining. In its coordinating and allocative functions the CRM replaces a product market.

(2) Given the inevitable human informational limitations the CRM requires for its operation a special organisational system. Its principal features are: the hierarchical subordination of the lower echelon managers to the superior state and party bodies (the nomenklatura mechanism)[1]; a highly developed central and intermediate administration; and an extreme organisational concentration whereby smaller enterprises exist mostly as parts of huge and centralised organisations.

(3) To maintain this system of organisation, the centralisation of rights to create, restructure and dissolve organisations is in turn necessary. Private individuals and enterprise managers are thus largely barred from taking these actions. This is especially true of creating new enterprises. Other mandatory features include the assignment of enterprises to specific branches; the prohibition of independent ties between different organisations and the elimination of enterprises through administrative procedures rather than through bankruptcy. This *centralisation of organisational rights* precludes the spontaneous evolution of the organisational system and ensures that it preserves the basic form necessary for the operation of the CRM.

The centralisation of organisational rights is an essential aspect of what may be called the closed or monopolising domestic property law, i.e. the law which tries to ensure the monopoly of one particular form of the ownership of the means of production by barring other forms (Balcerowicz, 1987). In the STES the favoured form is state ownership, but it could also be some type of the self-management solution as in Yugoslavia.

(4) Specific bureaucratic financial institutions carrying out the massive interenterprise redistribution of monetary means are a necessary supplement of (1) and (3) and a substitute for the capital market. These institutions include: (a) a non-commercial banking system (a monobank) which distributes credit according to the stipulations of the central plan and not to the criteria of financial viability; and (b) an overgrown state budget which could be automatically financed by the monobank. There is no place for a securities' market.

Various combinations of basic features lead to a number of interrelated derivative traits, for example:
— Administrative price fixing which in turn produces informationally defective prices;
— The isolation of domestic producers from foreign markets, stemming among other things from the domestic prices being unrelated to the world prices; the protectionist bureaucratic regulation of imports (licences, quotas, etc.) and a tendency for import substitution. They are, in my view, to a large extent by-products of command central planning, as planners seek to reduce the soures of uncertainty;
— Enterprises' soft budget constraint (Kornai, 1986) resulting from the extensive government intervention, defective prices, and the lack of commercial financial institutions;
— Extreme monopolisation due among other thing to the extreme organisational concentration, the centralisation of organisational rights (which precludes the free market entry), the lack of foreign competition, and the soft budget constraint which makes the suppliers insensitive to a possible drop in demand.

Basic and derivative characteristics produce, given certain psycho-social invariants (the dominance of self-centred motivation, informational limitations of the decision-makers), a number of typical features of economic performance under the STES: low cost efficiency, low innovativeness, chronic shortages, etc.

The indicated links within the basic features, between them and the derivative characteristics, and among the latter themselves, may be called the *functional necessities*.[2] For these links are in force regardless of the will of the human actors. For example, if the CRM is to be maintained, a special hierarchical organisational system must be preserved too, regardless of whether one wants it or not. Thus only the abolition of the CRM makes possible –

although in no way ensures – the transition to a radically different system of organisation. The functional necessities largely stem from human informational limitations, either directly or indirectly. An example of the direct relationship is that the CRM requires a hierarchical organisational system, as it reduces the informational burden on the central decision-makers. To maintain this sytem the centralisation of organisational rights is in turn necessary; this demonstrates how the informational limitations indirectly generate the functional necessities.

Besides these necessities there are also *motivational factors* that make the STES a highly indivisible whole. The problem here is that the STES – as with any other economic system – creates its own social structure, and that in the course of an economic reform certain powerful constituent groups are bound to lose some of their power, prestige or income, or be subject to additional effort. It is therefore reasonable to expect that these groups will try to prevent or obstruct the reforms, for example, by using the nomenklatura mechanism informally to maintain direct control over the enterprises. This is why radical systemic changes are needed at the very beginning, as they reduce the danger of the rejection of the reform by neutralising the groups which oppose it, and by creating or strengthening the groups which support it. But such steps are, of course, politically very difficult.[3]

THE REFORM THRESHOLDS AND TYPES OF ECONOMIC REFORM

From the 'constructional logic' of the STES we can now proceed to the reform thresholds. They are illustrated as 'stylised facts' in Figure 18.1 where r denotes the degree of radicalism of the economic reform,[4] e is the overall economic efficiency[5] and t is time measured from the start of the reform.

RT_1 signifies the first reform threshold. By definition it is passed when the CRM is largely replaced by other mechanisms of coordination but the remaining basic features of the STES are preserved. The second threshold, RT_2, is passed when all four basic characteristics are abolished. The left side of Figure 18.1 illustrates three types of economic reforms, or more precisely, their dynamic. On the right side, there is a function $e = e(r)$ which shows the maximum efficiency possible under the increasingly reformed econ-

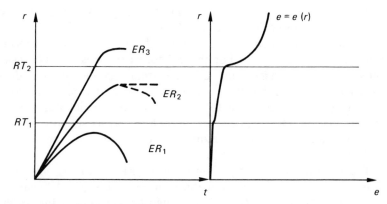

Figure 18.1   Reform thresholds

omic systems. The shape of this function illustrates the basic problem of the reform: only radical changes enable a substantial increase in e, i.e. the achievement of the most important economic goal of the reform. Small steps give very little or practically nothing.

Economic reforms of the first type, ER_1, are below the RT_1, i.e. maintain all the basic features of the STES. These reforms attempt, for example, to replace the gross indicators with the net ones – while preserving the command planning; to reduce the number of the binding targets; to shift some competence from the ministerial level to the regional bodies; to create new types of compulsory associations of enterprises, etc. (see Sik, 1987, pp. 82–5). ER_1 have so far largely prevailed in socialist countries.[6] As illustrated by Figure 18.1, ER_1 have two characteristics. First, the new systemic arrangements brought about by them are largely subject to inevitable rejection. For these arrangements create additional tensions which are dealt with by recourse to the old directive methods, and these are used because the reform, being so superficial, preserves the institutional possibilities for using them (the principle of the directive planning, party–state nomenklatura). A related reason for the rejection of the ER_1 is that it leaves virtually untouched the bureaucratic apparatus opposing reform. The main motive for this resistance is, in the case of ER_1, as distinct from more radical reforms, not so much the fear that the reform will infringe upon material interests, power or ideology but the fact that under the ER_1 the main function of the apparatus remains the balancing of the material flows in the economy. However, some elements of the ER_1 make the performance of this function more difficult (Kantorovich, 1988).

Second, during their short existence, the ER_1 can bring at most a minimal increase in e[7]. For these reforms preserve all the basic causes of low efficiency: the CRM, extreme monopolisation, distorted prices, soft budget constraint, etc. With the persisting low efficiency, ER_1 is not able to improve the economic situation of the population and cannot count, therefore, on its support. There is thus a link between the economic performance of the reform and its capacity for survival.

The reforms ER_2 largely abolish the CRM – without, however, doing away with all the basic features of the STES. The Hungarian economic reform of 1968 and the Yugoslav reforms in the 1950s and 1960s are the main cases in point. Figure 18.1 illustrates two main characteristics of ER_2. First, they are also susceptible to the rejection process, although perhaps not so inevitably as ER_1. The recentralisation in Hungary in 1973–9 and the hidden return to a quasi-administrative system in Yugoslavia in the 1970s (Mercinger, 1985) demonstrate that this is a real possibility. For the ER_2 still preserve a strong institutional potential for recentralisation, especially a party–state nomenklatura.

Second, the systems brought about by ER_2 can be more efficient then the STES and the short-lived systems produced by ER_1 (see e.g. Slama, 1984). The basic reason for this is, in my view, the abandonment of the CRM. However, the possible increase in e brought about by ER_2 is still quite small. For having preserved some of the basic features of the STES – e.g. party–state nomenklatura, centralisation of organisational rights, absent capital market – the ER_2 are still not able to eliminate two phenomena which rule out high efficiency: strong monopolisation and the pervasive rent-seeking, i.e. the tendency of enterprises to concentrate on bargaining with superior bodies for the most convenient terms of activity. Thus, even the more radical reforms are not radical enough to solve the efficiency problem of real socialism.

This brings us to ER_3: economic reforms which would pass the RT_2 and therefore replace all the basic features of the STES with market-type systemic arrangements. It is there that the solution to the efficiency problem seems to lie. The category of ER_3 is, however, so far empirically empty, and the big question is how to get there. Another important problem is whether ER_3 include only reforms based on massive privatisation, i.e. return to capitalism in the Marxian sense, or whether there is an equally efficient 'Third Way'. These questions require a separate treatment.

CONCLUDING REMARKS

The basic difficulty of the reform of the STES is that in order to be successful, i.e. to be able to survive and to produce a substantial increase in economic efficiency, it has to be very radical, or – in other words – it must pass a high threshold in a short time. One wonders, therefore, whether Popper's (1957, pp. 64–70) advocacy of 'piecemeal social engineering' applies to systems created by the previous 'holistic engineering'.

The concept of the reform thresholds suggests a useful approach to the analysis of the attempted reforms of the STES, one which could perhaps be better structured than some others. After establishing just what these thresholds are one should use them as a yardstick to assess the chances of the given reform, by inquiring whether the balance of socio-political forces is such that the necessary threshold can be passed. Space does not permit me to discuss this second issue. But it is obvious that the passing of this threshold requires quite extraordinary social and political circumstances.[8] Anybody familiar with the difficulties of introducing partial systemic changes, e.g. tax reforms in the West, will easily comprehend the political complexity of a successful economic reform of the STES.

The thesis about the high reform threshold suggests that in assessing the chances of the proposed reforms in socialist countries, one should be wary of using the hitherto popular formulation that a given proposal is 'a step in the right direction'. For this misses the essential issue of the magnitude of the step. It may well be that a proposed reform, although more radical than its predecessors, is still not enough to propel it beyond the minimum threshold. There would be then no difference between the two, as far as the final outcome is concerned: both would fail. Another popular idea to be avoided is that 'reform is a process'. This is a dangerous truism, as it may be taken to imply that the dynamic of the reform does not count. But we know that in order to be successful the reform must have a special dynamic: its first step has to be very big – if it is to get beyond the reach of the functional necessities within the STES and create a balance of socio-political forces favourable to the further existence and development of the reformed system.

Notes

1. Nomenklatura mechanism is largely operated by the party apparatus. It should be noted, however, that in the monoparty systems of the Soviet type the distinction between the party and state administration is a fiction. Party apparatus should be regarded, therefore, as a prominent part of a – conceptually broadened – apparatus of the State.
2. The study of these necessities belongs, in my view, to a hugely neglected field of the analysis of the economic systems, which should aim at establishing and explaining what country-wide combinations of the systemic arrangements are empirically possible, what are empirically impossible and what are necessary. The knowledge of these relationships is obviously relevant for the study of the possible evolution of the respective economic systems, and for building of their realistic typologies. It is also often necessary in explaining the impact of the selected systemic arrangements on the economic performance, since one should consider not only direct but also indirect influence of a given arrangement, i.e. an influence via other arrangements which are linked to it by the functional necessities.
3. This is why a radical economic reform is much more difficult to be introduced than to be maintained (disregarding the possibility of external liquidation of the reform). The reverse is true of the superficial reform.
4. The reform is, by definition, the more radical the wider is the application of the new arrangements and the more they depart from the STES.
5. As measured, e.g. by the potential long-run rate of growth of aggregate consumption (cf Schumpeter, 1947, p. 190).
6. The latest Soviet economic reform belongs so far, in my view, to ER_1. For analysis corroborating this assertion see Schüller and Peterhoff, 1988.
7. This assessment is on the safe side. Some observers (cf. Kantorovich, 1988) argue that the discussed reforms worsened the economic performance.
8. In the case of the smaller socialist countries, as distinct from the USSR, it is not only the internal political developments but also the external ones (i.e. the evolution of the Soviet constraint) which determine just how radical the economic reform will be.

References

Balcerowicz, L. (1987) 'Remarks on the Concept of Ownership', *Oeconomica Polona*, no. 1, pp. 75–95.

Kantorovich, V. (1988) 'Lessons of the 1965 Soviet Economic Reform', *Soviet Studies*, no. 2, pp. 308–16.

Kornai, J. (1986) 'The Soft Budget Constraint', *Kyklos*, no. 1, pp. 3–30.

Mercinger, J. (1985) 'Yugoslav Economic System and Performance of the Economy in the Seventies and Early Eighties', in P. Gey, J. Kosta and W. Quaisser (eds), *Sozialismus und Industrialisierung* (Frankfurt: Campus).

Popper, K. (1957) 'The Poverty of Historicism' (Boston: The Beacon Press).

Schüller, A. and R. Peterhoff (1988) 'Gorbatschov Reform – Modell für Osteuropa?', in H. Giger and W. Linder (eds), *Sozialismus-Ende einer Illusion* (Zürich: None Zürcher Zeitung).

Schumpeter, J.A. (1947) *Capitalism, Socialism and Democracy* (New York: Harper & Row).

Sik, O. (1987) *Wirtschaftssysteme. Vergleiche – Theorie – Kritik* (Berlin: Springer).

Slama, J. (1984) 'Empirische Prüfung der Wirkung der Reformen in den planwirtschaftlichen Ländern', *Jahrbücher für Nationalökonomie und Statistik*, vol. 6, pp. 537–56.

19 Strategic Reappraisal and Short-term Adjustment: The External Economic Policy of Socialist Countries at the Crossroads

András Inotai

Ideological and economic motives have been shaping the relation between socialist countries and the world economy in different ways in various periods of development. In the 1950s, this connection was considered a still necessary evil to be eliminated as soon as possible, because it demonstrated the dependence of the socialist economies on the world market and proved to be a disturbing element in the implementation of the closed, planned economy. From the second half of the 1960s relations with the international economy were regarded as an additional, supplementary growth factor, in accordance with the increasing exhaustion of the traditional domestic and regional factors of development, due to the changing international political framework. Nevertheless, these additional sources were meant to be used for maintaining the unchanged priorities based on national and regional (CMEA) autarky. Increasing trade relations, a large inflow of credits and technology and a limited transfer of manpower characterised this period. By the end of the 1970s the strengthening of international economic relations became one of the highest priorities in almost all socialist countries. Credit repayment obligations, increasing debt servicing intensified the necessity for exporting and looking for new resources. The creation of the institutional and legal conditions of attracting international direct capital is one of the high-lights of this development process.

In spite of these changes, opening up towards the world econ-omy has not been integrated either in the economic reform con-cepts or in the everyday economic policy, in an organic manner. The Hungarian economic reform considered the stability of exter-nal economic conditions as an indispensable factor to its own success and failed to recognise the necessity of adjusting to the international economy. Even the accelerated reform process of the 1980s seems to be determined by forced and superficial adjust-ments due to the worsening of debt servicing conditions, not by the creation of an adequate concept for long-term international adjustment. The same is true in the Polish and, most recent, Soviet cases.

Exports and imports and their connections to the domestic econ-omy remained structurally disrupted, and have disintegrated during the whole period. In earlier times, exports served to compensate for indispensable and not yet substitutable imports, while recently they appeared as a necessary means for financing debt repayments. At the same time, imports were expected to assure the continuity of internal production processes not linked to the world market, but rather as regional 'export-orientation' towards the CMEA market, thus alleviating domestic supply problems. Import require-ments emerged fundamentally from the economics of shortage; about two-thirds to three-quarters of the socialist improts for con-vertible currency can be rated as non-competitive, i.e. not compet-ing with any domestic products.

CHANGING CONDITIONS

In recent years, the modest results and increasingly manifest short-comings of a peculiar 'export orientation', as well as dramatic international rearrangements, call for an urgent reappraisal of the earlier economic policies and thinking.

Forced export activity – similar to the previous import-led 'inte-gration' into international economic processes – stressed again the growing vulnerability of Eastern European economies. A higher statistical figure or increasing share of foreign trade in GNP did not express a more organic, qualitative incorporation into the world economy. Socialist economies were not looking to achieve

conformity with the international economy in either their production pattern or the rules of the game to be applied. In order
to do so, they would need to restructure both production processes
and economic mechanisms. In reality, the opposite happened: the
increasing of exports at any cost only served to maintain a constrained method of procedure. In the first place, it helped to
conserve the old structure that was substantially responsible for
acute disequilibria and limited growth potentials, resulting in an
increasingly inefficient use of resources. Secondly, restricted
imports affected initially the inputs that should have generated
larger modernisation impacts, such as competitive machinery,
know-how and accessories (spare parts). Thirdly, the artificial
maintenance of inefficient and incompetitive exports led to substantial increases in the expenditures of the central budget. At the
same time, subsidies financed a redistribution of national income
to the benefit of loss-making production units and sectors. Last
but not least, the socio-political disadvantages of the short-term
response cannot be ignored: the short-term crisis management
strengthened the positions (and sometimes even the vital role) of
the conservative heavy industry lobby, characterised by general
opposition to any economic and political reform and by manifest
lagging behind in international competitiveness and restructuring.

Short-term efforts to restore external equilibrium showed only
limited success. The average growth rate of exports did not reach
the world average, while their pattern deviated considerably from
that generated by the international industrial division of labour.
In total, exports of the European CMEA countries in manufactured goods and machinery represented 31.1 per cent and 8.6 per
cent, respectively, in 1975, and 27.0 and 5.2 per cent, respectively,
in 1985. Dramatically decreasing shares characterise their position
in human capital- and technology-intensive fields. CMEA countries
accounted for 0.55 per cent of the total electric machinery imports
of the OECD region in the mid-1980s. The corresponding figures
were 0.3 per cent for scientific and measuring instruments, 0.20
per cent for telecommunication apparatus and 0.05 per cent for
data processing machinery. These shares made up 2.6, 5.4, 0.8
and 0.6 per cent of the corresponding exports of developing countries in the total imports of the OECD.[1]

Growing export constraints have disintegrated further the internal production processes and sharpened chronic tensions of the
so-called background (subsidiary) industries, already present as a

result of central administrative planning. In addition, the import pattern has worsened substantially. Energy- and material-intensive exports gave highest priority to energy- and material-intensive imports, always characteristic of socialist imports from the West. In respect of imports decreasing in absolute terms, the share of raw materials and semi-manufactured products that help maintain current production and traditional structures reached 50 to 70 per cent of the total, while machinery imports tended to fall to 19 to 35 per cent. Foreign trade and financial tensions were aggravated even more by the fact that restrained imports affected export dynamism adversely. Between 1980 and 1985 developing countries were able to double their machinery exports to the OECD while diminishing their corresponding imports from there by 9 per cent. At the same time, the socialist countries' machinery exports fell by 36 per cent while their imports decreased by only 19 per cent.[2]

The worsening performance of the socialist countries calls attention to the fact that the substantial sacrifices made to sustain the old production structure and the traditional economic and sociopolitical mentality proved incapable of directing the socialist countries towards a new path of world market oriented development. No real opening up based on strategic reorientation and readjustment occurred at a time when fundamental and far-reaching changes started to unfold in the international economy.

1. The technological revolution brings about substantial economic changes by exerting influence not only on some specific branches or activities but on the whole economy, interlinking production and service activities, and it brings new social, political and human values, too. It is dismantling old boundaries both among sectors and between national economies.

2. The world-wide liberalisation of various production factors (i.e. not only goods but services, capital, technology and manpower) is on the agenda, generating internationalisation and differentiation processes simultaneously.

3. Elements of national and international production cannot be separated; industrial production and services are growing together. Small- and medium-scale enterprises that for a long time had been producing for the internal market exclusively, are beginning to integrate themselves into the international division of labour. Several dozens of medium-developed and developing economies are trying to catch up with the decisive international economic pro-

cesses and patterns, whereas others seem to be irrevocably marginalised.

4. International competitiveness cannot be achieved by merely better prices and higher quality of particular goods, but through a set of factors only indirectly linked to the specific product. The whole chain of research-development-production-marketing, together with its economic and socio-political medium, will be reflected in the competitiveness of a given product and in the evolution of its market position. In this light, the socialist countries are not challenged by balance of payments problems but fundamentally by a historical peripherisation.

5. The socialist economies have to face this challenge since the previously dynamic development of CMEA seems to have stopped. Neither the structure nor the mechanism of CMEA cooperation meets world economic requirements. The economic strategy based, on the one hand, on the inputs of cheap, abundant and rouble-accounted raw materials and energy and, on the other, on the capital-intensive output of products oriented to the unsaturated Western markets at rather high prices and for convertible currency, collapsed on both sides. The prolongation of this strategy is increasing economic losses and strengthening historical marginalisation. It is well known that the central administrative planning, the distorted price formation, the bilateral quota system or the special accounting system within the CMEA are all products of this structure and could be applied as rules of the game only in this context.

INSTEAD OF SHORT-TERM RESPONSES . . .

It is probably not surprising that the new and evolving situation did not lead immediately to radical changes but rather to a more definite protection of traditional 'values' and structures and to just 'tactical' allowances, ignoring, the massive additional costs, the strategic impasse and the consequences of the peripherisation of such an artificially prolonged 'survival'. A number of deep-rooted conservative and autarchic reflexes have become manifested in this. Some of them will be mentioned in the following discussion.

1. The prevailing economic policy concentrated on the strengthening of direct central control and on the improvement of the efficiency of central planning, instead of on easing the movement

of various production factors and consequently liberalising the economy. The restrictions imposed by deteriorating balance of payments seemed to underline even more the inevitability of central intervention. This was in fact the only way in which traditional structures, outdated income redistribution patterns and input-determined yearly and five-year planning could be maintained.

2. Restrictive economic policies tried to redistribute the decreasing income on a lower and lower level, irrespective of the fact that basic problems could only be solved by urging income-generating processes. Restrictions are generally protecting outdated sectors and production responsible for the worsening economic situation. They are unable to support adjustment and adaptability, the only remedy to longer term development. Therefore, flexible smaller units (small- and medium-sized enterprises) should be given more emphasis.

3. Also the investment policy prioritises traditional sectors based on outdated self-supply and 'economic independence' concepts. The same holds good for the system of state subsidies or the customs policy which is not directed to making imports cheaper but to 'penalising' better-off companies and citizens, very much in accordance with the well-known model of levelling to the bottom.

4. The conservative planning concepts, troubled by supply and import difficulties in recent years, are increasingly and stubbornly sticking to maintaining the rapidly devaluing production and export pattern at ever higher costs, instead of deciding how, in which structure, and by which means newly opened up possibilities should be used.

5. Old, deep-rooted reflexes are clearly expressed by the declaration of 'export-orientation' in official top-level documents. At present, exports for convertible currencies have been taken out of the inseparable system of economic production processes, as had national autarky or socialist international division of labour in earlier times. Economic policy-makers seem to ignore the basic tenet that a modern economy cannot be managed in 'slices', and that campaign-mentality is producing substantial additional losses and damages which will have to be restored by future generations.

6. The less a certain production factor is available, the stronger central administrative interventions become apparent. However, such a shortage should be a decisive reason for letting market forces work, in order to achieve the most efficient use of this factor. Even in countries where companies were granted rights to

manage export and import deals freely, central import-licensing and foreign exchange monopoly remained practically unchanged, substantially limiting the effective use of this theoretical possibility.[3]

7. In order to achieve rapidly changing and sometimes increasing short-term objectives, many specific rules are necessary, creating an economic mechanism characterised by lack of clarity and dozens of irrational privileges.

In sum: recent developments have proved that the external economic equilibrium cannot be restored lastingly, and international competitiveness cannot be increased through conserving the traditional structure and mentality. The superficial treatment applied up to now does not change an economic structure which has brought about and keeps on feeding disequilibrium.

. . . A STRATEGIC REAPPRAISAL IS REQUIRED

Above all, the smaller socialist countries, more involved in the international division of labour, should drastically redefine their economic strategies. This cannot be limited to nice declarations, but it presupposes a set of new instruments, too. One cannot stress the necessity of an economic strategy following international trends and, at the same time, not introduce the integral means to achieve it. International competitiveness and catching up require the acceptance of internationally acknowledged rules of the game. Central elements of this set of instruments consist of the liberalisation of imports, the establishment of real exchange rates, the elimination of the foreign exchange monopoly position of the central banks, the transformation of export licensing and the shaping of a customs system serving technical modernisation. Imports should not be permitted that will only maintain the increasingly inefficient production, but should be of a kind to stimulate modernisation. At present, the official exchange rates of all socialist countries are – to a differing degree – overvalued, prioritising 'cheap' imports and neglecting exports. At the same time, economic policy generally aims at achieving export surplus . . . Modified conditions to acquire foreign exchange (retention quota, small amounts of freely sold foreign currency, etc.) cannot be considered as an essential change, since they are not emerging as an organic element of a well-defined development strategy, but express either socio-political priorities (improved domestic supply) or contribute to maintaining big loss-making companies. In other words, they represent a newly 'discovered' instrument of prolonging outdated patterns and mentality.[4]

The adjustment of external economic policy instruments to international requirements must take into account the following:
— the above elements should be introduced as a package;
— implementation should be rapid, if necessary, even shocking;
— the rules of the game should be made public, eliminating previous privileges and creating a clear framework for economic decisions.

Simultaneously, a new economic policy is needed, with special emphasis on a strict monetary policy (foreign currency could be bought only by companies having national currency) and on an improved general environment (instead of sectoral development priorities). This can attract more foreign resources, including direct capital, and ensure that the various means of support available wil be used more efficiently.[5] A bridge based on efficiency can only be linked to the world economy if socialist national currencies are made convertible. This step would be the real Copernican change – the point of no return in post-war socialist economic policy – since convertibility would not only link these economies to the international economy but would influence their whole economic life, from price formation via production to structural policy, according to world market rules.

Although the success of adjustment of socialist countries depends fundamentally on the reforms introduced or to be implemented, it cannot be separated from the broader economic and political environment. Here I do not have in mind a non-protectionist trade policy, freer transfer of technology or financing the credit- or interest-paying capacity of some socialist countries. The change in strategic issues and the adjustment to world economic rules on all levels are processes not without severe tensions and possible setbacks. Credits, loans, contributions to the maintenance of solvency or to structural readjustment have proved – according to experiences of the last decade – to be inadequate and insufficient means. Their inconclusive results and questionable impacts did not contribute to the implementation of international economic rules. Lacking these rules of the game, there is no chance for successful economic adjustment. It is highly probable that only compact financial packages would promise an overall improvement of competitiveness and integration into the world economy. The key factor of such 'package financing' is convertibility. There is, however, no country in modern economic history that could have achieved this goal without making a substantial external contribution.

POSSIBILITIES AND RISKS

Evidently, this sort of adjustment is not easy nor can it be carried out by all countries at the same time. Various socialist countries, bearing in mind such possibilities, will face a lot of serious domestic tensions – crushing the resistance of traditional lobbies, sharpening competition, elimination of monopoly positions, difficulties in creating an efficient labour and capital market, inflationary pressure, etc. No less important are some historical and international implications.

1. In contrast to the historically established path of development leading from an internal to an international division of labour, socialist countries have followed a different route. However, in a technologically and rapidly changing world, with manifest dangers of peripherisation, national and international division of labour should be implemented simultaneously.

2. Convertibility, generally and theoretically acknowledged to be the final, crowning stage of the adjustment and opening up process, should play a catalytic role and accelerate this process.

3. Individual socialist countries are prepared, to rather differing degrees, to effect fundamental changes in their external economic policies. But no unified behaviour can be expected and consequently no definite support can be planned by the West. Nevertheless, those countries that have achieved some progress in economic and socio-political reform may be able to formulate and implement strategic packages to be financed partly by external (Western) means, in order to become irrevocably integrated into the international economy and thereby implement the rules of the game in most fields of their economic activities.

4. The behaviour of individual socialist countries might be considerably influenced by the divergent development dynamism and adjustment capacities to be observed in Western and Eastern

Europe. In the European Economic Community, new ideas and practical steps in the fields of economic, technological, research and financial policy are tending to push integration towards a qualitatively new development stage, challenging practically every non-EEC country, but fundamentally the European economies. Analagously, even the most radical CMEA reforms are expected to fuel the socialist economies only after a longer period. This non-synchronism should be kept in mind when socialist countries are (re)defining their economic strategy.[6]

5. Last but not least, Western Europe (but probably the whole industrial world) and the future of East–West relations are fundamental influences on the outcome of the socialist experiments of opening up. Today, there is an obvious contradiction between increased political room and the lagging economic potentials in East–West relations.[7] Stagnating, structurally outdated economic ties contain several factors of insecurity. If new political developments cannot be backed up by clear economic results in a relatively short period, positive political processes might be endangered, giving way again to political instabilities on the European continent. Socialist, economic and socio-political reforms seem to be as inseparable from beneficial cooperation frameworks as are the basic aims of Western Europe. Any (Eastern) European instability would hinder Western Europe from catching up with present leading standards of the world economy. Consequently, a new, strategic cooperation with the better prepared socialist countries who are willing to open up and accept the indispensable rules of involvement in international economic processes – briefly, the financing of the aforementioned 'convertibility package' – can be regarded as of all-European, world economic and political importance.

Notes

1. A. Inotai, 'Competition Between the European CMEA and Rapidly Industrialising Countries on the OECD Market for Manufactured Goods', *Empirica*, no. 1, 1988, pp. 189–203.
2. A. Inotai, 'International Competitiveness and Imports', *Acta Oeconomica*, vol. 38, 1988.
3. A recent example of this short-sighted behaviour can be found in the treatment of direct capital imports. Joint ventures in some countries

are obliged to earn hard currency and show hard currency surplus from the starting of production.

4. Arguments that oppose import liberalisation because of trade imbalances and real exchange rates (i.e. partly drastic devaluations) because of inflationary pressures are further evidences of an outdated and distorted economic concept.

5. There is no reason for arguing that an economic system which cannot use materials, energy, capital and human skill efficiently, would do better using international loans, technology or direct capital.

6. It is evident that stronger world market (Western) orientation will increase the necessity of managing intra-CMEA relations in a different way. However, changes in approach, from a strict and centrally controlled bilateralism to a more relaxed and even partly convertible currency trade, are to be expected, according to the diversified interests and abilities of the individual countries.

7. For details see J. Nötzold, A. Inotai and K. Schröder, 'East–West Trade at the Crossroads', *Aussenpolitik* (Hamburg), no. 4, 1986, pp. 400–12.

20 The Technological Gap in the CMEA Countries: Missing Incentives

Friedrich Levcik

The technological gap in the CMEA countries[1] has evidently widened since the middle of the 1970s. There are many instances substantiating this statement which, besides, can be observed by every Western tourist visiting these countries. Looking at the commodity composition of East–West trade one will find that the share of manufactures, and especially of investment goods exported by the OECD countries to the European CMEA countries, is much higher than the respective import share. The CMEA countries have also persistently lost market shares in exports of manufactures to the West, partly because their export orientation was concentrated in fields where demand in international trade was weak but mainly because the goods offered could not compete in quality, technical standards or after-sale services. Some of the developing countries, especially the newly industrialised countries, were far more successful in penetrating Western markets and the CMEA countries had to accept severe price reductions in the face of competition from these countries.

Today, even official sources admit a falling behind technological world standards amounting to between ten to twenty years. This trend persists although high priority is given to technical progress in the national central plans, and in the multilateral programmes of the CMEA. The most industrially developed CMEA countries, the GDR and Czechoslovakia, placed great emphasis on technical progress in general, and on some high-tech programmes in the field of electronics and microelectronics in their five-year plans for the first and second half of this decade. Nevertheless, they lost market shares also in these priority areas.[2]

In December 1985, the CMEA adopted an ambitious multilateral programme of scientific and technological progress,[3] aimed at catching up with the industrially developed market economies in the main fields of technological standards by the year 2000. The coordinated efforts of the CMEA countries are to be directed at five priority areas: the usage of electronics throughout the national economy, comprehensive automation, accelerated development of nuclear energy, new synthetic materials and technologies, and the development of biotechnology. The implementation of the programme should be achieved largely by traditional procedures, i.e. by the coordination of the national five-year plans and by working out multilateral or bilateral agreements and treaties for specific projects. By now we know from the proceedings at the last (44th) session of the CMEA that the far-reaching expectations set in the programme have not been fulfilled.

Lastly, it should be added that the financial, material and manpower resources devoted to R & D, and to science education, measured as a share of the GDP, are comparable to those of Western market economies. The disappointing performance of the CMEA countries in the field of technical advance must therefore have causes other than unsatisfactory attention by government or insufficient resources earmarked for R & D.

This chapter concentrates on the motivation structure in the centrally planned economies, arguing that missing or poorly developed incentives to technical change (in products and technologies) are the prime cause for the widening technological gap in these countries and for hindering timely adjustment to structural change.

The influence of technical advances on structural change is not a new feature. Since the Industrial Revolution innovations have raised productivity by initiating new manufacturing processes and in creating new products. They have generated basic changes in production organisation and supported the opening of new markets. There are some indications that the influence of technological progress has gained enormously in weight in recent times. Timely and sufficient adjustment to technical advances will be even more important in the near future.

Initiating technical advance needs first of all the creative intelligence and imagination of individuals. In modern economies, based on the world-wide division of labour, creative work of individuals or of teams of scientists and engineers is a necessary but insufficient condition for bringing about technical change. In addition, capital and mainly the spirit and skill of enterprise is needed for using the technical innovation in the proper way, and for enriching it by adjustment in organisation and marketing. Only then will innovations lead to increase in production and sales.

In the market economies of the West, on the one side it is the expectation of profit and on the other the risk of losses or even bankruptcy in cases of lagging behind in relation to domestic or foreign competition which motivates enterprises in introducing innovations. Of course, in the world of today the entrepreneur is not only acting on his own.

Such a person will try by himself or with the help of associations or lobbies to enlist the support of the government in shaping industrial or technical policies which could increase his profit chances or diminish his risks. Very often it is due to the effort of entrepreneurial initiative that appropriate government measures are taken at all.[4] Nevertheless, in the first place it is profit and risk of the firm which stimulates technical advance.

In the CPEs technical change is determined mainly in advance by the central plan with its indicator system of output targets and input limitations. Adjustments take place only when the central authorities have grasped the need for change and make the necessary decisions. The enterprises lack the motivations for taking innovative actions because, bound by the central plan, they are unable to make the adjustments or are shielded from pressure to adjust. It may even occur that enterprises react to mandatory plan targets with a pattern of behaviour which may be hostile to innovation.[5] Cases have been noticed where possible technical improvements have been obstructed, when there was the danger that the introduction of innovative measures could hinder the fulfilment of mandatory plan indicators.[6] In other cases, advantageous technologies could not be introduced once the plan was set because the new processes or products would require intermediary materials or parts which were not foreseen in the plan of material-technical supplies.

Most of the reform concepts discussed or being introduced in some of the European CMEA countries envisage substantial narrowing down or even elimination of mandatory plan indicators, a widening of rights and responsibilities of enterprises, and an orientation of management and of the workforce towards profit incentives. Thus one hopes to stimulate the enterprises to a more efficient management of their own affairs. However, at least three further prerequisites bringing about innovative changes in the market economies seem to be missing, even in the partially reformed CMEA countries.

In a market economy an innovative push comes often from newly created enterprises which in the beginning operate frequently on a modest scale. In this case, potential for innovation and an enterprising spirit is more important than capital endowment. One can find creative and technically talented individuals also in the CMEA countries. They may also be keen on starting a new undertaking. However, the possibility of creating outside the established industrial organisation even small industrial firms is either very limited – as perhaps in Hungary[7] – or is practically non existent. Even if new legislation in some of the CMEA countries permits the foundation of small cooperative shops in trade and services under certain limiting conditions, the bureaucratic procedure in gaining permission for the intended enterprise is in many cases an insurmountable obstacle. The socialist countries of Eastern Europe are thus foregoing an important potential for innovation.

Incentives and pressures for introducing technologies or products developed within the enterprise or elsewhere exist also in established, large-scale enterprises in the market economies. Only in this way can they defend or even increase their market share by cost reduction and/or product innovation or improvement. The most important motor for these follow-up innovations is the competition at home and abroad. However, this potential and condition for innovative action hardly exists in the Eastern European countries. Domestic competition is practically non-existent in industry. The centralisation drive of the 1960s and 1970s led to an industrial organisation structure in which an enterprise is frequently exerting a monopoly position in its line of production.[8] This position is strengthened by the rationing system of material–technical supplies and of investments still existing in most of the CMEA countries which ties individual enterprises by plan to a given supplier. Given the conditions of a shortage economy, the monopolistic supplier can always sell his products without any innovative effort because he is in a far stronger position than the purchasing enterprise.[9] Even in the areas of food and light industry where monopolistic structures are less frequent, very often regional delimitations of supplies prevent effective competition between several producers. In addition, fixed prices set by the central authorities discourage enterprises in gaining market shares by price competition.

Enterprises in CMEA countries are in principle exposed to competition in foreign trade. One could assume that in this respect state enterprises are subject to incentives and pressures for innovative action. However, even in foreign trade competition proves to be ineffectual as a motor for introducing innovations. More than two-thirds of foreign trade is transacted between the CMEA countries themselves. Rules and instruments of intra-CMEA trade differ fundamentally from those applied in multilateral trade between market economies.[10] Foreign trade between CMEA countries is fixed by government agencies on a strictly bilateral basis by means of five-yearly intergovernmental trade agreements, worked out in greater detail in yearly agreed minutes. In these agreements and records, shipments and counter-deliveries of stipulated sets of commodities and items are fixed by government negotiators. Production enterprises do not have much say in these negotiations which anyway take on the shape of a package deal concerning goods produced in different plants. Prices negotiated in transfer-roubles, the inconvertible CMEA foreign trade currency, do not affect the enterprise results of the producers, or affect them only indirectly and in a limited way.[11] The real partners in intra-CMEA foreign trade are still, in most CMEA countries, specialised foreign trade organisations (FTOs) to whom the producing enterprises sell export commodities at domestic wholesale prices, and the price achieved in transfer-roubles by the FTOs is of little interest to them. In intra-CMEA trade, on the enterprise level, there is therefore hardly any innovative incentive initiated by foreign competition.

The CMEA countries are, however, subjected to fierce competition in trade with the developed market economies and with some of the developing countries. Since the middle of the 1970s the Eastern European countries have incurred considerable market share losses in manufacturing exports, to a large extent due to poor quality and lagging technical standards. All the same, these pressures were of little avail in inducing the producing enterprises to innovative actions. The seeming contradiction can be explained – in most of the CMEA-countries – by the above mentioned divorce of the producing enterprises from foreign trade transactions and therefore in most cases from the adverse effects of shrinking exports and low export prices.

This applies especially to those countries where the FTOs have the exclusive rights to foreign trade transactions. But also in those countries – where some producing enterprises now have the right to participate directly in foreign trade dealings and where, either by means of more realistic commercial exchange rates or by special internal conversion coefficients, export takings or import outlays affect the revenues of the producing enterprise – international competition has only a limited effect on enterprise behaviour.

In the case of imports the strained foreign exchange situation gives the ready excuse for restricting foreign competition, and in the case of exports losses incurred due to unfavourable prices will be covered by subsidies, arguing that the exports in convertible currencies are indispensable because of balance of payment difficulties. As to intra-CMEA trade, losses will be tolerated and neutralised by subsidies, if the delivery of an important import item, e.g. fuels, will depend on the agreed counter-delivery of industrial products at prices below domestic costs. Generally, it can be said that because of the prevailing 'soft budgetary constraints' one will frequently find excuses and reasons for covering losses incurred in foreign trade.[12]

This brings us to a further precondition which in the market economies forces enterprises to adjust in time to the global trends of technical progress, but which seems to be missing in the centrally planned economies. The enterprises in the West are often forced to introduce innovative rationalisation measures, so as to survive in the long run. These measures are usually followed by severe cuts in the size of the workforce and by other socially adverse results for the employees. Not only the carrot of profit but also the stick of possible losses and bankruptcy forces capitalist entrepreneurs to continuous innovative activities. The alternative is either to match prevailing technical levels or to perish.[13]

The CMEA countries can hardly reconcile this harsh alternative of capitalist competition with the socialist tenets they still hold. Even in those countries of Eastern Euroope where in the course of economic reforms enterprises are asked to achieve and to increase profits, and where management and the workforce are motivated by profit participation, an enterprise can hardly fail because of technological backwardness and concomitant losses. In the case of real danger of bankruptcy the State will invariably try to keep the state-owned enterprise going, disregarding the losses it makes.[14]

The scope and orientation of this chapter does not allow a considered value judgement whether, out of considerations of social or regional policy, the aforementioned behaviour of the owner – the State – towards the enterprise also has its merits. The fact remains that under these conditions the state-owned enterprises of the CMEA countries are lacking in an important condition which will force an enterprise, calculating strictly according to the rules of business administration, to adjust to the prevailing trends of technical and structural change if it wants to survive.

This should not be interpreted as an apology for the flawless working of the market economy. We know the social consequences of the relentless hunt for profits, of the rules of capitalist competition which eliminate the loser without mercy, and where the burdens of adjustment are shifted to the unemployed and the rank and file of the workforce, with no say in matters of enterprise strategy. The workers in socialist enterprises may have the advantage of job security regardless of performance, but this seeming advantage is being offset by lagging technical standards, poor supplies of consumer goods and a standard of living far below the possibilities.

What has been said so far pertains to innovative incentives and pressures on the level of enterprises. Industrial and technological policies on the macroeconomic level of national governments and even of regional groupings have gained in importance in the last two decades as it became obvious that structural adjustments initiated by technical advances in a wide sense cannot be left entirely to the working of the market forces. In this sense there is a certain similarity between central governmental industrial and technological policy in East and West.[15]

In the market economies, however, technical innovations first affect the enterprises where they are generated or where they have to be adopted – if developed elsewhere – in order to keep up with the new technical standards. Governmental or intergovernmental policies are meant, in addition, to speed up or, conversely, to slow down processes already under way.

In the centrally planned economies, structural change is, initially, determined in advance by the central plan. Adjustments take place in the East only when the central authorities have taken notice of the influencing force of technical advance and have made the necessary adjustment decision, either directly by changes in the central plan or by additional technological programmes.

In some ways, on the macroeconomic level the centrally planned economies seem to have an institutional advantage over the democratically governed market economies. In drafting the central plan they can largely disregard divergent views and concepts. Sometimes costly compromise solutions, frequently adopted in the market economies, to gain the necessary support, can be avoided in the centrally planned economies with their one party rule. On the other hand, just because of the absence of opposition, the possibilities of far-reaching misjudgements, the consequences of which will become apparent only after many years, may even increase. In addition, concepts of basic reorientations in technological policy will be only undertaken when the central authorities have already taken notice of the disturbances caused by obsolete or unadjusted industrial structures. As a rule, therefore, correcting measures taken by the central authorities come too late. But even if the central concepts of scientific and technical advance are logically and purposefully conceived, and will be integrated in time in the central plan or in additional programmes, the implementation will often fail because of the missing motivation of the enterprises. These will be guided rather by their short-term interest in meeting mandatory targets and indicators than by long-term considerations, taking on the burden of introducing new technologies, developing new competitive products or adopting new organisation settings.

In conclusion, it can be said that insufficiently developed profit motivations, the existing barriers to the entry of the market by gifted individuals or small enterprising groups, the lack of competition at home and abroad, and lastly, the absence of the danger to fail, are characteristics of the CMEA countries which place them at a disadvantage with regard to the necessary adjustment to technical advance and structural change, compared to enterprises in the setting of a market economy.

Only if and when in the course of a determined reform process the barriers to innovation incentives are overcome, the CMEA countries can hope to develop an economic mechanism suited to meet the challenge of the global trends in technological advance and structural change.

One could even speculate that an economy with predominantly public enterprises, with a workforce motivated to identify its own aims with those of the enterprise, and with pluralistic, democratically arrived at choices of macroeconomic concepts may be better suited for adjusting in time to innovations than market economies in a capitalist setting.[16] However, if at all feasible, this can't be the aim of a medium-term 'perestroika' but of a long drawn out development process reaching far into the twenty-first century.

Notes

1. CMEA = Council for Mutual Economic Assistance, sometimes called COMECON. The term centrally planned economies (CPEs) will also be used. European CMEA countries: Bulgaria, CSSR, GDR, Hungary, Poland, Romania and the USSR.
2. WIIW, *Mitgliederinformation*, 1987/1.
3. *Neues Deutschland*, 19 December 1985.
4. C.T. Saunders (ed.), 'Industrial Policies and Structural Change', *East–West European Interaction, Workshop Papers*, vol. 9 (London: Macmillan, 1987).
5. J. Kosta and F. Levcik, *Economic Crisis in CMEA Countries* (Cologne: Index, 1985).
6. M. Gorbatchev, *Political Report to the 27th Congress of the CPSU* (Moscow, 1986).
7. Zoltán Roman, 'Industrial Organisation in Hungary', *Ipargazdasági Szemle* (Review of Industrial Economics, Special Issue in English) (Budapest, 1985).
8. Ibid.
9. Ota Sik, *Wirtschaftssysteme. Vergleiche-Theorie-Kritik* (Berlin/Heidelberg/New York/London/Paris/Tokyo: Springer Verlag, 1987).
10. F. Levcik and J. Stankovsky, 'East European Countries' Trade Problems: Between Ties to the USSR and Ties to the West', in, J.P. Hardt and C.H. McMillan (eds) *Planned Economies Confronting the Challenges of the 1980s* (Cambridge: Cambridge University Press, 1988).
11. J.M. van Brabant, 'The USSR and Socialist Economic Integration – A Comment', *Soviet Studies*, no. 1, 1984; G. Fink, 'Verrechnungssystem und Hartwährungshandel im RGW', *WIIW*, Reprint Series No. 74, 1984; F. Levcik, 'Transferable Rouble and Convertibility', in *Unités et monnaies de compte* (Paris, 1977).
12. Kornai, J., 'The Soft Budget Constraint', *Kyklos*, vol. 39, fasc. 1, 1986.
13. E. Streissler, 'Strukturelle Innovationsanreize – ein volkswirtschaftlicher Ansatz', in Z – Perspektiven – Berichte, Analysen, Forschung und Innovation – Möglichkeiten und Hemmnisse (Wien, 1985).
14. Kornai, 'The Soft Budget Constraint'.
15. C.T. Saunders, 'Editor's Introduction', in C.T. Saunders (ed.), *East–West European Interaction, Workshop Papers*, vol. 9, 'Industrial Policies and Structural Change' (London: Macmillan, 1987).
16. Sik, *Wirtschaftssysteme*.

PART III

The Evolution of Planning Systems: (2) Evolution as Reforms in Eastern Countries

21 Innovation as the Crucial Problem of Perestroika

Harry Maier

In the early 1970s, the phase of rapid economic growth which had lasted since the end of the 1940s came to a world-wide end. All countries were confronted with the problem to manage the change-over to a new 'technological–economic paradigm'.[1] As historical experience shows, this is a complicated social process of search which can only be successful if a flexible approach to technological, economic and social structures and a new equilibrium of interests between the different social groups is reached. The basic innovations constituting the new 'technological–economic paradigm' not only offer a new efficiency potential for economic development, but they also devaluate and destroy existing products, processes, production and power structures, as well as traditional decision mechanisms.

In socialist countries, the bureaucratic decision mechanism proved to be the decisive obstacle to achieving the change-over to the new 'technological–economic paradigm' and the required flexible approach to economic and social structures. Since the mid-1970s it became apparent that the same economic mechanism, which in the 1950s and 1960s had been able to keep pace with the technological advances of the Western industrial countries, proved to be completely incapable of finding a productive access to the new fields of innovation. Particularly frightening was the fact that the socialist countries did not have a position worth mentioning in any of these new fields of innovation – neither in microelectronics, information and communication technology, nor in the field of new materials, laser technology and new biotechnology, and this in spite of the fact that there is quantitatively more than a quarter of the world's research potential in the Soviet Union.

In a situation where basic innovations destroyed the traditional economic–technological equilibrium and set in motion a radical change of structure in direction of a new equilibrium, the existing system of leadership and planning became a 'brake mechanism' (Mikhail Gorbachev).

Though the main goal of central planning in socialist countries is to secure a 'balanced' ('planned proportional') development, it became apparent that this was more and more difficult to achieve in an economy becoming more complex and being affected by structural change.

The USSR's vast planning apparatus with a staff of more than 2 million people, which makes strenuous efforts to allocate the country's scarce resources to the production units by means of 50 000 product balances[2], proved to be powerless in view of the problems entailed with the new push of innovation. The inevitable result was – as Joseph Schumpeter put it – an 'improper equilibrium',[3] i.e. a state of equilibrium which causes the entrepreneurs' economic activities to remain permanently far below the attainable economic rationality.

As balance is never achieved, the production units have to acquire the resources they still lack by means of an archaic exchange economy in order to reach the quotas imposed on them. To be able to participate in this exchange trade, they hoard scarce resources. The result is paradoxical in that the more is produced, the more shortages increase. The inevitable result is that the stock of products and materials in socialist countries has continued to rise, as opposed to the situation in Western industrial countries. In the Soviet Union, they have even increased twice as fast as the national income between 1971 and 1985, and are likely to have reached a figure of more than 470 billion roubles at present.[4]

It becomes apparent that the enormous simplification of the economy by the abolition of the market, as Marx and Engels had hoped for, did not take place. Neither did Lenin's idea that economic action without a market would be so simple that even a female cook could direct state and economy efficiently. Even the unprejudiced Joseph A. Schumpeter stated: 'The socialist form of organization has the advantage that it emphasizes the economic connection of things more clearly than capitalism.'[5]

It may be that Schumpeter's prediction will come true at some time but the present situation of socialism shows just the opposite. Even under particularly favourable circumstances, as in the GDR, it is apparent that it becomes more and more difficult to plan and direct a complex economy without the coordination of the market.

THE NEW 'TECHNOLOGICAL–ECONOMIC PARADIGM' AND PERESTROIKA

In a bureaucratic economic mechanism, radical innovations must inevitably be undesirable[6] as they considerably increase the risk of not accomplishing the programme. First, because they are very hazardous and may lead to an economic disaster for the management in case of failure. Another reason is that if radical innovations are effective their success may be very hard to repeat the next year.

At a point of time when the new 'technological–economic paradigm' began to make headway in the leading industrial countries, such an economic mechanism inevitably produced a technological gap between East and West which increased rapidly. This became apparent very soon in the decreasing growth rates of productivity in socialist countries, as well as in the deterioration in terms of foreign trade in industrial goods. According to Aganbegjan, industrial production has not grown at all from 1979 to 1982. For 40 per cent of the product groups it has even decreased.[7] In Abel Aganbegjan's opinion, the rates of growth shown by official statistics were either the result of shifts in types of goods or of price increases.

The metal-working industry, especially mechanical engineering, is particularly affected by the processes of devaluation. The proportion of high quality mechanical engineering products decreased from 50 per cent in 1975 to 12 per cent in 1984.[8] The annual rate of innovation in Soviet mechanical engineering is 3.1 per cent at present, and approximately 2.5 per cent overall.[9] This means that Soviet mechanical engineering updates its classes of goods only every twenty-three years, and Soviet industry generally every twenty-eight years. In the same sector of Western industrial countries, products are updated every three to four years.

As a result, the OECD market share of Soviet mechanical engineering exports decreased from 5.8 per cent in 1973 to 1.5 per cent in 1986. In contrast to this, the threshold countries managed to increase their market share in OECD countries considerably. In 1973, South Korea with 5.9 per cent had the same market share as the USSR. In 1986, South Korea's share was already ten times as high as that of the USSR. In 1986, Taiwan's share was thirteen times as high.

Though the USSR's number of employees in research and development increased from 354 thousand in 1960 to 1.5 million in 1984, i.e. by more than four times, the share of research-intensive goods in total exports into OECD countries is less than 8 per cent, while it is 54 per cent in Western European countries.[10] The share of CMEA countries in the OECD market for research-intensive import goods decreased from 2.5 per cent in 1965 to less than 2 per cent in 1986, in spite of the rapid expansion of the research potential.

The innovation weakness of the Soviet economy became particularly apparent when oil prices began to fall in 1986. The Soviet Union exports hardly any of the competitive products of its civil manufacturing industry which were able to compensate for the decline in oil prices. The result was a considerable growth of net debts, which increased from $18.3 billion in 1985 to $25.3 billion in 1987. This is 25 per cent of the debts of the CMEA countries.[11] Due to the renewed fall in oil prices from $18 in 1987 to $14 per barrel, the debts of the USSR will very soon reach $30 billion.

DIFFERENT CONCEPTS FOR OVERCOMING THE STAGNATION TENDENCIES IN THE SOCIALIST ECONOMY

Without any doubt there is a far-reaching consensus between the different social groups and centres of leadership in the Soviet Union and in other socialist countries on the necessity to overcome the economic stagnation. But this consensus is jeopardised again and again by diametrically opposed opinions on the way, the goal and the manner of the reform of the socialist economy and society. There are three basic positions which reflect the present interests and conceptions of different social groups:

The Conservatives

They think that a fundamental reform of the economy and society is not necessary, though they do, of course, want to overcome economic stagnation. In their opinion, the problems are the result of subjective failure; the central authority's lack of ability to get its way, as well as insufficient working discipline, morals and increasing corruption.

The Technocrats

They accept the need for reforms but want to restrict it to the economy. They try to make the existing planning and decision-making mechanism more clear, flexible and efficient.

The Radical Reformers

They proceed on the assumption that the stagnation of the socialist economy and society is the inevitable result of a rigid political system, of a bureaucratic planning and decision-making mechanism (command economy), of the antiquated property and production conditions, and of a sterile intellectual climate. In their opinion, the basic structures of the command system are still a heritage from the Stalin era. To remove them would mean to finally put an end to Stalinism.

These three currents do not only exist in the USSR, where the radical reformers' group around Mikhail Gorbachev succeeded in October 1988 in strengthening its position considerably *vis-à-vis* the conservatives and technocrats. While the Hungarian and Polish leaderships support the radical reform conception of Gorbachev, though for different reasons, those of the GDR and Romania firmly reject it. The CSSR leadership supports the Gorbachev conception verbally, but leaves no doubt that it is not willing to follow th way of radical economic reform.

In the centre of the present conflict about economic reform there are four basic aims:

1. The establishment of complete economic independence of enterprises and associations. This includes the creation of general economic conditions by which production units are force to face economic competition in domestic and foreign markets, to work out their own strategies of innovation, and to bear the risks involved on their own.

This requires the elimination of the supply monopoly of big enterprises and associations. The creation of these enterprise associations (in the GDR they are called industrial combines) was the technocrats' reply to the challenges inherent in the new 'technological–economic paradigm'. In the GDR, 3526 enterprises were merged to form 224 industrial combines in the early 1980s, and have an unlimited supply monopoly on the domestic market for the goods produced by them.

As opposed to the technocrats, the radical reformers, however, regard the supply monopolies of the enterprises as the main cause for the economic stagnation and decreasing innovation capacity of the Soviet economy. At the party conference, in June 1988, Mikhail Gorbachev objected to making it possible for big enterprises to have a supply monopoly.[12] He was supported by Georgi Arbatow, director of the North American Institute of the USSR, who pointed out that there 'is an appalling monopoly economy' in the USSR, though 'the monopoly always causes decay, also in socialism'. He added that 'competition is needed, socialist competition'.[13]

2. The abolition of the directive–command economy of central planning, which is, according to the radical reformers, the main cause for perpetual shortages, the limitation performance and the innovation inertia of the enterprises. The central authority should concentrate its activity on strategic fundamental processes of the economy, structural policy and the setting of general conditions for innovative action. This is only possible if the present dual structure of the decision-making and planning mechanism can be removed. Besides these elements of the economy bureaucracy, the party has built up its own economic apparatus which, being a 'neutral force', is designed to solve the conflict of interests between the central economic bureaucracy and production units. The result is a double bureaucracy which not only requires a great deal of energy and money, but also multiplies in an extreme way the usual defects of a bureaucratisation of economic life.[14]

At the party conference, Mikhail Gorbachev has therefore rejected the thesis of the increasing role of the party, designating the 'concentration of economic conduct in the hands of the party leadership' as 'contra-productive'.[15] The GDR leadership, however, adheres to the thesis of the increasing role of the party in the economy and would not think of withdrawing from the economic decision-making process. At the December conference (1988) of the Central Committee of the United Socialist Party of Germany,

Otto Reinhold, one of the mouthpiece economists of the GDR leadership, rejected the idea that the party should give up this leading role, seeing it merely as an attempt 'to reduce the party to a debating club'.[16]

3. The establishment of functioning market relations with an efficient price, finance and credit mechanism. A first step should be the change to wholesale trading with capital goods.

In this field, the radical reformers have not yet realised many of their ideas. At the nineteenth party conference in June 1988, Gorbachev pointed out that the technocrats have tried to save the command system by taking advantage of the possibility offered by the 'law on enterprises' to impose directions on the enterprises by means of government contracts (more than 60 per cent). 'Under the cloak of government contracts, the old system of liabilities relating to the extent of production has virtually been maintained.'[17]

4. Integration into the world economy and the opening of the system to Western industrial countries. It speaks for the far-sightedness of the reformers' group around Mikhail Gorbachev that it has recognised the importance of opening the system to the West for the purposes of reform. One of the causes of failure of the reforming attempts in the 1960s was that economic reform was supposed to be practicable without any overtures to the West. But experience has shown that it is not possible to establish a productive relationship with the newly developing combination of productive forces and support of basic innovations without striving for economic, scientific–technological and cultural relations with Western industrialised countries. On the other hand, contact with the West will not last without a reform of the economic and social system, as experience in the GDR has recently shown.

However, integration into the world economy requires a change-over to free convertible currency. The group around Gorbachev wants to achieve this goal in two steps: the introduction of a convertible currency in the CMEA by the beginning of the 1990s, and then the establishment of a full convertibility with world currencies. At the party conference in June 1988, Mikhail Gorbachev stated plainly: 'We see the prospect of the future lying in the change-over to the free convertible rouble.'

THE NECESSITY OF ECONOMIC REFORM IN THE GDR

In agreement with the conservative group in Moscow, the GDR leadership states that there is no need for reforms. However, there have been several attempts to increase the innovation level of industrial production within the framework of the present economic mechanism. In 1983, the politburo decided to achieve an annual rate of innovation of 30 to 40 per cent in the GDR's enterprises, and this was confirmed at the eleventh party congress in 1986.

Up to that time, the annual rate of change in GDR industry was only 3 per cent, i.e. types of products were renewed every twenty-three years. Now the industrial combines have to renew their products every two to three years, even if Western enterprises such as Philips and Siemens manage to change theirs at an annual rate of only 9.6 per cent. But these unrealistic product renewal rates proved to be very favourable for the industrial combines, because they were thus enabled to enforce price increases of 30 to 40 per cent of annual production, therefore experiencing high growth rates of net production, profits, labour productivity as well as a lower consumption of material and energy per unit, together with the benefit of the respective bonuses. On the world markets, however, the situation was different since the alleged increase of the net product was not acknowledged, and the value added achieved by the new products was often lower than that of the previous products. Foreign exchange earnings decreased, indebtedness increased, and the process of devaluation of the produced goods expanded. A country like the GDR, which has to sell more than 50 per cent of its products on the world market, is, of course, particularly affected by this development.

The declining level of innovation of the GDR product becomes particularly apparent in that the value added per unit of delivery achieved by the GDR in foreign trade with the Western industrial countries continues to decrease. The GDR has to export more and more products in order to achieve the same value in foreign trade with industrial products. This development can be also seen in the GDR's trade with the Federal Republic of Germany. While, in the case of basic and producer goods the value added achieved by both German states (e.g. for steel and iron) developed only slightly in favour of the Federal Republic, there is a rapidly increasing gap as far as technology-intensive goods are concerned.

While the value added for mechanical engineering achieved by the Federal Republic in 1970 was 1.8 times higher than that of the GDR, it was even 6.0 times higher in 1987. This means that the GDR has to use its resources sixfold in its most productive sector of industry – mechanical engineering – in order to achieve the same value added as the Federal Republic. This relation is more strongly marked in the field of office machines, where the employment of microelectronics is decisive for quality. In this sector, the value added per unit of delivery achieved by the Federal Republic in 1970 was already six times higher than that of the GDR. Due to the falling back of the GDR in the field of microelectronics, the value added of the Federal Republic increased 11.4-fold in 1987. Even where the GDR once had an advantage over the Federal Republic, e.g. in fine mechanical optics, it has been lost long since. While the added value per unit of delivery achieved by the GDR in this field was 1.1 times as high in 1970, it attained only 33.0 per cent (1987) of the Federal Republic's value added in inter-German trade.

In all major technologically relevant product groups, such as mechanical engineering and plant construction, electrical engineering, chemistry, as well as measuring and control engineering, the proportions of the value added achieved by both German states developed according to the same pattern.

It is evident that all ideological stunts in the long run cannot veil the fact that the innovation level of the GDR's industrial products is declining and cannot be increased within the framework of the present economic mechanism. Therefore, it is not difficult to predict that, after the forthcoming change in the GDR leadership, this development will become the starting point of an extensive discussion on the radical reform of the economic mechanism.

Notes

1. See also O. Sik, R. Höltschi and C. Rockstroh, *Wachstum und Krisen*, (Berlin, 1988); C. Freeman and C. Perez, 'Structural Crisis of Adjustment: Business Cycles and Investment Behaviour', in G. Dosi (ed.), *Technical Change and Economic Theory* (London/New York, 1988), p. 38; H. Maier, 'Basic Innovations and the Next Wave of Productivity Growth', in T. Vasko (ed.), *The Long-Wave Debate*, (Berlin, 1987), p. 46 ff.

2. L.M. Sor, *Economic Relations under the Circumstances of Experiment* (Moscow, 1986), p. 25 (in Russian).
3. J.A. Schumpeter, *Konjunkturzyklen* (Göttingen, 1962), p. 51.
4. O. Lacis, 'Über die Umgestaltung des Wirtschaftsmechanismus', *Sowjetgesellschaft* (Berlin (East)), no. 1, 1987, p. 24.
5. J.A. Schumpeter, *Konjunkturzyklen I* (Göttingen, 1961), p. 251.
6. Also in this case, Joseph A. Schumpeter's assumption has not yet been confirmed that in a 'socialist community' it will be more easy to bring about basic innovations than in a 'capitalist society'. He states: 'In a socialist community it would be obvious that periods of innovation – compare Gosplan – are also periods of effort and sacrifice, of working for the future, while the harvest will take place later' (J.A. Schumpeter, *Konjunkturzyklen*, vol. I, p. 152).
7. A. Aganbegjan, *Perestroika in der Wirtschaft der UdSSR*, (Moscow, 1987), p. 3 (in Russian).
8. E. Sapilov, 'Economic Incentives for the Introduction of New Technology', *Voprossi Ekonomik*, no. 4, 1986, p. 46 (in Russian).
9. A. Aganbegjan, *Bahn frei für den Innovationsschub* (Green Light For the Push of Innovation) (Moscow, 1986), p. 14.
10. See also H. Maier, *Innovation oder Stagnation* (Cologne, 1987), p. 119; J.B. Donges, *Kritische Anmerkungen zum Ost-West-Handel* (Kiel, 1988), p. 13, Working Paper No. 324.
11. *Economic Survey of Europe in 1987–1988* (New York, 1988), p. 309.
12. M. Gorbachev, 'Die Verwirklichung der Beschlüsse des 27. Parteitages und die Intensivierung der Perestroika' (The Realization of the Resolutions of the 27th Party Congress and the Intensification of Perestroika), in *Offene Worte* (Nördlingen, 1988), p. 23.
13. *Offene Worte: Beiträge und Reden der 19. Konferenz der KPdSU* (Open Words: Contributions and Speeches of the 19th Communist Party Conference) (Nördlingen, 1988), p. 172.
14. See also Maier, *Innovation oder Stagnation*, p. 167 ff.
15. M. Gorbachev, *Die Verwirklichung*, pp. 83–4.
16. Otto Reinhold, 'Das Programm unserer Partei hat sich im Leben bewährt' (The programme of our party has been proved in life), *Neues Deutschland*, nos. 3–4 December, 1988, p. 5.
17. M. Gorbachev, *Die Verwirklichung*, p. 20.

22 Gorbachev's 'Radical Reform' and the Future of the Soviet Planning System

Hans-Hermann Höhmann

Ever since Stalin's death, successive Soviet leaderships have endeavoured to improve the functionability of the USSR's planned economy system by way of a variety of reforms from 'within the system'. Khrushchev's unsuccessful attempt at administrative decentralisation on a regional basis was followed in the 1960s by Brezhnev's broad-based but half-hearted and inconsistent programme of reforms. More recently, Brezhnev's attempts to 'muddle through' with 'improvements' to and 'perfectings' of the administration of the economy (Nove, 1982, pp. 17–44) instead of embarking on any real reforms have given way to Gorbachev's ambitious project of a 'radical reform'. While the periodic repetition of attempts at reform only presses home the fact that it has still not proved possible to give the Soviet planned economy a modern, efficient structure, Gorbachev's unprecedented determination underlines the realisation that the need for effective reform has by now become so urgent as to brook no further delay.

THE PERCEPTION OF CRISIS AND THE STARTING POINTS FOR REFORM

Any appraisal of the current status of and the future outlook for the latest Soviet attempts at reform must commence with an analysis of the circumstances occasioning their inception. These circumstances and the way in which they were and are still perceived by the Soviet leadership were the motive forces that triggered the reform process and continue to determine its further momentum. The principal factor initiating the perestroika drive was a multidimensional crisis of development in the Soviet Union which in fact goes back a long time, but had clearly been growing more and more serious since the late 1970s. Gorbachev himself has spoken on several occasions of a 'pre-crisis', thereby making use of a concept that makes sense only if it is accepted in principle that crises are possible within socialism, too. But 'crisis' – or 'pre-crisis' – does not imply that the Soviet system as such is on the point of collapse. System and leadership have adequately effective political and economic instruments at their disposal for assuring their survival and viability. Instead, the crisis lay – and continues to lie, even after four years of Gorbachev – in the fact that, if current trends are allowed to persist, there will soon no longer be adequate resources available for the vigorous articulation of Soviet great power policies at home or abroad.

The most important descriptors for the economic aspect of the crisis are low economic growth, stagnation of productivity and standard of living, and a widening gap in economic competitiveness with the Western industrialised nations. This situation is relatively new. Though there had in earlier periods been drop-offs in growth and multifarious functional disturbances, nevertheless resources had always increased enough to be able to satisfy investment, consumer and armaments demands, and the USSR had always been able to catch up in the field of international economic competition. At the turn of the 1980s, however, the situation changed profoundly. Economic growth fell to historic lows – possibly even to zero. Since the Western industrialised nations were at the same time achieving some limited but nevertheless constant and technologically innovative growth, the USSR found itself caught up in a 'scissors-movement' crisis: on the one hand, the discrepancy between the level of domestic expectations and the country's economic performance capacity was becoming more and more pronounced, and on the other, the performance gap separating the USSR from the Western industrialised nations was widening again, too. To this day, it has still not proved possible to regain control of the economic situation. In particular, the persistent problems affecting the supply of goods are generating an urgent need for action in the field of economic policy.

After Gorbachev had, in the initial period following his coming to office, attempted to tackle the country's economic problems with the aid of a rather conventional 'policy mix' consisting of labour policy and structure policy elements, as time went by elements of economic reform policy became more and more prominent (Höhmann, 1987, pp. 112–32). This economic reform policy was not, however, geared towards any new model of socialism. Instead, reform attempts were restricted from the very beginning to combining various measures directed against the many dysfunctions of the old system into a package which, as a result, is by no means consistent and also reveals no clear-cut objective in terms of system policy. Four sectoral reforms, in particular, can be singled out in this context: the reform of the state sector, and especially of industry, the reform of foreign trade, the agricultural reform, and finally the creation of an as yet small but rapidly expanding sector of cooperative economic activity outside agriculture, too. First and foremost among the new elements in Soviet reform policy are the changes in the *foreign trade and payments system* to relax the traditional state monopoly on foreign trade (Meier, 1987, pp. 190–2). These included transferring to twenty-one ministries and more than seventy large-scale enterprisees the right to carry on independent, even if still administratively supervised, foreign trade activities as of January 1987, and giving them the right to free use of the 'foreign currency funds' generated in the course of those activities as an incentive to improving the efficiency of export trade. Also worthy of mention is the newly granted possibility of forming joint ventures with Western firms, introduced with the intention of improving access to foreign capital, technological know-now and managerial skills. Further effects aimed at are the promotion of exports and the substitution of imports. In *agriculture*, the freedom of the agricultural production units to market produce in excess of their planning targets was extended as early as in 1986, and stronger emphasis was placed on the use of so-called 'group contracts' with a view to encouraging the individual to improve his performance in production within the *kolkhozi* and *sovkhozi*.

These reforms brought only limited success. Since the summer of 1988, the introduction of the 'leasing system' has been propagated with new emphasis, widespread application of which would amount to the *de facto* abolition of collectivisation. Also of importance are the new legal provisions for *cooperative and individual economic activity*. The new Cooperatives Act, in particular, affords considerable freedom for quasi-private group economic activities. The cooperatives are intended to perform three major functions: to improve the supply situation in deficit sectors of the economy such as the consumer goods and services sectors, but also to boost innovative activity; to create employment reserves as a catchment for possible large-scale redundancies in the administration and in industry; and finally it was hoped that they would perform a system–policy function by affording organisational alternatives and displaying a more competitive attitude than the more rigid state sector of the Soviet economy. The practical significance of the cooperatives is still slight, however. And they are facing opposition, especially from the bureaucracy.

The most significant feature of the reform as a whole, however, is not so much the modifications outlined up to now, for all their importance from the point of view of changing principles and increased dynamism, but rather the *reform of the Soviet state economy*, focused on the industrial sector. This new stage got under way with the resolutions of the June 1987 CC Plenum and the passing of the Enterprises Act at the subsequent session of the Supreme Soviet (cf. 'Osnovnye polozheniia', *Pravda*, 27 June 1987). The starting point for the reform is to be the changed status of the production unit in the economy as a whole. Up to now the performance of the production units has suffered under inexpedient steering from above, inadequate coordination between the production units themselves, and lack of economic motivation. In a largely administratively dictated production process, the production unit likes to be given 'easy' plans and to organise a costly, qualitatively inadequate, and not very innovative production process that is geared towards the formal fulfilment of the targets established in those plans. Unsatisfactory technological progress, in particular, is one of the main grounds for criticism of the old system and one of the main reasons in favour of reform.

The production unit is in future to become more of an 'enterprise' in the true sense of the word. On the basis of the new Enterprises Act, its autonomy is to be extended, the role played by planning directives is to be restricted, and, where external planning is still to be carried out, the production unit is to be given a greater say in it. Coordination between the production units is preferably to take the form of contracts between them, and even requirements by the authorities are to be established in state contracts specifying the reciprocal obligations of the production unit and the administrative body – instead of being mandatorily imposed by the directive indicators used up to now. The production unit is to gain access to the means of production mainly via a wholesale trade. Furthermore, the traditional principle for measuring the success of the production units, the criterion of fulfilment of planning targets, is to be drastically curtailed. Within the terms of reference of so-called 'full economic accountability', much greater emphasis is placed on profit as the objective of the production units' activities and as an indicator of their performance. Remuneration and investment activities are also to be profit-related. And finally, the decision-making process within the production units is to allow for extended self-administration.

The new role to be played by the production units also entails changes in the functions of the planning and economy administration system. In future, the five-year plans are to consist essentially of 'control indices' that are no longer to be of a compulsory nature, but instead are to be implemented in production unit activities via indirect (or 'economic', as they are called) instruments such as taxes, norms and limits, and the state contracts referred to earlier. All this brings progress but also gives rise to as yet unsolved problems. What, for instance, could be more tempting, in the event of 'economic methods' failing to grip or of intensifying performance pressure from state priority areas, than to extend the system of state contracts or to reconvert control indices back into mandatory planning directives? Developments in 1988, the first year of the reform, showed that the administration was often unable to resist this temptation. Progress coupled with problems is also becoming apparent in many other areas, for instance in the supply of means of production to the production units, in the pricing system, or in the financing and credit system. Everywhere, a departure from the prevailing centralism is envisaged. Everywhere, the trend is towards a freer economy. But everywhere there are doubts as to whether the changes introduced or under consideration to date are going to be adequate.

Finally, the Gorbachev leadership further proceeds on the assumption that, in order to ensure the performance capability of a more strongly decentralised economic system, it will also be necessary to reform the structures and functions of the ministries that administer the economy. The ministries are to be relieved of their functions of operative economic management and are to be turned into 'general staffs' for the promotion of technological innovation in their respective sectors. Since, however, the administrative apparatus remains essentially intact, at least for the time being, a potential for bureaucratic intervention is preserved that can be expected to come into action especially if the instruments of indirect steering should fail and shortages emerge in the satisfaction of state demand in priority sectors.

PROBLEMS OF IMPLEMENTATION: HOW REFORMABLE IS THE SOVIET PLANNED ECONOMY?

The Soviet leadership itself assesses the status achieved in restructuring with reservation: we are still at the beginning, the phase of implementation has only just started, the next two to three years are going to be crucial to its success. In actual fact, the results of perestroika have been greatest where words have already been followed by deeds (Brahm, 1987), specifically in the case of glasnost (Mommsen, 1987) and the new foreign policy initiatives. The next lower stratum of change, the level of institutional restructuring, has hardly been touched upon as yet. Much less have any significant improvements become apparent to date in the economy. On the contrary, economic growth, somewhat livelier in 1986, flattened off again in 1987. If restructuring is not to lose its momentum, more institutional change, and above all an improvement in the standard of living, are crucially urgent at this time.

The principal motive forces of perestroika continue to be the unsatisfactory situation in the USSR, the fact that the leadership around Gorbachev perceives that situation as requiring urgent action, the General Secretary's own resolve, and support by some of the Soviet intelligentsia, by authors, scientists, progressive officials, engineers and managers, who all, of course, represent a disparate and at times also an importunate following.

The forces in opposition to the policy of restructuring are likewise of diverse composition. Part of the braking effect is connected with *political risks and conflicting objectives*, which even the General Secretary has to take into account. These include sensitive social problems such as the looming danger of inflation or unemployment, but also the problematic interdependencies between reform and armaments policy. Even if success is achieved in arms control, i.e. even if it is able to relieve the load on the economy, the burden of defence expenditure remains heavy. A market-oriented reform that goes too far would jeopardise central access to resources for arms purposes, which the leadership also considers important and which serves more than just the interests of the military-industrial complex. The latter, of course, itself represents a barrier to reform, not so much in the field of technological modernisation (Schröder, 1987), but certainly when resources and decision-making authority are at stake. Another aspect to be taken into consideration is the nationalities problem. In this area, progress made in decentralisation threatens to lead to further instability, at least to loss of Russian control, which, on the other hand, could perhaps – but by no means with certainty – be accompanied by an improvement in the legitimacy of the Soviet Union as a true multinational state with equal rights for all nations. Reform also harbours risks in terms of relations within the USSR's hegemonial sphere in Eastern Europe.

Both inside and outside the USSR, the discussion about the chances and problems of 'restructuring' centres around the *role of the Soviet bureaucracy*. The resistance it poses is indeed substantial. This foot-dragging has a variety of causes, and it is expedient to examine them with discrimination, especially for the purposes of discussing strategies for overcoming bureaucratic impediments to reform. One first reason for opposition on the part of the officials is that the strategies for change are incomplete and inconsistent. The reform of economic management is comprehensive in that it covers all relevant fields of economic activity. However, the reform strategy package is by no means an integral and consistent entity, and this enables the bureaucracy to circumvent it. The economy administration is not only expected to promote the introduction of the new steering mechanism, it is at the same time held responsible for ensuring that the desired acceleration of economic growth is achieved. It is thus not surprising that the officials for their part give growth priority over reform and continue to apply the old administrative methods with which they are just as familiar as with the associated reactions on the part of the production units. Thus, much will depend on the leadership's ability to implement the reform rapidly and emphatically and on its willingness to respond with institutional corrective actions when – as is inevitable – the inconsistencies outlined become evident. The bureaucracy's opposition to 'restructuring' is also linked – for such is human nature – with the bureaucrats' struggle to preserve their status, power, prestige and incomes. In reform lurks a threat to vested interests, for one of the purposes of the reform is to cut back the inefficient and costly steering apparatus. On the other hand, the aim is not an all-round reduction in the administration as a whole. Even a 'restructured' Soviet Union will remain an interventionist system with large numbers of functionaries, whose personal status might even be improved in the wake of the broadening of functions that would result from the numerical reduction of the apparatus. The aim should be – according to a theory propounded by the sociologist Tatiana Zaslavskaya – to use a strategy of social contracts to win over the performance-oriented section of the bureaucracy in support of the leadership and perestroika (Zaslavskaya, 1983).

On the whole, Gorbachev's perestroika has up to now attained only its first launching stages. The attempted take-off is both ambitious and limited. It is radical in that for the first time in recent Soviet history a comprehensive, even if not fully complete and consistent, strategy has been developed with the aim of breaking out of decades-old forms of politics and economy – but not out of the Soviet system itself. On the other hand, the limits to the reform are also clear. This becomes apparent, for instance, in a comparison with those socialist systems in which really profound changes are in progress or have already been implemented, in particular with the Hungarian system. But an analysis of the reform resolutions passed in the USSR itself also gives grounds for doubt as to the likelihood of any impending radical change in system policy. Though the reform does constitute a departure from the old status quo, a new, stable, effective system has yet to be found. There are serious conceptual, political and social obstacles standing in the way of any functional blend of planning and market, of single-party system and social pluralism.

Consequently, if a new, efficient system balance is to be achieved in the USSR, there are other preconditions that will first have to be satisfied. These are only partly of an economic and above all of a political nature. First, the resolutions passed must be implemented without delay and the gaps in the overall strategy filled in. Many of the reforms of the past ran aground because of a lack of political determination and a half-hearted conceptual definition. Further crucial factors are going to be whether Gorbachev can continue to expand his power base and consolidate his authority in the future, too; whether, within the framework of the political system of the USSR, democratic mechanisms can actually be transformed into pressure from below; and whether, in the long term, glasnost is able to change popular awareness. Western observers are voicing scepticism. At times, they even speak of 'system traps' in which the Soviet Union is ensnared, no matter how good the intentions of its leadership. But to go that far is perhaps unjustified. After all, there are signs of progress being made: the Soviet Union has changed politically, Gorbachev has managed to stabilise the foundations of his rule despite opposition from many sides. Nevertheless, the obstacles still to be overcome are many and varied, especially since the consent of leadership groups is only part of the problem and must be accompanied by cooperation on the part of the bureaucracy and acceptance of the reforms by the population at large. This acceptance is a prerequisite for the success of the reforms, but is hardly likely to be granted until positive improvements in the economic situation have made themselves felt.

Finally, another major factor is whether Gorbachev as the central political leadership personality is himself open to new and more far-reaching conceptions. If, in particular, the 'New Economic Mechanism' in its present form proves to be no more than a functionally weak hybrid, what new ideal for far-reaching, really radical reforms in economy and politics will then be available? The General Secretary's personal evolution from a technocratic moderniser to a reformer of socialism by all means attests to his conceptual versatility. What is more, glasnost is promoting the discussion on economic reform, possibly tending to establish a better theoretical basis for further evolution of the economic policy strategies of the future. Nevertheless, the question remains as to the inherent fundamental limits to any reform that is confined to within the system. In the final analysis, this question boils down to whether far-reaching economic and social reforms can or cannot be reconciled with the single-party regime of the CPSU, with the socialist system of ownership, and with a still prevalent underlying understanding of economic policy which refuses to grant the economy of the USSR autonomy to the benefit of the people but insists on keeping it available for use for political ends.

References

Brahm, H. (1987) 'Glanz und Grenzen der Glasnost', *Sowjetunion, 1986/87* (Munich: Hanser), pp. 103–11.
Höhmann, H.-H. (1987) 'Sowjetische Wirtschaft unter Gorbatschow: Auf

der Suche nach neuem Profil', *Sowjetunion, 1986/87* (Munich: Hanser), pp. 112–32.

Meier, C. (1987) 'Sowjetische Aussenwirtschaft auf neuen Wegen?', *Sowjetunion, 1986/87* (Munich: Hanser), pp. 186–96.

Mommsen, M. (1987) 'Von "Kritik und Selbstkritik" zu "Glasnost"', in M. Mommsen, H.-H. Schröder (eds), *Gorbatschow's Revolution von oben* (Frankfurt: Ullstein), pp. 23–27.

Nove, A. (1982) 'USSR: Economic Policy and Methods after 1970', in A. Nove, H.-H. Höhmann, G. Seidenstecher (eds), *The East European Economies in the 1970s* (London: Butterworth), pp. 17–44.

Schröder, H.-H. (1987) 'Gorbatschow und die Generäle. Militärdoktrin, Rüstungspolitik und öffentliche Meinung in der "Perestrojka"', *Berichte des Bundesinstituts für ostwissenschaftliche und internationale Studien*, vol. 45 (Cologne).

Zaslavskaya, T. (1984) 'Studie von Nowosibirsk', text (German translation) published with introduction and commentary by H.-H. Höhmann and K.-E. Wädekin, *Osteuropa*, vol. 1.

23 Success and Failure: Emergence of Economic Reforms in Czechoslovakia and Hungary

Tamás Bauer

The market-oriented economic reform of 1967, of which Professor Ota Sik was the main architect, turned out to be a brief episode in the post-war history of Czechoslovakia. On the one hand, it remained a matter of nostalgia for reform-minded economists both in the country and in exile; on the other hand, it continues to be a butt for fierce criticism for those in power since April 1969 up to now, within the country. Was the reform of the late 1960s a move into a blind alley which resulted in a collapse of the economy instead of bringing about the promised improvement in economic performance, or was it a sound set of measures whose successful implementation was only prevented by the foreign intervention?

This question would be extremely difficult to answer, if the Czechoslovak reform were the only one of that type. However, a fairly similar reform blueprint was drafted and, to some extent, implemented at the same time in Hungary. The reform process in Hungary was not broken by foreign intervention but developed on its own logic. Despite all inconsistencies in the blueprint and compromises in the implementation, it has been considered a success story both within and beyond Hungary. It seems, therefore, adequate to raise the question whether Hungary's successful experience during the late 1960s and early 1970s has been the one that Czechoslovaks might also have experienced had the foreign intervention been avoided. The reform blueprints and their implementation in the two countries will be compared in this chapter, and an attempt will be made to explain the difference in the outcome.

245

A comment on the period under review is valid at this point. In discussing economic and political reforms in Czechoslovakia, authors often focus on developments in 1968–9 and neglect the fact that *economic* reform was already introduced in 1967. In comparing *economic* reforms in Czechoslovakia and Hungary, it seems more appropriate to focus on the Czechoslovak reform in its 1967 form, as implemented under the conditions of political stability. Similarly, only the first two years of the implementation of the Hungarian reform will be considered.

SIMILAR CAUSES

The Czechoslovak and Hungarian reform endeavours of the mid-1960s were both part of the second wave of economic reforms and, as such, products of the second considerable downswing in post-war economic development in Eastern Europe.

Following the 'second wave of industrialisation' in Eastern Europe, connected with the Khrushchev's seven-year plan and Mao's Great Leap Forward, all countries experienced some recession in one or two years between 1962 and 1966. This time, it was Czechoslovakia where the downswing was the deepest (not only was investment cut considerably, but industrial output and national product also declined, a development without precedent in centrally planned economies up to that time). In Hungary, economic disturbances did not seem so serious (economic growth slowed down in one year only (1965) and output continued to grow), but sensible economists and officials realised that serious problems were concealed behind the moderate disturbances in the economy.

The governments (party leaderships) of both countries reacted, among others, with readiness to reform the economic systems. In Czechoslovakia, the party leadership had decided by 1963 that something in this direction should be undertaken. In Hungary, when Rezsö Nyers was elected secretary of the Central Committee in charge of economic policy in late 1962, he initiated the establishment of an informal advisory body for brain-storming in that direction. In doing so, one could rely on earlier experience in both cases. In Czechoslovakia, a first comprehensive attempt to reform the control system was undertaken in 1958–9 but collapsed, due to the tensions resulting from the second wave of industrialisation and to inconsistencies within the reform measures apparent by 1960. In Hungary, a far-reaching reform blueprint was drafted following the 1956 uprising but rejected by the Kádár government after having been consolidated surprisingly rapidly in 1957. Instead, partial improvements in the system were introduced but proved to be inefficient during the late 1950s and early 1960s. Aware of such experience, experts suggested more comprehensive reforms in both countries.

The leading bodies of the two communist parties passed resolutions concerning the reforms of the economic management systems. The Central Committee of the Communist Party of Czechoslovakia passed a resolution on the 'Main Directions of Perfecting the System of Planning and Management' in January 1965. In Hungary, the Central Committee passed a first, more general resolution in December 1965 and a more elaborate one, 'On the Reform of the Economic Mechanism', in May 1966. Work by experts on the details followed these resolutions to arrive at workable measures.

SIMILARITY IN MAIN POINTS

A comprehensive reform of the economic system was introduced on 1 January 1967, in Czechoslovakia, and on 1 January 1968, in Hungary. One of the most important common features of the two reforms was their *comprehensiveness*. Changes concerning all important aspects of the system were introduced simultaneously and overnight. This makes an important difference in comparison with earlier efforts to perfect the system in the two countries, as well as in several other centrally planned economies during the 1960s. The designers of both reforms drew the conclusion from their respective earlier experiences that partial changes have little impact on the operation of the economy.

The *abolition of mandatory planning as a system* was the central element of both reforms. Mandatory target planning and quotas were abolished in both countries overnight, on 1 January 1967 and 1968, respectively. (In the Czechoslovak case, an important exception should be mentioned: export targets and import quotas were maintained in 1967 and were formally abolished on 1 January 1969 only.) Up to that time, decentralising reforms implied the reduction of only a number of mandatory targets in both countries and elsewhere; this time it was realised that the preservation of even one mandatory target could result in the preservation of the traditional attitudes of enterprises and major bodies that undermine efficient economic activity. As a result, the breaking down of the plan as a central feature of traditional Soviet-type planning was eliminated and has not been experienced (at least in the classical form) since then in Hungary. That has, in my view, made the Hungarian economic system fundamentally different from the classic form of planning prevalent in the rest of the centrally planned economies.

The abolition of mandatory targets was a precondition for and a result of the *lifting of centralised resource allocation*. Centralised allocation was abandoned except for a few items in both countries. Again, this is something that continues to be a dream for economists and managers in other centrally planned economies.

A comprehensive *price reform* was the third key element of the reforms in both countries. The simultaneous resetting of industrial wholesale prices in every five to ten years is a well-known concomitant of Soviet-type planning. Reshaping of the bureaucratic price system, e.g. the replacement of one pricing paradigm with another within the framework of bureaucratic pricing, has been part of the attempts to perfect the economic systems in several countries. The price reforms in both Czechoslovakia and Hungary represented something different: an – at least partial – shift from bureaucratic pricing to market pricing, and the introduction of a mixed price system with the coexistence of different forms of fixed and free prices. Free prices were to be subject to market interactions. They were assumed to fluctuate according to market conditions, and suppliers obtained a certain freedom in setting these prices according to their evaluation of the market situation. To create the conditions of such pricing, a first big step had to be made in equalising profitability between sectors and subsectors in the economy (particularly in manufacturing industry). This, however, necessitated another simultaneous resetting of wholesale prices (organised and implemented once again, but, and this was emphasised in both countries, for the last time by the centre).

This resetting of prices was necessary, among other things, to create favourable conditions for the new system of *enterprise motivation*. Plan fulfilment as the key motive for enterprise management had to disappear and be replaced by interest in higher enterprise incomes. The higher the actual income of the firm (and not the overfulfilment of the incomes plan), the higher the remuneration of the staff and the investment possibilities of the firm – that was the leading principle in both countries, be that income the *net income* (Czechoslovakia) or the *profit* (Hungary) of the firm. To create a clear link between a firm's actual income and the remuneration of the staff or the investment possibilities of the firm, a more or less uniform tax system was created in both countries. This replaced the earlier system of money transfers between enterprises and the state budget based on enterprise-specific arrangements, always subject to enterprise-specific considerations and bargaining between firms and state administration.

An interersting similarity in detail deserves mentioning here. The introduction of uniform rules could be very unfair in a world of enterprises supplied with capital in varying amounts due to arbitrary decisions of the bureaucracy in the past. To avoid this, the starting conditions of firms were equalised in both countries under the reforms: in Czechoslovakia, firms were to 'buy out' their capital assets in the course of seventeen years, while in Hungary the transfer of the depreciation allowance to the state budget was differentiated in accordance with the age of the firm's capital assets.

Both Czechoslovakia and Hungary are small countries highly dependent on *foreign trade*. The economic forms of and conditions for foreign trade activity were transformed in the same direction. Numerous industrial firms obtained direct export rights. Domestic prices were linked to actual export and import prices by means of a quasi exchange rate – the uniform price equaliser in Czechoslovakia and the foreign trade price multiplier in Hungary.

Investment was a field of economic activity where serious compromises seemed unavoidable. Still, a considerable part of investment was formally decentralised to enterprises. Different categories of investment projects were introduced in both countries from large projects approved by the government, and included within the national plan by item, small ones being decided on by the firms themselves. Investment in firms was to be financed, to a great extent, by self-financing and bank loans.

Planning, resource allocation, pricing, motivation, foreign trade and investment, these were the most important aspects of economic reforms. The reformers in the two countries followed essentially the same course regarding these key aspects.

SIMILAR COMPROMISES

The reforms were initiated by the same kind of governments under very similar economic and social conditions. No wonder that not only reform blueprints but also their shortcomings and compromises in implementation were similar.

Although the reform blueprints envisaged the reshaping of the price structure and allowed for a considerable liberalisation of *price setting* in both countries, they did not break with the autarkic orientation in pricing. The reformers intended that *domestic* costs and, to a limited degree, *domestic* market conditions should influence prices, but world market prices were not assumed to have a considerable impact on domestic prices. Since a quasi exchange rate was introduced in both countries, systems of 'financial bridges' between foreign prices and domestic cost and market conditions had to be created. After all, the introduction of uniform rules overnight would hit a great many firms and, consequently, the whole economy very strongly. In Czechoslovakia, a system of rebates and surcharges (*cenové srážky a přirážky*) was introduced, while in Hungary customs duties and export subsidies called government refunds (*állami visszatérítés*) had to play a similar role. Their gradual reduction was promised in both countries but, in fact, this could only partly be implemented. As a consequence, cost-plus pricing continued to prevail, and prices did not turn into reliable means of judging scarcity of goods and performance of firms under the new conditions.

Investment was the other area where changes were particularly limited. Big projects which, as is usual in centrally planned economies, required the bulk of investment outlays continued to be approved by the governments. Projects already in process when the reforms were introduced were continued and financed accordingly. Little remained for new projects initiated by the newly emancipated firms. Planning offices and ministries were still considered necessary to control this minority area of investment to assure the desirable structural proportions. They could argue that, because of unreliable price adjustments, enterprise profitability is an inadequate indicator of the desirability of investment. Bank loans for investment were, therefore, allocated more or less according to plan priorities in both countries.

Autonomy of enterprises was also endangered by the *continuous changes in the 'rules of game'*, the economic regulators in both countries. In Czechoslovakia, the system introduced in early 1966 for three years was replaced by a fundamentally different system in early 1967, implying much more fundamental changes. While the government promised to leave the system essentially unchanged for a few years, new restrictions were introduced in May 1967 (directly linking wage increases to labour productivity growth, freezing 25 per cent of profits, hardening the crediting of working assets, etc.). The system was modified in January 1968 again. In Hungary, too, the system introduced in early 1968 was revised a little by January 1969 (though essentially in the same spirit as promised: prices were somewhat liberalised, subsidies and tax exemptions reduced, etc.), but the changes which were decided on in late 1969 contradicted the main parameters of reform. (The rules of the distribution of bonuses were revised, the auxiliary industrial activities of agricultural collective farms were subject to restrictions, the principle of 'responsibility' of enterprises 'for supply' (*ellátási felelösség*) was proclaimed and enforced.)

DIFFERENCES IN IMPORTANT DETAILS

Most of the differences discussed in the following pages are of secondary importance compared to the similarities described above. This does not apply to the first difference to be discussed: the approach to the *organisational structure* of the economy. This was, in the two reform blueprints, fundamentally different.

In Czechoslovakia, state enterprises were grouped into associations during the late 1950s (under the preceding attempt at reform). The whole industry, controlled by ministries, was organised in 252 associations (*VHJ*), with a branch directorate at the top. Now, to achieve 'strong units' which are allegedly more suitable for greater autonomy, the associations (and the firms under them) were further amalgamated and the number of associations was reduced to ninety.

In Hungary, in the early 1960s, instead of forming associations, 'nation-wide big enterprises' were set up with numerous branches. Trusts were organised in some other branches. However, in some industries, medium enterprises and industrial directorates in the ministries were preserved. The latter and some trusts were abolished by 1968. As a consequence, although Hungarian industry was as highly monopolised as in Czechoslovakia, medium-level control bodies were eliminated from the system. Together with big firms prevailing in some industries (mining, steel, building materials, food processing), medium and small enterprises coexisted with large ones in machine-building and in light industries. In fact, there existed only two levels of control in Hungary (government and enterprises), even if the enterprise level often meant very big monopolies. Therefore, industrial lobbies that were strong in certain industries in Hungary as well as in Czechoslovakia were considerably weaker in others. Enterprise managers might feel freer in Hungary than in Czechoslovakia, particularly because Czechoslovak branch directorates were entitled to reallocate funds between enterprises (and made use of this right very widely), while in Hungary even ministries were deprived of that right.

This difference in the organisational structure certainly contributed to the difference in *planning practices*. As mentioned above, the abolition of mandatory planning targets was not implemented so consistently in Czechoslovakia as in Hungary: export targets and import quotas were preserved in 1967 and 1968. More important was the fact that Czechoslovak enterprises were obliged to present their plans to higher authority using uniform formulas with numerous 'oriented targets', essentially non-existent in Hungary. The elimination of medium-level intermediaries prevented Hungarians from returning to the comprehensive breaking down of plans even during the years of 'freezing the reform', while in Czechoslovakia the restoration of mandatory planning in 1970–1 proved to be easy.

The difference in the *procedure of the resetting of prices* was really only an important detail. The Czechoslovaks decided in 1966, with the intention of accelerating the introduction of reform, to accomplish the resetting of prices in a simplified way with the aid of computers, simultaneously calculating prices at various levels. The Hungarians, in turn, insisted on the traditional way of resetting prices which was much slower but somewhat less risky. Critics often explain inflationary tensions in Czechoslovakia during 1968–9 as a result of the resetting of prices. True, wholesale prices increased by roughly 30 per cent instead of the 22 per cent envisaged. Gross profits in prices amounted to about 70 per cent of wages instead of 22 per cent. But in Hungary, too, average profitability in industry achieved 10 per cent instead of the intended 6.5 per cent.

The difference in the 'overfulfilment' of profitability increased because of the different system of *taxation*. In Czechoslovakia, a system of resource taxes (*odvody*) was introduced and levied on capital and wages. The main tax was the linear 18 per cent tax on 'net income', essentially a tax on the wage fund. Such a system of taxation necessarily *enlarges* the differences between firms in terms of profitability and also the deviations from planned incomes. A linear tax in respect of net income is a regressive tax in respect of profits. Net income consists of wages and profits; wages are the more stable while profits are a more unstable and dynamic component. This tax system causes differences of income among firms, but also leaves them with more profit than the envisaged (planned) amount and relatively less is thus transferred to the state budget. The system is strongly stimulative (that was the reason for introducing it) *provided* prices are exogenous for the firm. However, this was not the case when the new system was introduced and enterprises could influence price-setting quite considerably. On the other hand, the system has a strong destabilising effect on domestic financial balances, and this was strongly felt in Czechoslovakia. The disponible incomes of firms were considerably higher in 1967 than planned: rather than having a deficit amounting to 16–40 billon crowns, they had a surplus of 3 billion in the first half of 1967. Instead of being strongly dependent on external finance, they presented additional demands in the marketplace.

The Hungarian tax system was based on a progressive profit tax. Wages were controlled separately while profits were divided into two parts (one used for remuneration and the other for investment); the first part was taxed progressively and the second by a linear tax rate. This system was much less stimulative but had less differentiating and destabilising effects.

Correspondingly, the two reform blueprints differed also in respect of *investment financing*. In Czechoslovakia, enterprises were supposed not to have money for investment, the bulk of this (60 per cent, according to the reformers' intention) being financed by bank credits (for the rest, 15 per cent came from the state budget, 24 per cent from amortisation allowances and only 1 per cent from enterprise incomes.) State control of the allocation of investment should have been asserted by means of credit. In fact, however, the enterprises were richer and could cover 40 per cent of investment from amortisation allowances and their own incomes. Under such conditions, the importance of the so-called 'selection procedure' (*výběrové řízení*) of investment proposals gained in importance and became more or less independent of the granting of bank credits.

In Hungary, the reform blueprint assigned a much lesser role (up to 20 per cent) to bank loans than in Czechoslovakia. Though Hungarian enterprises also proved to be richer than assumed, the difference *vis-à-vis* the blueprint was less striking. Even with higher incomes, most enterprises were unable to cover investment outlays without external financing. Consequently, state influence could be asserted by means of granting loans and government subsidies.

Summarising what has been said above, we can say that, on the one hand, the Czechoslovaks made more compromises in the field of organisation and planning which made the survival of old behavioural patterns easier. On the other hand, in the area of taxation and financing, the Czechoslovak solution was more selective, more stimulative but also more sensitive to deviations from the envisaged proportions, consequently making the whole system somewhat more vulnerable.

CONCLUDING REMARKS

What *explains* the differences? The main cause lies in the different political conditions for preparatory work. In Hungary, both the party leadership and the experts involved in the work remembered the lessons of the 1950s. They decided to undertake substantial changes in the system but at the same time were ready for sensible compromises. Adequate time (two full years) was made available for preparatory work and academic economists, government officials and managers were brought together in the groups of experts. Leading reform principles were made sufficiently clear and also accepted by the vast majority of the administration. The reform was introduced in 1968 after satisfactory preparatory work, with consistency in the main principles and care taken over the details. As a result, no acute tensions emerged in the first years and no spectacular retreats turned out to be necessary (the only exception being bonus distribution). In Czechoslovakia, the struggle between government officials and academic economists continued. The first compromise resulting in the transitional system introduced in January 1966, was so poor (numerous mandatory targets were preserved, financial relations individualised, etc.) that it was immediately attacked by reform-minded economists and had to be abandoned within a year. The next version was prepared in half a year with too many compromises (associations were maintained, new prices were frozen, etc.) and insufficient care for important details. Again, after a few months of operation, in May 1967, a substantial retreat took place (binding wage increases to the growth of labour productivity). The political turn of January 1968 gave the next positive impetus to reform.

Still, the differences presented above do not explain the different *outcome*. Despite all its weaknesses, the Czechoslovak system introduced in January 1967 was viable. If, in 1966, tensions in the Czechoslovak economy increased (partly due to the prereform expectations of firms, as well as in 1967 in Hungary), the restrictive policy of the government in 1967 was nearly as successful as in Hungary in 1968. Growth slowed down in both countries and domestic and external balances were consolidated. The achievements of the two reforms were also similar: supply followed demand considerably better than before. In Czechoslovakia, the unprecedented explosion of consumer demand in 1968–9 was well absorbed by the growing supply of consumer goods.

True, tensions increased during these years in the economy, but one has to keep the following in mind. The new economic system created by the reforms both in Czechoslovakia in 1967 and in Hungary in 1968 eliminated most of the traditional mandatory planning, without allowing for the operation of a competitive market. Market constraints have not become really relevant for firms. Under such conditions, the formal and informal authority of the government, the feeling of dependence on superiors, plays an important role and can have a paralysing effect in the long run but a stabilising effect in the short run. In 1967 (and in the first quarter of 1968), this factor was fully in force in Czechoslovakia, as well as in 1968 and later in Hungary. From March to April 1968 onwards, with the simultaneous growth in political power of the party leadership, the authority of the government over the economy gradually collapsed. Wage and investment demands, which the government could no longer resist, cumulated. The vulnerability of the system was seen to be particularly acute under such conditions.

24 The State of the Debate on Planning in Hungary

Jan Adam*

INTRODUCTION

The 1968 reform in Hungary meant great progress over what had existed before, but it was still far from what was needed to bring about a definite turn-round in the economy, one reason being that the space carved out for the working of market forces was quite narrow. 'We have abandoned the command planning system but we have not anchored in the port of regulated market,' wrote Bauer (1982). In addition, the reform came to a halt in 1972–3. Only under the pressure of the worsening economic situation did the authorities again start, at the end of the 1970s, to consider changes in the management system. It took some time for the Party (in 1984) to come up with a package of suggested changes which meant not only a return to the principles of the 1968 reform, but in some respects an advance beyond them. The promised changes were implemented slowly and inconsistently. Only when the situation started to worsen again, after a short recovery, did the authorities devise a stabilisation programme in 1987 (for more see Adam, 1989, p. 129); at a 1988 conference, the Party carried out far-reaching changes in its leadership and promised further reforms in the economic as well as the political field. In the economic field, the reform was to create 'conditions for the working of a socialist market economy' (see the Standpoint of the Conference of the Party, Supplement to *Népszabadság*, 23 May 1988).

The 1980s were marked by debates revolving around the problem of ensuring the proper combination of planning and market. These debates had quite a significant influence on the activities of the authorities. The aim of this chapter is to give an insight into

* I would like to thank the Social Sciences and Humanities Research Council of Canada, Ottawa, for the extended research grant which enabled me to work on this study.

the development of the thinking of Hungarian economists about the role of planning.

THE ROLE OF PLANNING

The debate on planning has revolved around the following questions: what should the function of planning in the management system be, what should be planned, what should the role of annual, medium-term and long-term plans be, what is the relationship between planning and economic policy, how should state and enterprise plans be harmonised, how should the planning system be democratised? – just to mention the most important ones.

The length set for this chapter does not allow me to discuss all the problems mentioned. I will confine myself to the most important ones and, in addition, to the 1980s. I will start out with the debate in the Planning Office in 1983 which was attended by many of the best known reformers.[1] With some simplification it can be said that two groups of views crystallised in this debate. In one group, the role of planning, as designed in the 1968 reform, was seen as correct in substance and not in need of change. According to Ákos Balassa, who represented this view, the planning's function is, among other things, to detect the possibilities of economic development, and to determine the growth rates, equilibrium conditions and the main proportions. The State should help to implement the most important structural changes, primarily by research, but also by investment activities. Balassa believes that, in energy and basic material production, government intervention should be direct, whereas, in the competitive sphere, both indirect and direct methods should be used. In brief, Balassa's views were in line with actual government planning activities at the time.

The second group included quite a broad range of views. All agreed that planning should play an important role in the expansion of the infrastructure and in some non-competitive branches such as energy. As to the competitive sphere, some took more or less the position that the government should stay out of production. To Márton Tardos, the government role in the development of the competitive sphere should be limited to the setting of priorities and 'the determination of the degree of their support' (1984, p. 189). In other words, if the government feels that a certain branch or line of production should be developed preferentially, that should be publicised and organisations which are willing to involve themselves in such projects should get government support.

Tardos's views are in line with his opposition to centralisation of decision-making about allocation of resources in the hands of government or the national bank and with his favouring the development of a capital market.

The 1983 debate took place as the political leadership prepared for new moves in economic reform. The Party resolution of April 1984, mentioned above, brought no important changes in planning itself: 'The national economic plan is the instrument for the assertion of the societal interest and the basic instrument of management' (*Népszabadság*, 19 April 1984).

The appearance of the 'Turning Point and Reform' in 1987, which had a powerful effect on Party and government and on intellectual circles above all, because of its sharp criticism, regarded by many as justified, and because it came from well-known reformers,[2] was an important milestone in the debate about the economic mechanism, including planning. The study gives a critical analysis of the dire economic situation in the country and suggests how to overcome it. It calls for the establishment of a market economy and a radical overhaul of the planning system. According to the study, the new planning should be based on a macrofinancial plan. The departure point for such a plan is to be the determination of internal and external equilibria. The main instrument of management should be money supply regulation, which should play the central role in the regulation of aggregate demand and will, in the long run, the authors hope, open the door to an efficient restructuring of the economy. This refers to the competitive sphere. As to the non-competitive sphere, mainly the infrastructure, the role of planning should be greater and direct (1987, pp. 653–6).

The 'Turning Point and Reform' was published with some modifications in *Közgazdasági Szemle*, accompanied by a 'standpoint' written by some members of the economic work-team, an advisory group of the Central Committee of the Party (Standpoint, 1987).[3] The writers of the 'standpoint' reject mainly the part of the study which deals with planning and which adds up almost to a rejection of planning. They maintain that the study overestimates the importance of monetary policy, and that it alone cannot solve such current problems as a restructuring of the economy. Government coordination policy is indispensable and cannot be given up. Neither can the government leave to the market and to representative interest groups the harmonisation of conflicting interests. On the other hand, the writers of the 'standpoint' recognise the need to revitalise and modernise planning, and call for a greater role for financial instruments in planning. 'It is necessary to create a planning system which would be more open, flexible and willing to accept and absorb the impacts of the market' (ibid., p. 667).

The adoption of the stabilisation programme in 1987 and the promise of an acceleration of the reform gave a new impetus to the debate about planning. Interest in the subject was substantially enhanced in the aftermath of the Party conference which brought about the ousting of the old guard, headed by J. Kádár, from the leadership, and promised new changes in the management system.

The debates on the role of planning are proceeding at present mostly in non-public meetings of government officials and experts. From what has penetrated to the public arena, it can be assumed that some important changes in the functions of planning will occur. It cannot be otherwise since recent changes, whose purpose is the expansion of market forces, such as reorganisation of the banking system, provisions for the establishment of a capital market and the introduction of joint stock companies on a large scale, have reduced the possible role of planning.

The ministry of finance, whose former research institute played the leading part in the final formulation of the study, 'Turning Point and Reform,' supports, in substance, the demands in the study and is pushing for a substantially reduced role for planning and for a larger role for monetary policy. The Planning Office, to judge from K. Lóránt's article (1988) and other documents, still sees an important role for planning. According to Lóránt, planning should be focused on what he calls strategic planning, government management and coordinative activity. By strategic planning he means the determination of the goals of the economy, especially with regard to structural changes, and also of the development of the management system of the economy. By economic management (*gazdaságmenedzselés*) he understands the implementation of the strategic goals. This does not mean that he favours a return to operational planning; what he wants is for the government to focus only on important processes. The coordinative activity should lie in coordinating regulative activity with regard to pricing, wages, forcign trade, etc. (ibid., pp. 86–7).

Judging from the latest reports from Hungary (*Népszabadság*, 11 October 1988), it seems that the market will become the main coordinating mechanism, whereas planning will be limited to areas where the market is not efficient enough or is not acceptable.

TYPES OF PLANS

All the participants in the 1983 debate agreed that the main focus of planning should be on the long-term plan. Róbert Hoch (1984, p. 24), for example, maintained that the annual plan was a remnant of the traditional system and therefore had no justification. In his paper, written for the debate, László Antal (1984, pp. 48–9) argued that the annual plan has not been a real plan, but rather an analysis whose purpose is to figure out whether the strategic goals and priorities are realistic. In normal times, its scope should be limited to influencing variables, mainly of a monetary nature, which have an effect on the business cycle in the short run. The rest, including changes in the regulation system, should be left to the decision of Parliament. A similar idea has been expressed by Tardos (1984, p. 196).

The debate about the role of plans of different duration entered into a more important phase recently due to serious considerations about changes in the function of planning. The debate has concentrated primarily on the middle-term and annual plans. Some would prefer a shorter, three-year plan. This would make the plan more realistic, open and flexible, since a shorter period would allow the expected developments inside the country and abroad to be estimated more accurately. However, other considerations, such as the coordination of plans with CMEA countries, and the political cycles – Party congress, parliamentary elections – favour five-year plans. In the event, the five-year plan is retained – which is probable – and it is suggested that goals for the first three years should be worked out in detail at the beginning, and later, the second half should be elaborated upon.

Many argue against the continuation of the annual plan. The main objection is that the plan is too short to be relevant for the needed structural changes. The fact is also alluded to that the state budget could take over some of the functions of the annual plan. The Planning Office maintains, however, that the annual plan, though in a modified form, is still needed for its coordinating role (Illés, 1988; Bossányi, 1988).

DEMOCRATISATION OF PLANNING

According to one author (Huszár, 1987), democratisation includes two things – on the one hand, participation in decision-making about plan objectives, and, on the other, harmonisation of the interests of different segments of the population. Many economists prefer to use the term 'social control over planning' instead of 'participation in planning'.[4] The change in term is the result not only of a push towards a general democratisation of political and economic life, but also of planning's recent dismal record. Planning is blamed for the very slow adjustment of the economy to needed changes in its structure and for the increasing lag in technological progress. This state of affairs has been caused to a great extent by the fact that in the distribution of funds for investment, power relations in the Party have often played a more important role than economic considerations.

In order to ensure that control over planning is not reduced to a formality, many preconditions must be met. One is that the plans must be worked out in more than one variant, which has already been happening for some time. Some economists would like to see that the hypotheses and figures which are essential for the working out of the variants are accessible to the public, primarily to experts, social organisations and, of course, Parliament (see Kovács, 1984). Only by making accessible all the materials pertinent to successive stages of planning will the public and experts have a good idea about the opportunity costs of different variants of the plans and be able to pass competent judgement. It is especially important that Parliament, whose role has substantially increased recently and will continue to increase, get the plan variants in a package which will enable it to scrutinise them in an expert fashion (see Nyers, 1986).

Unlike the traditional system which was based on an illusive idea of identity of interests between society and its segments, the system advanced in the 1968 reform had as one of its points of departure recognition of the divergence of interests between different groups in society. One of the tasks of planning is to detect these divergencies and harmonise them. To achieve this goal means giving representatives of the different social groups a say in the formulation of the aims of plans as well as their targets. At present, the representatives still come from the known mass organisations; however, quickly spreading, new pressure groups must also be given a hearing. The practice of planning hitherto has shown that it is easier to detect the divergence of interests than to find a proper harmonisation (see Huszár, 1987).

The expected changes in the role of planning will surely bring about a change in the role of the Planning Office. Those who push for management of the economy primarily by monetary policy would like, of course, to see the Planning Office stripped of many of its functions and turned into an agency concerned with prognoses and concepts of economic development (see Bossányi, 1988). Some would like a transfer of at least short-term planning to the ministry of finance (see Antal, 1984, p. 31). Needless to say, the Planning Office and all those who would like to see planning play an important role oppose such ideas. Nevertheless, the Planning Office will have to share the planning activities to a greater extent than before with functional ministries and central agencies as well as with branch ministries (Lóránt, 1988).

COMMENTS ON THE DEBATES

Due to limited space, comments must be short and will be confined to a discussion of monetary policy and the democratisation of planning.

Considering the great disappointment with central planning, it is understandable that the authors of 'Turning Point and Reform' are looking for indirect methods for managing the economy. It is, however, not entirely clear why they put such stress on monetary policy, unless it is only meant as a part of the present austerity policy. One reason for the great stress may be disappointment with fiscal policy (the inability of the government to restrain subsidies and tax breaks and to maintain a balanced budget) and another, related to the first, the belief that monetary policy can be carried out independently of the government. (And this may be one of the reasons why the authors asked for independence for the national bank.) It is an illusion to assume that any government can afford to give up completely its influence on monetary policy. Most Western governments exercise influence on the monetary policy carried out by the central bank (e.g. in Canada, the Minister of Finance, after approval by the Cabinet, can give written instructions to the Bank of Canada with regard to monetary policy). In addition, economic policy cannot be successful if monetary policy is not combined with other policies, primarily fiscal. It is, for example, impossible to ensure full employment or even low rates of unemployment combined with a low rate of inflation by monetary policy alone.

Even if the importance of government in distributing funds for investment purposes dramatically declines, the government will continue to influence the direction of economic development. As a result, there is a difficult problem which has not yet been addressed, namely, making sure that economic considerations prevail over special interests in conditions where the government is not fully controlled by the public, and outsiders do not have the necessary information to make an expert judgement.

Notes

1. The papers presented there as well as the debate were published by the Economic Institute of the Hungarian Academy of Sciences in its *Studies* (*Vita . . .* , 1984).
2. This is a collective work written by social scientists, primarily economists, from various research institutes, the media and communications, and edited by research fellows of the former research institute of the ministry of finance.
3. The writers of the standpoint are well-known economists and party and government officials. To mention the most important: Iván T. Berend (President of the Academy of Sciences), B. Csikós-Nagy (former chairman of the Material and Price Board), I. Hetényi (former Minister of Finance), R. Nyers (former and present member of the Politbureau).
4. For example, in the summary of the debate in the Planning Office, this term has been used (*Vita . . .* , 1984, p. 29).

References

Adam, Jan (1989) *Economic Reforms in the Soviet Union and Eastern Europe since the 1960s* (London: Macmillan; New York: St Martin's Press, 1989).

Antal, László (1984) in *Vita . . .* (Budapest).

Balassa, Ákos (1984) in *Vita . . .* (Budapest).

Balassa, Ákos (1987) *Tervgazdasági Fórum*, vol. III, no. 3, pp. 65–78

Bauer, Tamás (1982) *Mozgó Világ*, vol. VIII, no. 11, pp. 17–42.
Bossányi, Katalin (1988) *Népszabadság*, 13 April.
Hoch, Róbert (1984) in *Vita* . . . (Budapest).
Huszár, Józsefné (1987) *Tervgazdasági Fórum*, vol. III, no. 3, pp. 120–9.
Illés, Iván (1988) *Figyelö*, vol. XXXII, no. 14, p. 5.
Kovács, János (1984) in *Vita* . . . (Budapest).
Lóránt, Karoly (1988) *Tervgazdasági Fórum*, vol. IV, no. 2, pp. 83–90.
Nyers, Rezsö (1986) *Tervgazdasági Förum*, vol. II, no. 2, pp. 7–18.
Tardos, Márton (1984) in *Vita* . . . (Budapest).
The Standpoint of the Conference of the Party (1988), *Népszabadság*, 23 May.
The Standpoint of the work-team by the Central Committee of the Party (1987) *Közgazdasági Szemle*, vol. XXXIV, no. 6, pp. 664–70.
Tinbergen, Jan (1964) *Central Planning* (New Haven: Yale University Press).
Turning Point and Reform (Fordulat és reform), (1987) ed. by L. Antal, L. Bokros, I. Csillag, L. Lengyel, Gy. Matolcsy, *Közgazdasági Szemle*, vol. XXXIV, no. 6, pp. 642–64.
Vita a népgazdasági tervezés feladatairól az 1980-as évek Magyarországán (1984), Publication of the Economic Institute of the Hungarian Academy of Sciences (Budapest).

25 The Evolution of Socialist Economic Theories and the Strategic Options of Reform in China

Jinglian Wu

The course of China's economic reform in the past thirty years witnessed a gradual evolution from traditional Stalinist economic theory to a socialist market economic theory that makes full use of modern economics. In the course of this evolution, the following schools came into being: (i) the traditional, 'classical' theory of centralised socialism; (ii) decentralised administrative socialism; (iii) 'revised' administrative socialism; and (iv) socialist market economic theory. These four types constitute competing schools of socialist economic theories.

'CLASSICIAL' ADMINISTRATIVE SOCIALISM: RIGID 'COMMAND ECONOMY'

From the time when the Chinese Communist Party was founded to the initial period of the People's Republic, 'classical', centralised administrative socialism was in an absolutely dominant position. For a long time it was taken as the cardinal truth, following Marx's and Engel's theory, that after public ownership is established, the whole economy will be managed as a nation-wide factory without the existence of a market. After the People's Republic was founded, the Chinese government, with the help of 'Soviet experts', based the economy solely on Stalinist 'political economy of socialism'.

Chinese society had been predominantly a small-holding peasant economy. Just as Marx, in *The Eighteenth Brumaire of Louis*

Bonaparte put it, in countries there was a long and solid tradition that administrative power was in a dominant position. Therefore, during the first five-year plan period, China's socialist economic system was more centralised and dependent on administrative coordination than that of the Soviet Union. Because this facilitated the concentrated use of scarce resources to satisfy the government's preference, and to develop sectors so as to increase state strength, it had much appeal for developing socialist countries that were trying to 'catch up with and bypass' Western developed nations. Even today, whenever disorder and difficulties arise from economic reform, some officials and labourers recall those 'golden years' – the first five-year plan.

DECENTRALISED ADMINISTRATIVE SOCIALISM: 'DELEGATING OF POWER TO LOWER LEVELS'

Just as the highly centralised administrative command economy embraced the entire society in the 'socialist high tide' in 1955, its defects were thoroughly exposed. Beginning at the end of 1955, all departments under the government made a systematic summation of the work they had done in the first three years of the first five-year plan. But this analysis was conducted almost completely within the framework of the conventional 'socialist political economy', except for an additional theory of 'mobilising people's initiative' which was used as a new weapon in making the analysis.

Chinese leaders, having realised the shortcomings of the Soviet system, began to do their best to 'find a path for building socialism in accordance with China's specific conditions'. Mao Zedong further developed this line of thought of 'mobilising people's initiatives' as a key difference between his and Stalin's models. It was this emphasis which gradually helped to formulate the so-called 'socialist general guideline' of 1958, which had as its starting point 'attaching importance in the masses' socialist enthusiasm' and had 'actively mobilising all factors and building socialism in a faster, better and more economical manner' as its basic principle. Most of the conclusions of the analysis on conventional socialism were incorporated in Mao Zedong's speech, 'On the Ten Major Relationships', he gave to the politbureau of the Chinese Communist Party in April 1956. The speech held that the major shortcomings of the traditional Soviet system were the 'overconcentration of decision-making powers' which was harmful to the production of initiative of local governments, production units and producers. Therefore, this system must be reformed. The general orientation of the reform should be to give local governments, production units and workers more power and more benefits.

In accordance with these approaches, China launched an economic reform in 1958 for the first time since the socialist economy was established. Since the reform was conducted in an unusual political atmosphere, i.e. after the 'Anti-Rightist' Campaign in 1957 and during the movement of 'criticising Yugoslav revisionists' in 1958, only the following reform measures were taken: (i) The great majority of central ministry enterprises were transferred to local control. (ii) In production planning, the system of unified balance achieved through the State Planning Commission was transformed into one based on regional planning and bottom-to-top balancing. The number of products under the control of the State Planning Commission was greatly reduced, and local authorities were granted important planning and allocative powers. (iii) In investment planning, a subcontracting system was adopted: the central authorities distributed funds to the local authorities, who added their own funds and then chose investment projects on their own. (iv) Reforms reduced the amount and the categories of materials inventories distributed by the State Planning Commission and the ministries, leaving the rest to be distributed by local government. The local authorities could reallocate centrally rationed materials to enterprises in their region, including central ministry enterprises, and could also share in the surplus output produced by local enterprises. (v) The financial system was sharply decentralised: taxes were assigned to provincial government for collection, with various tax retention rates, fixed for five years. Meanwhile, the central government gave the power to reduce, exempt or increase a tax to the local authorities. (vi) The former highly centralised credit system was replaced by 'delegating credit control to lower levels and controlling only the debit–credit differential'.

The general framework of administrative socialism (the administrative coordinated command economy) remained unchanged, only separated into several smaller and more or less independent command economies, with enterprises remaining as subordinates to administrative organs at various levels. This decentralising administrative socialist system which, together with the rural People's

Commune, constituted the institutional foundation for the disaster of 1958.

After the disorder of 1958, the Chinese government undertook a series of recentralising measures. However, the intended recentralisation has never been completely achieved. The ideas and practice which has been termed 'administrative decentralisation', from the East European reform experience, had a profound impact in China. Since 1958, words such as *chengbao* and *baogan*[1] often appear in Chinese economic documents and refer to the relationship between the superior and the subordinate in the decentralised administrative socialist economy, determining their respective commitments through bargaining. On the other hand, in the consquent reforms the policies of administrative decentralisation were adopted again and again.

After the Cultural Revolution, although decentralised administrative socialism was no longer the mainstream of China's reform, it did not lose all its influence. For example, in 1980 China lauched the reform of *fen zao chi fan* ('eating in different canteens'), requiring enterprises to turn over income (taxes and profits) to government agencies according to their jurisdiction, and a 'contract' system into setting of financial, credit and foreign trade targets level by level was adopted by the central government.

'REVISIONISTS' OF ADMINISTRATIVE SOCIALISM: THE INTEGRATION OF PLANNING AND MARKET

Administrative decentralisation leads to the cycle of 'decentralisation – confusion – recentralisation – stagnation'. This makes more and more people realise that administrative decentralisation is bound to cause disorder in the national economy. An effective solution should be found to improve the socialist economy.

In 1961, Sun Yefang, a noted Chinese economist, pointed out that the crucial question of economic reform was not the distribution of power among various levels of administrative organs, but the relationship between the autonomous enterprises and the State. Proceeding from this view, Sun Yefang, on the one hand, did not agree with 'natural economic theory' which refused to acknowledge enterprises' independence and right to exchange commodities in accordance with the 'law of value', refusing the practice of material balance planning. On the other hand, he opposed the 'commodity economic theory' which stated that the law of market and equilibrium prices was still playing a role in the socialist economy. Because he maintained that enterprises should have full decision-making power over their daily operation and stressed the importance of the law of value, Sun Yefang became the first victim in the purge of 'revisionists' that began in the mid-1960s.

After the Cultural Revolution, Sun Yefang's economic theory won support from more and more people, becoming a prevailing theory for economic reforms. The basic framework projected by this theory for the socialist economy is to combine the strengths of a planned and a market economy and that the major relations in the national economy are determined by central planning, but daily operation activities are left to enterprises; the State, using 'economic levers' including prices, to guide the economic activities of enterprises. After the Third Plenum of the Eleventh Central Committee, this line of thinking became the theoretical foundation for economic reform in cities, especially among state sectors. Between 1979 and 1983 the prevailing reform slogan was 'integration of planning and market'. Many Chinese economists – myself included – were active supporters of this approach.

Of course, there were several different understandings of 'integration of planning and market', but to the majority of Chinese reformers, their views were formulated under the influence of Sun Yefang's idea that 'major decision-making power should be monopolised by the State and minor decision-making power should be delegated to enterprises', and W. Brus's early 1960 model of planned economy with a built-in market mechanism. In practice, this approach evolved into a reform strategy that had, as its fundamental starting point, 'delegation of power' and 'invigoration of enterprises' for the urban economic system reforms. The main measure, to 'invigorate enterprises', was to relax physical control over them and to 'delegate power and relinquish revenues to them'. After the fall of the Gang of Four in 1976, economic reform in China was carried out along this line.

However, due to a lack of supporting reforms in other aspects, and especially in the price system, the enterprises which had a certain amount of autonomy were not bound by fair market competition. Therefore, the mobilised initiative of enterprises did not correspond to the interests of the entire national economy; on the contrary, it caused disorder in the macroeconomy. As a result, an austerity programme and readjustment had to be carried out in the national economy in 1981.

In 1984, reform regained momentum and the State Council promulgated the Provisional Regulations Concerning Further Extending the Decision-making Power of State-owned Enterprises in May. These regulations made it clear that state-owned enterprises had the following powers: (i) To set production according to market demand, after fulfilling state plans; (ii) To sell, on their own, a certain part of their production; (iii) To set prices on the products they sell on their own; (iv) To utilise the profits retention funds; (v) To rearrange their staff, and appoint middle-level administrative cadres.

The above reform helped state enterprises to move away from merely passively fulfilling the mandatory state plan. There has been a clear reorientation towards growth and the pursuit of profit. Enterprise management is active and full of initiative. The invigorating of the economy can be seen from the rising industrial growth rate, although output growth was not due to improved efficiency. Our calculations show that between 1981 and 1984, the annual TFP growth rate was only 0.6 per cent. The share of total factor productivity in the sources of 1981–5 was only 8.2 per cent of total industrial growth, far lower than that of the major industrial countries. Meanwhile, a rising trend in both the budget deficit and the inflation rate was becoming more and more obvious.

With regard to the above mentioned phenomenon, Chinese economists have drawn different conclusions. Some reformers, who regarded 'delegating power and relinquishing revenues to lower levels' (DPRR) and 'invigorating enterprises' as the major objectives of reform, believe that the rapid GNP growth shows the success of this strategy. If endeavours continue along this path, a new economic system will be established. Moreover, they did not think the present inflation was worth considering. According to their understanding, international experience had proved that an appropriate inflation contributes to economic growth with little risk.

Some of the reformers (myself included) draw a completely different conclusion. They maintain that the major causes for the economic fluctuations after 1984 are the 'fundamental shortcomings in the present economic structure and system' resulting from the existing 'dual system', which is neither a planning nor a market system but a monetary economy coordinated by administrative power.[2] The inherent defects of this system cannot be overcome by further DPRR and 'invigorating enterprises', because this is not enough to help the promotion of efficiency.

SOCIALIST MARKET ECONOMY: 'THE STATE REGULATES THE MARKET AND THE MARKET GUIDES ENTERPRISES'

The criticism of the above mentioned socialist economic theories and the reflections on China's reform in the past few years have given rise to the theory of the socialist market system, and the approach of reform whose objective is to marketise the entire economy.

As early as the 1956 'Thaw' period, Gu Zhun, an outstanding economist, pointed out that an alternative model would be one under which enterprises make decisions freely according to market price changes. However, very few economists raised questions as he did, and his opinion did not have much impact and was soon forgotten.

It was not until 1980 when economic fluctuations occurred, that Xue Muqiao, a prominent economist and leading member of the Economic Reform Office under the State Council, pointed out the limitations of previous reform that attached importance only to incentive mechanisms. He maintained that emphasis should be placed on the 'reform of the system of price administration' and the 'reform of commercial channels' so as gradually to abolish the administrative pricing system in favour of a commodity market and a financial market. Xue Muqiao's opinions and those of Ota Sik, who was then visiting China, about building an aggregate planning and independent enterprise guided by the market, opened a new horizon for Chinese reformers. Some of the Chinese leaders called for price reform. However, mainly because of the hostile attitude of the conventional communist ideology towards market, the price reform failed to win the support of the majority of the leadership.

The second economic fluctuations of 1984 made more people consider seriously the shortcomings in China's reform theory and reform strategy. Their reflections gave rise to the 'coordination reform group' or the 'comprehensive reform group' (with which I fully associate myself). Their main points are as follows:

— The major defects of the old system is that scarce resources
are allocated by means of administrative directives and a
mandatory plan. Because of the major shortcomings in the
information and motivation mechanisms, the system cannot
function effectively. If this way of allocation remains
unchanged, measures for 'strengthening incentives' can only
introduce chaos and are not capable of achieving their desired
goals.

— The only system which can be substituted for administrative
coordination is the market system. Therefore, it is not enough
to monetise the economy. The important thing is to make the
market the chief allocator of scarce resources and the chief
coordinator of decision-making. Of course, as the market allocation system exercises guidance after the event, it may easily
give rise to fluctuations. This calls for necessary social guidance
and management of the market.

— A market economy with macromanagement is an organic
system that comprises three aspects: (i) independent enterprises; (ii) a competitive market system; and (iii) a macroregul-
ation system based on the market. Unless these three have
been basically established, the system cannot function
efficiently. Therefore, economic reform must proceed in a coordinated and synchronised way in these three interrelated
aspects.

— The market system can be based on various ownership patterns
with public ownership as the dominant form. Under this
system, the government only functions as a social administrative
body rather than the owner of public assets, let alone as manager of the enterprises. In those companies, ownership and
management are completely separate, with managers fully
entrusted with the authority to control the companies.

— Socialism does not exclude the market system. This is not only
because, according to socialism, a good system is the one that
has higher productivity, but also because the market system is
not naturally antagonistic to socialist principles.

In accordance with those theories, the conclusion was drawn
that if a competitive market system was not established until
long after the direct administrative command system was dis-
mantled, then there would not be an effective socialist market

economy, but an 'administratively regulated monetary commodity economy'. Sooner or later, this would lead to investment expansion, sluggish growth of supplies, runaway inflation and difficulties for further reform. They also drew up a series of overall scenarios for China's reform and plans to implement them, which revolve around the following main points: determined measures should be taken to speed the reform of the price formation mechanism and lift the control of prices. In the meantime, supporting reforms should be carried out in areas ranging from the types of enterprise organisations, the taxation system, the financial system, the banking system, and the system of both domestic and foreign trade in the economic system in three to five years.

Necessary conditions must be created for these long-step comprehensive reforms to be carried out smoothly. It is essential to adopt the stategy of 'taking control of currency and lifting the control of prices', to ensure that no serious inflation will occur in the course of the reform.

Keeping the above mentioned reform approaches in mind, the economy should be put on the new track at the earliest date, so as to make it possible for the economic system under which 'the state regulates the market and the market guides the enterprises' to begin to work. After all this is done, efforts will be made to seek improvement and perfection. Because piecemeal reform has caused more problems than it has solved, a comprehensive reform approach has gained momentum since 1984, the main aspects of it being accepted by the National Congress of the Chinese Communist Party in September 1985 and incorporated in the 'Proposals of CPC Central Committee for the Seventh Five-Year Plan'. In accordance with the Proposals, the Chinese government planned, while continuing to improve the environment and initiate comprehensive reforms in the pricing system, the taxation system, the financial system, the banking system, and the system of domestic and foreign trade. But it is very difficult for the majority of people to understand socialist market economics immediately. For this reason, the comprehensive reform approach of 1986 was defeated in the winter of that year as it was severely opposed by economists and those with vested interests in the current dual system.

Although this approach was not adopted, it seems to us that it is the only road to success.

CONCLUSIONS

From the winter of 1986 to the spring of 1987, the government decided to avoid price reform and focused instead on enterprise reforms together with reforms in planning, investment, materials supply, finance, banking and foreign trade as supportive measures. Evidently, this strategy failed to achieve the anticipated results because economic contradictions and conflicts accumulated. In May 1988, the Chinese government once again mentioned the necessity of implementing price reform and other supporting reforms in the three links of the system of enterprises, market and macromanagement. Because China has missed several golden opportunities for launching comprehensive reform, the defects of a monetised economy dominated by the administration, became even more obvious; economic structure and efficiency suffered and budget deficits and inflationary pressures mounted. The economic environment for reform is very tense at present. In order to guarantee the smooth progress of the reforms, the Chinese government adopted an austerity programme in the Autumn of 1988 to stabilise the overheated economy and controlling aggregate demand. The future of China's reform and the progress of the modernisation drive depends, to a great extent, on how well the economy is stabilised and reform is deepened.

As can be clearly seen from the tortuous course of China's reforms, it is of great significance to the progress and realisation of the economic objectives to be clear (in theory) about the market orientation of the reform, and genuinely to understand how the market economy operates under socialism. Therefore, in order to make reform a success, it is essential, on the basis of the integration of theory and practice, to make a careful and systematic summation of the reforms carried out by socialist countries in the past few decades, to develop economic science and to establish socialist market economic theories. This is the only way China can improve her understanding and base the market-oriented economic reform on a more scientific foundation.

Notes

1. In Western documents, *bao* is usually translated as 'contract', but this is not accurate and may lead to misunderstanding. This is because in a modern economy, a contract is signed by two legally equal entities, but in the *bao* system, although the transaction takes the form of a contract, it is between a superior and a subordinate. According to some Western observers, the *cai zheng bao gan* (fiscal contract system) in China is quite similar to 'tax farming' in Europe in the eighteenth century.
2. In the course of their reforms, socialist countries are often in danger of being side-tracked into 'administrative coordinated monetary economy'. Janos Kornai called this economic system 'the indirect bureaucratic'. For a market-oriented reform, the administrative coordinated monetary economy is only a blind alley.

References

Jinglian Wu, Zhou Xiaochuan *et al.* (1988) *The Integrated Design of China's Economic Reform* (Beijing: The Prospect Publising House).
Liu Guoguang (1984) *Selected Works* (Taiyuan: Shanxi People's Publishing House).
Sun Yefang (1984) 'On the Financial Question of the Economy Under the Ownership by the Whole People', in *Selected Works of Sun Yefang*, Chinese edn. (Taiyuan: Shanxi People's Publishing House).
Xue Muqiao (1984) *An Anthology of Xue Muqiao's Economic Essays*, Chinese edn. (Beijing: The People's Publishing House).
Zhou Taihe, Gao Shangquan *et al.* (1984) *Economic Structural Reform in China Today* (Beijing: The Publishing House of Social Science of China).

26 The Evolution of Economic Systems: A Summary

Karl-F. Raible

The Evolution of Economic Systems tries to arrange into some kind of pattern several totally different ways of theoretical thinking and practical experiences from both the East and the West. This, we believe, is the only way of expressing the common interests, the differences, but also the common problems which affect all of us.

Even if, at first sight, the West seems to be in a much better position – our material situation and our standard of living are much higher and even Third World countries are overtaking the Eastern economies – we nevertheless have to realise that our society is also suffering from stagnation, bureaucracy, cyclical economic crisis, etc. The term 'eurosclerosis' was an attempt to describe the lack of dynamism in Europe a few years ago. In this context, *Ernst Heuss* talks of 'sclerosis of association and law'. Rent-seeking pressure groups, lobbying, distributional coalitions slow down the diffusion of new technologies and reduce the productivity and efficiency of our economy. Monopolistic structures and increasing protectionism jeopardise free world trade, yet free trade can only be of benefit to all participants. This enumeration could easily be continued, and it is indeed surprising how well our economy is doing despite all these influences.

Besides these negative factors, we have to acknowledge new challenges which might jeopardise our standard of living: the ecological, environmental issue, unemployment, Third World conflict, income distribution, the humanisation and democratisation of our working sphere, etc., but also changing values, changing paradigms, the change of *Weltbild*, questions which are gaining more and more importance.

Jan Tinbergen points out that the priority of socialism has changed due to the threat of nuclear weapons. Nowadays, mutual security, tolerance, and peaceful cooperation of all are required. Only if the security of all societies can be guaranteed, can the former socialist priority – social justice – be realised. Tinbergen shows us the way of further cooperation instead of confrontation. He regards the common threat as a chance to overcome the tense relationship between East and West. The common problems and challenges of mankind, such as the pollution of the environment, the Third World crisis, etc., can only be solved by cooperation and mutual trust.

Gerhard Schwarz highlights the interdependence between political and economic conditions. Social, political and economic life are closely interrelated and causal reciprocity of the respective systems may be noticed. Though, according to him, a market economy and an undemocratic government can hardly coexist over a long period of time, the interdependence has to be seen in historical terms. Pure forms of political and economic orders cannot be implemented and tensions between both are inherent in them.

The pollution of our environment is caused by the reduction of nature to simple factors of production, as *Hans Christoph Binswanger, Malte Faber and Reiner Manstetten* demonstrate. Time as a limiting factor has been abolished by modern economics, the fascination with 'progress' has replaced God. The Faustian element has taken over the regime, mankind creates a new world of his own, of his own freedom.

Leonhard Bauer and *Herbert Matis* emphasise that humans are not autarkical, but have to be regarded as part of their social environment. New concepts, changes of behaviour, of the living process are tested for their effectiveness and are decisive parts of the system's reproduction.

Gerhard O. Mensch focuses on the 'historical moment', i.e. the structural readiness for basic innovations and the necessity of the right time for reforms in order to succeed. There are 'cumulative causes . . . to both the emergence of new needs . . . and the emergence of sufficient conditions for their favourable . . . reception'.

The interdependence between political life and economic science is the subject of the survey by *Alfred Meier* and *Susanne Haury*. Communication problems often exist between economic advisers and politicians. Their different interests are not always compatible and lead to misunderstandings. Therefore, the economist should participate in political life: he should be part of the political system and think and behave like a politician.

Entrepreneurship is the driving force behind capitalism. There is permanent innovative pressure, according to *Jochen Röpke*, either to invent new technologies and to introduce new products or to lose one's foothold in the market. The limit of this process can be found in rent-seeking and institutional constraints. Technological change, as *Ernst Heuss* states, leads to the cracking of old, obsolete structures and to a transformation of the technological, social and economic framework. Stagnation is caused by the probable loser from transformation. *René Höltschi* and *Christian Rockstroh* talk in this context of a temporary 'mismatch', which has to be overcome in a process of adaptation to the new conditions by evolutionary change.

Despite some obvious advantages of market capitalism, *Alec Nove*, as well as *J. A. Kregel*, stresses the need for governmental planning. Since the market will not provide a sufficient number of public goods, only a credible, consistent and coherent long-term plan will allow an efficient outcome of the economic process and will prevent a disallocation of goods. However, the State must not take over the risks which are involved in entrepreneurship. The sanctions of mismanagement are loss or even bankruptcy. If this pressure is reduced or taken over by the State, then according to Kregel a situation of moral hazard will occur. The allocation of goods and loans will no longer depend on risk-minded thoughts of productivity or market chances.

The transformation of our society is a permanent process, and the economic, political and social sciences are challenged to search for new, appropriate solutions. A monocausalistic view, however, seems to be increasingly outdated, a critical point of mainstream economics, of the neo-classical approach. Alternative, interdisciplinary approaches are considered necessary in order to express the unity of social, political, and economic aspects.

Michael Hutter introduces 'soft factors', as for example communication skills and education. For him, an economy is just one of many other different 'plays'. The 'single element' has to be in a position to communicate and to take part actively in these plays.

Bertram Schefold demands a new economic style reintroducing a classical basically neo-Ricardian approach. 'Social and institutional changes . . . must be reflected in the theory itself, not only in its data,' he states. Schefold argues that new forms of formal and informal controls have to be designed and introduced in order to find solutions to the growing and alarming problems of society.

For *Marc R. Tool* the availability of knowledge, the ability of a society to absorb and to adapt new knowledge and new technologies determine the 'progressiveness' of evolutionary change. Society is constantly transformed in order to solve problems, whereas norm related criteria like rules, morals, values and institutional boundaries may decrease the speed of necessary change.

Of course, change seems in many ways more pressing in the Eastern economies. Not only since Mikhail Gorbachev pronounced the words 'perestroika' and 'glasnost' has it been very obvious that a dramatic and profound transformation of the economic as well as of the political system is inevitable.

The present situation of the existing Soviet-type economic system is indeed frustrating. The dream of catching up with the West or even of overtaking Western economic performance has failed completely. On the contrary, the situation has worsened in the last few years. Analysis shows that the progress made has been financed by Western banks. Debts are increasing and not even the payment of interest can be guaranteed by export surpluses. The decline of world market prices of some of its major export items and huge budget deficits are even shaking the foundations of the Soviet Union. What are the reasons for this development?

All authors agree that the present situation does not have merely subjective causes, i.e. the failure is less the result of personal mistakes, insufficient working discipline, morale, imperfect planning, etc. On the contrary, there are obviously fundamental, objective defects inherent in the political system which cause the stagnation of economic life. Central governmental planning, monopolistic production structures, decreasing productivity, waste of resources, lack of quality, etc., on the one hand, bureaucratic structures, an ideological framework, an infallible party, on the other – all these facts hinder a democratic exchange of opinions, of decisions and experiences, and contribute to a dropping standard of living, which cannot be hidden any longer. The lack of motivation for workers seems to be not only a vicious circle with the resulting shortage of consumer goods, but also a consequence of resignation, of political and social agony. Therefore, the central issue of all contributions is not whether socialism should be reformed or not, but how to realise this challenge.

After all, has socialism failed or should it be considered as being in a transitory crisis? For *Branko Horvat*, 'real socialism' as it exists in Eastern European countries has to be characterised as etatism, which thoroughly discredits socialist ideas. For him, 'project socialism' remains alive, the dream of equality, justice and democracy still has to be realised, a spirit which always stimulated the scientific work of Ota Sik as well, as *Jiří Kosta* points out.

Harry Maier gives a very explicit and detailed description of the state of innovation, of the decline in technological transformation which is apparent in the decreasing growth rates of productivity, despite similar efforts in research compared to those undertaken in Western countries. *Friedrich Levcik* stresses, furthermore, the important influence of individual incentives and market pressure on an entrepreneurial level in the context of introducing new technologies and products. Both agree that foreign competition and international economic and scientific–technological relationships are crucial for economic reforms.

This view is supported by *András Inotai* who demands far-reaching steps towards an integration of socialist economies into the world economy. He urges a long-term strategic reappraisal in order to prevent a historical peripherisation of Eastern societies.

In general, there is wide agreement among the authors that the central planning mechanism has to be replaced by market prices, market allocation and market competition. These are the only possibilities of gaining profitability and productivity. Nevertheless, it has been made clear that despite all the faults of present real socialism, a pure capitalist economy cannot be regarded as a solution. A certain combination of plan and market is worth striving for. The present state of debate in Hungary is described by the contribution of *Jan Adam*. The central issue is what instruments should replace the plan and how to ensure democratic and social control over economic development.

Tamas Bauer gives a historical review of the introduction of economic reforms in Czechoslovakia and Hungary, starting in the late 1960s. Bauer concludes that the political restraints and conditions for preparatory work were totally different and partly responsible for the success and respectively the failure of the reforms. Bauer emphasises that these economic reforms can only be seen as a first step, as a sort of take-off, which would have required further far-reaching changes in Czechoslovakia as well.

However, is the one-party, governmentally planned economy

reformable at all, or are the thresholds, the bureaucracy, the nomenclatura too strong, too well established to be overcome lastingly? These sceptical questions are asked by *Leszek Balcerowicz* and *Hans-Hermann Höhmann*. Balcerowicz demands a policy of great strides in radical reform and argues that a piecemeal transformation is condemned to fail since in the latter case the conservative forces will be allowed to gather and strike back – efficiency is lost, the old interest groups, who are going to be the losers in any reform, will unite and prevent any further change. These arguments are supported by the Chinese experience, as *Wu Jing Lian* points out. Half-hearted attempts at change will always fail, since the creation of incentives without real market conditions will not lead to a permanent improvement, but to chaotic circumstances, which are used to justify any steps backwards.

A fundamental, far-reaching economic, political and social development of planned economies is certainly a challenging task for a political leadership. The remedies may be bitter, often painful or even brutal. Nevertheless, all authors agree that radical change has to take place as soon as possible, if the long-term development of the socialist countries is not to be jeopardised.

The evolution of systems seems to be a never-ending process. As in nature, a human society has to adapt to a higher, more feasible state in order to survive, even if for political and institutional reasons such a change might be prevented for a while.

Index

accumulation, 10–12, 148–52

banking, 16–17, 133–9, 148, 253–4
behaviour, 168–73
bureaucracy, 96–8, 126–8, 187–91,
    193–200, 226–9, 241–3, 265–73

capital, neutralised, 15–17, 181
centralisation, 194
change, *see* transformation
Classical theory, 141–53
communication, 101–9
communication problems, 84–6
competition, 94, 229–30
competitiveness, international
    202–11, 214–21, 225–8, 236
conflicts, international, 26–31
conservation of nature, *see*
    environment, natural
consumption, 10–15, 145
convergence, 30–1
convertibility, 208–11, 231
cooperation, 28–30
crisis, 66, 156, 225–33, 236
cycles, 72–6, 121–8, 183, 187

demand, aggregate, 11–12
democracy, 16–17, 21–3, 36–9, 181–4,
    186–91, 261–2
development, 93–6
distribution, 11–12, 148–50, 181
dynamics, 53, 61, 199–200

ecology, *see* environment
economic growth, *see* growth
economic reforms, *see* reforms
economy, dynamic, *see* dynamics
economy, planned, *see* planning
economy, market, *see* market
efficiency, 6–10, 45, 191, 196–9,
    204–9, 270–1
entrepreneurship, 112–19, 183–4
environment, cultural, 63–7
environment, economic, 100–9
environment, social, 2, 4, 59, 63–7
environment, natural, 2, 43–57, 65,
    152–3

equality, 21–3, 187–91
equilibrium, 5–15, 59, 95, 156–8, 226
etatism, 186–91, 280
eternity, 53–6
exploitation, 187–9
exports, 202–11
external effects, 48–51

Faust, 52–7
Faustian activity, 53–7
Faustian dynamics, 56
freedom, 35, 45

Gorbachev, Mikhail, 27–8, 69, 71,
    226, 229, 235–43
governmental planning, *see* planning
growth, 53–7, 65, 122–8, 183, 204–5,
    225–33, 236–41

Hayek, Friedrich, A., 35–7
hierarchy, 194–6
hierarchy of needs, 3, 7
historical dimension, 59–67, 91–3,
    122–8, 145–6
historical concept, 59–67
historical moment, 73–6

imports, 202–11
incentives, 214–21, 266
innovation, 69–71, 73–5, 93–6,
    112–19, 123–8, 205–8, 214–21,
    225–33; *see also* technologies
institutions, 116–19, 165–73
interdependence, policy–economics,
    28–31, 32–9, 77–86
interests, 3–5, 44, 65, 97–8, 181
interventions, governmental, 135–9
inventions, 73–6, 93–6
investment, 10–17, 158–61

Keynes, John Maynard, 7, 10, 60,
    133–5, 183
Kondratieff cycles, 121; *see also* cycles

labour, 60
labour movement, 22–4, 66

Lenin, V. I., 22, 155, 187, 226

market, capital, 16–17, 133–9, 148, 253–4
market economy, 66, 91–4
market mechanism, 133–6, 179–82, 231, 268–73
market pressure, 216–18
market prices, 48–51
market process, 7, 187
market theory, 5–9
Marx, Karl, 2, 5–8, 21–5, 60–3, 155, 179, 187. 226, 265
Marxian reproduction scheme, 10–15; *see also* reproduction
Maslow's hierarchy of needs, 3, 7
Mephisto, 52–7
mismatch, 123–8
monopolies, 160–4, 180–1, 195, 216
moral hazard, 137–8
motivation, 214–21

needs, 2–4, 6–8, 181
nuclear weapons, 26

October Revolution, 22, 187

paradigm, technological–economic, 72–6, 111–19, 123–8, 225
Pareto-optimality, 45, 151
planning, 32–9, 94–6, 133–5, 155–64, 179–84, 193–6, 256–63
policy, economic, 77–86
policy, foreign economic, 202–11
policy advising, 84–6
policy rituals, 80
pollution, *see* environment, natural
preferences, 3, 7–8, 44
price adjustment, 6
price mechanism, 43–4, 57, 195
price reform, 248–50, 269–74
price rigidities, 6
property rights, 34–8, 179–84
public goods, 48–51, 160–64

radical reforms, 196–200, 274
reform failure, 196–200, 227, 265–74
reform process, 68–9
reform threshold, 196–200
reformability, 193–200, 240–3
reforms 69–71, 178–84, 193–200, 203–11, 228–33, 235–43, 268–74

relations, socio-economic, 60
rent-seeking, 117
reproduction, 10–15, 59–67, 73
Ricardo, David, 141–7
rituals, 80

Schumpeter, Joseph, 9, 37, 113–19, 121, 226
sclerosis, 96–8
self-management, 191, 194
self-organisation, 100–9, 114
self-referentiality, 100–9
self-reproduction, 100–9
Smith, Adam, 3, 91, 100, 111, 135
social aspects, 145–8
social development, *see* transformation
social processes, 61–2, 165–73
social systems, 64–7, 100–9, 189–91
social environment, 100–9
socialism, 22–9, 189–91
socialism, 'project socialism', 190–1, 280
socialism, 'real socialism', 186–9
stagnation, 96–8, 113–16, 193–9, 225–33, 236, 240–1, 246–7, 268–73
stock exchange, 69–70, 148
subsidies, 194–6, 218
supply, aggregate, 11–12

technologies, 111–19, 123–4, 171–3, 213–21, 225–33, 238; *see also* innovation
Third Way, 1–17, 32, 37, 177–84
time, 6, 39, 68, 75–6
trade, foreign, 202–11, 213–17, 231, 249
transactions, 102–5
transformation, 71–6, 102–9, 126–8, 167–8, 191, 193–200, 214–21, 225–23

values, 44–8, 65, 169–72

waste, *see* environment, natural
war, 26–7
waves, 72–6, 121–8, 183, 187
workers' participation, 16, 179–84, 220–1
world economy, 202–11